LETHE

For Gary & Connie
Thank you for all you do
for me -

Anthony N. Warren

— Tony —

LETHE

The Life and Times of
Dr. John de la Howe

ANTHONY NEIL WARREN SR.

TATE PUBLISHING
AND ENTERPRISES, LLC

Published by Tate Publishing & Enterprises, LLC
127 E. Trade Center Terrace | Mustang, Oklahoma 73064 USA
1.888.361.9473 | www.tatepublishing.com

Tate Publishing is committed to excellence in the publishing industry. The company reflects the philosophy established by the founders, based on Psalm 68:11,
"The Lord gave the word and great was the company of those who published it."

Published in the United States of America

ISBN: 978-1-62994-288-9
1. Biography & Autobiography / General
2. History / United States / State & Local / South
14.01.30

DEDICATION

To my wife and to all the other students, teachers, and all those who worked in a support capacity and leadership positions at the John de la Howe School. Without you, we would have no school and no story.

CONTENTS

FOREWORD

In 1982, I had just begun my career as an archaeologist. I was working on a survey project in McCormick County and we were tasked with examining Badwell Plantation, home of James L. Petigru. He is known for being one of the few politicians in South Carolina to take a stand against secession and the Civil War. His most famous quote was that South Carolina was too small to be a nation yet too large to be an insane asylum. Through this I learned of the French settlement of New Bordeaux and of Dr. John de la Howe. Having seen the ravages of erosion caused by cotton agriculture in the area, I was intrigued by the de la Howe property, because the area around the doctor's homesite had been left untouched since his death in the 1790s and should be in pristine condition. Thus it should tell us what we were missing in other areas.

Along with my boss and the rest of the field crew, I visited the de la Howe tract and was amazed to see the largest short leaf pine in the country there, along with the second largest and probably the third, fourth and so on. I also learned more about Dr. de la Howe and his interesting life. Here was a man who came to the United States late in life and who never really fit into the stereotype of the planter lifestyle. He was married in Charleston, yet ended his life in a remote wilderness living with another woman. He didn't have children or other heirs so when he died he left his estate to found a school for the poor and orphaned children of the area.

Having an interest in how people express ethnicity and social identity in their use of material things, I kept the site in mind because, after all, here was a man who would have been distinctly French in many ways, and a site that should be undisturbed enough to let this show. Most archaeological sites in South Carolina seem to have been continuously occupied, with succeeding generations tearing down the old and building anew, generally disturbing and messing up what came before. The contributions of a person who was clearly French should be obvious here and the uniquely undisturbed property should let this show through unambiguously.

So in 1992, I got a small grant from the state humanities council. I contacted the school and with the help of staff, faculty, and two groups of students, did a couple of weeks' work at the site. At this point, I met Tony Warren. Tony came to the de la Howe School at a crucial point in his life, and the experience allowed him to rise above an adverse situation and go on to lead a productive life. Tony is not a man to blithely overlook such a contribution, and to this day he is still active in supporting the school and its students.

Tony came out and helped with the fieldwork in 1992 and encouraged me to seek further funding. In the meanwhile, he began the kind of historical research that only a true devotee can do. In those days, historical records were nearly all on paper or even worse, microfilm, and except for the rare instances where collections were indexed or cataloged, the only way to find what you wanted was to spend hours going through old newspapers, government records, and handwritten papers. It had to be a labor of love, and for Tony it was.

In 1995, I got another small grant from the State Historic Preservation Office and again, with the help of Tony and the school, did some more fieldwork. Tony gave me his historical research to use in preparing my project report. It was so thorough that I felt I had to include the full document as an appendix to the report. It's not that there is a tremendous amount of documentary evidence of his life and actions, but that I feel confident that Tony had turned over every stone and found pretty much everything there was to find.

And what an interesting story! In this novel, Tony has taken the few direct references and fleshed them out into an intriguing tale. No, not every word is true, and we in the present cannot hope to truly understand why he did the things he did, or what he thought, or how he felt about any given thing. Tony has tried to link together the few references in a framework that reflects the times and the little we know of John de la Howe, the man. Most of what he says is speculative, but the story he tells is plausible and well considered. It would be possible to interpret things differently, but Tony has done the job as well as he could and the impetus for correcting any errors and doing a better job is on us now. Thanks Tony for telling this story and for all of your help and support over the years.

—Carl Steen

INTRODUCTION

This is my first attempt at writing a novel. I was raised in Charleston, South Carolina, most of my life. I loved growing up being a lifeguard at Folly Beach and shagging on the strand. I lived downtown and loved Charleston history. I remember as a young lad, taking tourist on walking tours in the old section of town. I barely made it out of elementary school and then in high school I had a very hard time. I knew that I was not stupid, but I had great difficulty with academics. One day, I shot a little firecracker in the yard at recess, and the principal expelled me for setting off a bomb and being unable to learn. I had a friend that was attending John de la Howe School in McCormick, South Carolina. My mother and I went to bring him home for Thanksgiving in 1958. While I was there, Dr. Erwin Finley Gettys, the superintendant, told me that he knew that I was having trouble and asked me if I would like to come there and try it out for a while with no strings attached. I was fighting with my parents and I was lost on the streets probably heading to jail. I told Dr. Gettys that I would love to get away and be a part of the school. I really did not qualify because my parents were very well-to-do, but Dr. Gettys made a pilot program so he could recruit boys with leadership potential so the other boys could emulate. He always found a way to help children. We had 120 boys and 120 girls.

I fell in love with the school right away. The boys worked at the farm and the dairy, and the girls worked at the kitchen and the laundry. I was given responsibility and I flourished. I met and dated my wife there and made many lifelong friends. I will always consider it home.

In order for me to go to the state school, I had to take an Intelligence Quota test and I scored so high that the psychiatrist called my mother and told her that I either cheated or that they had made a mistake. They rescheduled me and I took an oral I.Q. test in front of a panel of psychiatrist and again I scored in the 99.7 percentile of the world's population. Then the professionals said that I was just lazy, obstinate and rebellious, a typical 50's diagnosis. My youngest son was born with the same affliction but by the 80's, he was treated in special schools and he did fine. If I had not passed the genes on to him, I would have always wondered what was wrong with me. I found out later in the 80's that my short-term memory brain cells did not develop until I was about fifteen or sixteen while at de la Howe. I made up for lost time and went on to graduate from Southern Institute of Technology in Marietta, Georgia. The reason I went there is because I qualified to go to any college, but Southern Tech had the highest paid graduates in the nation. I attended the University of Georgia School Of Graduate Studies for one semester when my second son was born and I left to go to work.

I returned to Charleston after completing three years in the US Army paratroopers and attending school on the G.I. Bill and eventually started my own hydraulics repair business. I came back to John de la Howe School and served on the Alumni Board. I have been on the board for upwards of thirty years now and served as its president in 1996–1998 during the two hundredth anniversary of the school. The trustees have elected me as the school historian, and I served as the parliamentarian for the Alumni Board of Trustees.

I spent my spare time in Charleston when I was not busy with the Masons and the Shrine, searching records at the South Carolina Historical Society and the Charleston Library Society. I found hundreds of papers and reports that were not known at that time. I faxed the superintendant and started keeping records.

In 1996, I was invited to join the governor's Bicentennial Book Committee to be published in 1997. I turned over my records to Mr. Al Loftis who was chairman of the committee for the book. Mr. Loftis did an excellent job correlating the material, but due to time constraints, there were many gaps in the story.

I have searched many records and I have not been able to find any data predating Dr. de la Howe coming to Charleston in 1764. I have read reports of second hand information, but nothing solid. I knew he was a surgeon in the Seven Years' War and there is no ship record of him coming to Charleston. I have some ideas of what could have happened but most of the information in this book is fiction. I have tried to be as accurate as possible concerning the chronology of the events in the book, and I have quoted the ads in the newspaper and other reports such as the wills and inventories as they were written. I have copies of the originals, but I had to fill in many gaps in the life of Dr. de la Howe and that is why I must enter the word "fiction" on the cover.

Even though the story is historically accurate, the story between the facts is completely made up out of my imagination.

My hope is that the story will motivate a child at the school to become interested in his or her heritage. It is said that John de la Howe School is for the "underprivileged" child but I always felt "privileged" by attending.

I will always be indebted to the school and the state for allowing me the honor of attending John de la Howe School. Because of them and the foresight of Dr. John de la Howe, I went from a burden to the state to a business owner and productive member of society.

I have worked on two archeological digs on the Lethe site. I have built a trail from Dr. de la Howe and Rebecca's tomb to the home site. We found at least sixteen structures and I have erected a trail and signage at each site. The archeologist Carl Steen and I have published a book with color pictures of the artifacts. Contact Carl at the Diachronic Research Institute in Columbia, South Carolina. Lethe is open to visitors; just check in with the office when you come into the campus.

Living in Charleston for sixty years and living at John de la Howe School for four years coupled with my natural interest in history makes it seem like this was destiny for me to author this book. I will never stop researching Dr. de la Howe's life, and I will always be involved with the school. I hope that with the advent and progress of the computer information highway that we will learn more as time goes by.

Disclaimer: The main character of this story is true, and the events surrounding him may or may not have happened.

THE EARLY YEARS AND THE
SEVEN YEARS' WAR

"All this in the name of vanity," I whispered to my assistant Mr. Hendrick Seles. There had been over a million casualties during this world conflict and it seemed like I had attended them all over the last seven years.

"You are correct Dr. Jean de la Howe," he answered "and I have been here to assist you and learn from you from the beginning."

Dr. de la Howe answers, "Here it is 1762 and I will be forty-five years old my next birthday and I have been here for almost seven years. There must be more to life for me than this." I was thinking about how we got into this mess. I was living a comfortable life in Hanover under English rule when this war started. I believe King George must be obsessed with land acquisitions. He and Fredrick, the ruler of Prussia, seem to think that with English ships and Prussia's army, they can control the world. France and Spain have other ideas, especially concerning the lands in the new world of America. The French are now fighting the English in Canada and Ohio territories, and the Indians are supporting them.

I am standing here in this operating room thinking how much I hate war and all of its by-products. Here are hundreds of young men in the prime of their lives awaiting hospital space, some to die, and others to carry on with their farms and businesses with parts of their bodies missing. Worse than that, they will suffer the agonizing memories of battle in their minds for the rest of their lives. They will look at the moon on a clear spring night and remember their best friend or family member, getting their face shot off or a cannonball exploding near them, ripping their sons and neighbors to shreds in front of their eyes. This will not pass. It will affect their lives in so many ways. Their marriages will often fail because their wives will not understand why they are often lost deep in thought of the horrors they encountered. When they are disturbed, they will snap back as if to say "please take it all away!" but the wives and girlfriends will not know what to do and all they can do is stand helplessly by their men hoping that they will not completely be lost in that unseen numbness of oblivion.

Medicine and languages came easy to me as I studied in the finest schools of Europe. I attended the best schools as a boy in Flanders and medical school in Hanover. My favorite subject was mythology, both Greek and Roman. I learned French from my native land, German and English from school in Hanover and Latin from prep school and medical school. I studied and learned other languages also. At the time, I thought I was preparing myself to be a "proper gentleman," to take my place in polite society. I had no idea that God was preparing me to communicate with casualties of war. I become so efficient in speaking different languages and dialects that I actually could think in whichever language I choose.

I was thirty-five years old when I was practicing medicine in Hanover when I was approached by the French government to go to the American colonies and practice Physick. There is a great shortage of formally trained doctors aiding either side of this awful unpleasantness taking place in the American Ohio Valley. I thought It would be a chance to learn the most modern techniques in treating all sorts of wounds and diseases that I could use in my practice in America when the French, German, English, Prussian, Hanoverian, Austrian, Swedish, Saxony, Russian and Spanish governments, and kings realized that a few acres of speculative land was not worth one soul, much less the thousands that are maimed and wounded every day here in Nova Scotia. I was picked due to my reputation of being able to speak in many languages and my skill and intelligence as a doctor. I am definitely not political. I see the way politicians make themselves submissive to a principality in order to attain some of their goals. By their caviling and groveling, they crawl and now wallow in their ineptness to govern intelligently. The effect is they act in a servile way demeaning themselves, their countries, and their constituents. Because they were born rich and privileged, they think that they are better than anyone else in every way. Now thousands die for a cause of which they are not aware. May God have mercy on us and give us grace.

I came to the new world in April of 1756 with the new French commander Marquis de Montcalm and about twenty-five thousand men. The British had about the same number. Allied with the Indians, we had several battles around Lake Ontario and he eventually captured forts at Oswego on Lake Ontario thus controlling the Great Lakes. We then captured Fort William Henry on Lake George, and the British decided to get dedicated to winning the war. I told my assistant that there is a difference between being involved and being dedicated. If you had ham and eggs this morning for breakfast, that chicken was involved in that breakfast by laying the eggs, but that pig that was made into bacon was definitely dedicated. England sent Maj. Gen. James Abercromby here who came to battle with twenty-five thousand men. He turned the tide of war by capturing forts and blocking French supply ports. By 1759, the British sent Maj. Gen. James Wolf with nine thousand men to the front to capture Niagara and Quebec. My regiment has lost the Battle of the Plains of

Abraham and has retreated to Montreal. We have buried many young men and left behind those who were not ambulatory.

Thank goodness War Hawk William Pitt was driven out of the office of Defense Minister of England and new King George III is negotiating a peace agreement. Things have calmed down somewhat and we are enjoying a lull in the fighting, awaiting the peace treaty that will be forthcoming next year.

As I was taking my evening meal with the officers last night, I met a most extraordinary gentleman. His name is Henry Laurens from Charles Town in the colony of South Carolina. He is here visiting the generals, making plans to continue his business interest after the war. For some time now, he has supplied the French and the English armies with bread and other supplies from his shipping company. He has made a fortune in the slave trade industry by specializing in those from Sierra Leone on the African west coast. Mr. Laurens explained that Sierra Leone and Charles Town climate is much alike and the slaves have been growing rice for hundreds of years in Africa. Since Charles Town was founded in 1670 on Albemarle Point a money crop was sought by the settlers. The colony was moved to the peninsula of present-day Charleston in 1680 when it was discovered that the conditions were right for growing rice, cotton, indigo and other staple crops. Since the Sierra Leone natives were already well versed in cultivating rice, the slaves brought a premium price to the plantation owners. Soon rice exports were the major source of income for the colony.

Mr. Laurens proceeded to show me an advertisement from the Charles Town newspaper, *The South Carolina & American General Gazette* in which he advertised a shipment of slaves to be sold at Ashley Landing in the city. He made sure that everyone knew that they were from Sierra Leone. He left me a copy.

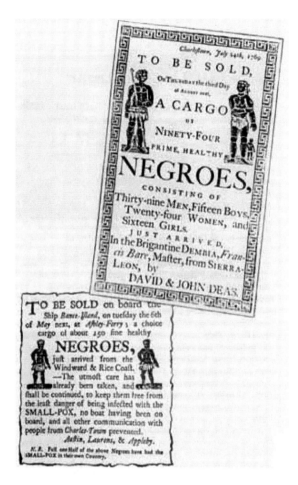

I noticed Mr. Laurens' signature at the bottom of the advertisement.

Mr. Laurens told me, "To give you an idea of how much rice, which is called 'Carolina Gold' is affecting the economy, you must take into consideration that the average cost of a slave is about $600.00, which is a year's wage for an average middle class worker. Most farmers or wealthy business families have two or three slaves, but Mr. Arthur Middleton owns about 1,700 slaves. He even purchased a mile long strip in Charles Town and built sheds so the slaves could raise money by selling their wares such as sweetgrass baskets, vegetables, and meat which they grew independently of their normal slave duties. Some of the slaves have actually purchased their freedom doing this. In 1700, Charles Town exported ten thousand pounds of rice and this year we will export over two million pounds, and the demand is growing every year."

I later figured out that Mr. Laurens had not found me by accident. He had been talking to leaders on both sides in trying to find a skilled and well-versed doctor who had the proper documentation, necessary credentials, and a reputation for being an accomplished gentleman. He was here to offer me a position under his auspices to meet a group of French Huguenots that were due in Charles Town sometime in the spring or summer of 1764. Mr. Laurens was a direct descendant of these Huguenots and had learned of their awful persecution and torture at the hands of the Catholics in France, especially near his ancestral home of Abbeville. With the signing of the treaty, England will open new lands to settlers in hopes of gaining wealth from their bountiful exports of goods. Mr. Laurens has offered me passage to Charles Town and has arranged with the King of England to grant me four hundred acres on Long Canes settlement in the backcountry of South Carolina. This land was to adjoin the lands he received as a grant of fifty thousand acres to form a new township which he named Hillsboro. He has already arranged for one of his ships, *Friendship*, to bring over 168 Huguenots to come to Charles Town and eventually to settle the area. Rev. Peter Gibert is to be leader of the Huguenots at Hillsborough and has expressed a desire to form a new township there and call it "New Bordeaux."

I was very flattered at his offer and under the present circumstances, I could see nothing that would prevent me from starting over in the new world and finding some peace at last.

My friend Hendrick Seles dined with me that night. I was deep in thought and Hendrick, who had been with me since my days in Hamelin, Hanover, has assisted me in my practice. He has become my confidant and my friend. He has the skills to become a fine doctor; however, he came from a poor family and lacked the funds to gain a proper education.

"Dr. Jean, I feel that you are far away tonight as you have been many times we have broke bread together. Is there something wrong?" Hendrick asked.

"Thank you for your caring, my good friend, but nothing is wrong. I was approached by Mr. Laurens today who offered me an opportunity to start a new life in Charles Town in the colony of South Carolina. He has offered me passage and expenses to Charles Town where I can set up a medical practice and tend to his Huguenots when they arrive."

I took a sip of my tea and continued "I will then accompany them two hundred miles from Charles Town to the backcountry of South Carolina and attend to their medical needs as long as they need me. Along with the expenses, he will arrange for King George to grant me four hundred acres in the backcountry near the Huguenots in order to start a plantation."

I stirred the fire and took another sip of my tea and continued "I am seriously considering taking him up on his offer. It will establish me in a large city with very wealthy clientele. I can live in Charles Town and be an absentee landlord. You can be my overseer. My given name is Jean and my Latin name is Johannes, but I think I will change it to English John which would be better suited for the environment to which I will enter. Many of the Huguenots will have changed their names to keep from being persecuted or followed to the new world and attacked."

"Please take me with you, Dr. de la Howe. I have been with you for all these years and I can find no better friend and companion to enter into such an adventure. I have no place else to go. I find myself in the perdictiment of lacking the finances to start over," he said with a sigh of desperation.

"Don't worry about that," de la Howe replied. "I will finance you and you can pay me back as you are able to do so."

Hendrick replied, "I had rather not take advantage of our relationship by receiving charity from you."

"Then you can legally indenture yourself to me and we can maintain our friendship. Then you would be under bond to pay me back someday."

"You, sir, are too kindhearted. I will accept your offer and become your indentured servant."

"You will have a hard time getting rich with that kind of attitude."

"Yes," replied John, "but I can live with my choices. I pray to be a blessing to someone every day of my life and today it is you. I am confident in my skills and ability to see me through. I am not afraid to take a chance, and besides, how can I put a price on your companionship while traveling in a strange land. I will feel safer and better occupied by discussing philosophy and bouncing new ideas off you to see if it is feasible. I do not possess your skill and ability to communicate with the world around you and with others. I see things more as black and white and with reason and logic. You can teach me people skills and I can make you smarter and more learned."

"Let's do it!" replied Hendrick.

The next morning, I wrote a letter to Mr. Laurens informing him that I would agree to the terms he set forth to me personally. I also mentioned that Mr. Laurens, by virtue of his wealth and politics, could obtain a discharge for me and arrange transportation to Charles Town. I also wrote a letter to my relatives in Hanover and in London to send me what money I had saved from my practice there. I asked that they send it in the care of Mr. Laurens in Charles Town. Mr. Laurens would write a letter introducing me to the local gentry.

GOING TO CHARLES TOWN

It is a distance of 1,650 miles from Halifax, Nova Scotia to Charles Town, South Carolina. Do I want to go by carriage and see my newly adopted country or do I want to go by sail direct to Charles Town? By carriage, it will take about three or four months of traveling, stopping occasionally to rest and see the sights. By ship, I can be in Charles Town in about five days. Mr. Laurens has a supply ship leaving port in a few days and then returning to Charles Town with a cargo of cobblestones. He has unloaded most of his cargo of rice, cotton, and indigo in England and the rest here to feed and clothe the British and French armies. In England, he filled most of the voided cargo space with cobblestones which he will use as ballast to steady the ship. It is the middle of March, still early spring and the hurricane season is five months away and this would be a good time to sail. If I were to go by carriage, I might miss the arrival of the Huguenots. I need to be there to certify that they are not carrying any diseases into the new world. I understand that the South Carolina government is very strict about this since some ships have come into port with small pox, cholera, flu, leprosy, and other contagious diseases. I guess that there is no real decision to be made here. Mr. Laurens said that if I desired passage on the ship, he would leave word with Captain Francis Charles Worley that I may be traveling with him. The captain will arrange the sleeping quarters and a place for me to relax during the voyage. Of course my friend Hendrick will accompany me. I will give him orders to pack up my medical supplies, medicines, clothes and other possessions then proceed to the wharf where the ship is moored.

"Good morning, sir," I said to the ship officer on watch. "I am Dr. John de la Howe with my servant Hendrick Seles; I believe Captain Charles Worley is expecting me."

"Yes sir, please wait while the captain is informed."

Within a few minutes, Captain Worley came to the gangplank with a big smile on his face. "Welcome, sir. Please come aboard and make yourself at home. I will have the men bring your gear aboard so you may get settled into your quarters. Mr. Laurens has told me a great deal about you, and we are very excited and honored that you grace us with your presence. May I get you anything?"

"Thank you very much, but I have everything I need until dinner. Your reception is gracious and your hospitality is appreciated. I wish to extend my appreciation to you and to Mr. Laurens."

"Will you grace us with your presence this evening at dinner?" he asked. "I would like to introduce you to the officers of this ship."

I thanked him for the invitation and told him that I would be delighted to join him.

That afternoon, Hendrick and I unpacked what was necessary for the voyage, but left nonessential items packed up for when we entered the city. Mr. Laurens had made sure that there were servants there who attended to all of our needs. I was particularly impressed by one such slave. He appeared to be in his twenties, very good looking and healthy with a bright smile and personality. He seemed very intelligent and was very amiable. He had a way with people and is a descendant of a family of slaves taken from the

Gullah tribe in Sierra Leone. He had been trained as a personal attendant for the head of the household and was very good at executing his duties. I made friends with him immediately even though I understood the boundaries of rank and privilege. There was always that line to which he was not to cross nor could I. Society would not allow it and being a stranger in this land, I did not want to do anything that would cause waves. I asked him his name and he said in his Gullah dialect. "Massa Laurens just calls me 'boy.' Massa say he gwain to give me ta you as a present for 'greein ter kear fer hizzon friends. Massa say you is a goot main and yo will tek goot care o'me. You gwain call me Boy?"

"No, if you will be my charge, we need to come up with a proper name, one of status and awe. Since you will be serving me and my guests wine and meals, how about Bacchus?" I asked him.

"Souns lack sumtin yo smok or chaw," he said.

"No my friend," I replied. "Bacchus was the Roman name for the God of Wine. Dionysus was his Greek name. He was the god of wine, revelry, and drunkenness. Dionysus was, naturally, a very popular god with quite a few people. His festivals were among the most interesting and most wild. His father was Zeus and his mother was the mortal princess Semele, his wife was Ariadne, and his son was Priapus. Unlike other gods, Bacchus had no obvious, fixed character. He could be masculine or effeminate, young or old, human or animal. In crossing such boundaries, he personally took on the central attribute of the cults centered on him—the transgression of social norms, traditions, and boundaries. Dionysus is also the only one of the Greek gods who had a mortal parent. The offsping of mortals and gods usually became demigods or heroes, not full-fledged members of the Olympian pantheon."

"I don't rekon mos'ter whet youse say, but hit sounds lack he a portant main. I lack dat; bein' namd atter a god. Bacchus, my own name fer ta nowon. Thankee massa, I lack dat a lot."

"I will have you address me Doctor and not massa. If I have earned a name, it is Doctor and not massa. Massa is a purchased name and not an earned name. As distasteful as slavery is it remains the lawful staple of the society of which I am to become a member. I will treat you with respect and you will honor me because I have earned it and not because I own you. Do you understand?"

"Yessur, Docter, I does," he replied.

"We can work on your English as we grow old together. I know it is against the law to formally educate Negros in America, but I will teach you to be a gentleman's gentleman. You will be refined and learned."

Hendrick smiled in a knowing way. "I guess everyone is a servant to someone or something; you with your Mr. Laurens and the Huguenots and your patients; me with you, Captain Worley with his ship and now Bacchus with us."

And with that, we heard the snap of the sail unfolding and filling with wind and the ship pulling away from port. I hoped that the war part of my life was forever over, and I was excited and eager to start a new chapter in my life.

There was a knock at my door. I answered the door and a yeoman said, "With compliments from Captain Worley, sir, would you please be so kind as to join him in his state room at 6:00 p.m., for dinner?"

I answered, "Thank you sir, I would be delighted." I noticed that he did not ask Hendrrick to join us. I then realized that Hendrick was legally my indentured servant, and I did not know the proper protocol for such matters, so at 5:45 p.m., I left Hendrick going to the ship's galley and went to the captain's quarters. I have on one of my suits that Bacchus and Hendrick cleaned, pressed, and readied for me. I am a man of somewhat small statue. I stand about five feet six inches tall and of slender to medium build. The cuffs on modern coats have gone, and now the sleeve is left unbuttoned at the wrist. The coat is long and full-skirted, but not stiffened. The cravat is loosely tied, and the frilled ends stick out. These frills were made on the shirt, and were called chitterlings. I am also wearing black silk knee breeches and stockings which are very common today. I am wearing a tight-brimmed hat and buckled shoes, and my hair is in a twisted roll. It feels good to dress for dinner again and enjoy company that is not talking about war. It will be good to talk about the latest fashions, news, and learn some things about my new home.

I arrived at the captain's quarters just before 6:00 p.m. I always wonder if "dinner at six" means we start eating at six, or do I allow time for pre-dinner drinks and conversation, or do the pre-dinner conversation start at six. And to be socially fashionable, how much time should I allow. I believe that the captain understands that I am just returning from years at war and I think they would be gracious enough to excuse some of my ineptness. *Do I knock on the door or do I walk in? How loud do I knock? Am I really this nervous?* I have always prided myself to be able to conform to my surroundings. I am comfortable in any circumstance so what am I afraid of? To thine on self be true. I will be myself and, as always, everything will be fine.

As I approached the cabin, I noticed that there is a greeting servant standing at the door so all my anxiousness was for naught. I smiled at myself and thought how vain can you be? The Negro servant said, "Good evening, sir. May I take your hat and get you an aperitif?"

I replied that a glass of Cognac would be appreciated.

The captain came over to me and bowed. He was wearing his formal captain's uniform and looked quite dashing. He said, "Dr. de la Howe, it is such a pleasure to see you again. I pray that you found your accommodations adequate and acceptable."

I replied, "Yes, thank you. Your hospitality and everyone associated with it has been most helpful and kind."

Then a servant proclaimed, "Dinner is served."

During the dinner, the officers of the ship were very cordial to me. I am beginning to see the effect of the influence that Henry Laurens has not only on the people in his employ, but also on the public in general. Captain Worley offered me a pipe and tobacco and a digestif. He considered the Grappa wine, purchased on his last voyage to Italy, the perfect digestif. He explained that it was made from skins, seeds and pulp left over from wine making and was an aid to the digestive system as well as good tasting. " We we can talk while we smoke and sip," he suggested. Being from the wine making area of France, aperitif and digestif is not new to me. In fact, I have enjoyed them all of my adult life. It is the hospitable thing for a proper host to offer.

As we made ourselves comfortable in his huge but soft leather chairs, we sat by a potbellied stove and while puffing on my long stemmed pipe, sipping my wine and contemplating the flames inside the stove. Captain Worley said, "Did you know that Nova Scotia is very nearly one half the distance between the equator and the North Pole? Just a little known fact to get our conversation started. I thought I would tell you a little about our employer. Mr. Laurens, even though he is only in his fortieth year, has amassed a fortune from several of his businesses. He is an American merchant and he owns his own rice plantation. Laurens had earned great wealth as a partner in the largest slave house in North America, the name of which is "Austin and Laurens." In the 1750s alone, his Charleston firm oversaw the sale of more than eight thousand enslaved Africans. He is not only a self-made very rich Huguenot, he is also a very powerful politician. He is working behind the scenes for America to become a free and independent nation. You were very blessed to have been sought out by him. You will find him a very caring and generous man. I think it is ironic that his brother who is in the army with Col. Washington is against slavery in any form. He once asked Henry why he should fight for America's freedom while we enslave others. Henry respects his brother's opinion. I keep a drawing of him on our wall to ever remind me to carry out my duties with equal precision and dignity," as he pointed in the direction of the picture.

"You seem to have done well for you and your family. What is your secret?" I asked him.

Captain Worley replied, "There are thirty-one proverbs which is one per day for each month. They were written by the wisest and wealthiest man that ever lived in this world, except Jesus Christ. I try to read one each morning, before work, and apply it to my business. If I do that and attach myself to the shirttail of Mr. Laurens' rising star, I feel that I cannot fail."

"You sir are a wise businessman. I hope to do the same in my Charles Town practice. Our conversation has been most enjoyable, and it will be a pleasure to see you again in Charles Town. Mr. Laurens is finding me a place to live and to work. Please find me the next time you are in port that I may return your graciousness."

Due to endowments from from my father and grandfather, who were also doctors in London, my monetary concerns are few. Returning to my room there is a greater appreciation of my circumstances. Being further blessed by my association with Mr. Laurens, I look forward to see what the future holds for me. I pray I may be able to be a blessing to others in return.

I was walking on deck with Hendrick one afternoon six days after we departed Halifax when Captain Worley came up to us and bowed and said, "Good afternoon Dr. de la Howe. How are you and your fine friend doing today?"

"Hendrick and I are doing well and enjoying the salt air and the blustery sea breeze. Since you told me that we might see land this afternoon or tonight, I thought we would take a look at our new home."

Captain Worley replied, "It has been a pleasure meeting with you for supper each night. I know proper folks call it dinner, but I believe that Jesus attended the Last Supper and being a Christian from Charles Town most of us call it supper. Please forgive me if that sounds vulgar."

"Not at all, sir," I replied. "There is wisdom in what you say. I too have learned much from our conversations about people with whom I will have dealings and especially about the local culture. I believe you may have saved me from some embarrassing moments while getting settled in my new environs."

With that I heard from the crow's nest, "Land-Ho, Dewees Inlet two points off the starboard bow!"

Captain Worley said, "Please excuse me, Charles Town Harbor is fairly shallow, and there is a certain way we must approach the harbor to miss the shallows. We needn't be too concerned but our cargo of cobblestones makes our attention necessary."

Then Captain Worley yelled to the helmsman, "Come ten degrees to the south west and head for Morris Island by way of Folly."

I said, "What a strange name Folly. What does it mean, Captain?"

Captain Worley replied, "It is a barrier island that we will pass by. It was originally called "Coffin" island because when you look at it from a ship it is shaped like a coffin. It is full of scrub oaks and other foliage and has since come to be called Folly because of the foliage on the island. We are about ten nautical miles from Charles Town Harbor and we need to swing to the left of the harbor because there is a shipping channel that lays off Folly and Morris Island leading into the harbor. Anywhere else is shallow from all the drainage from the Ashley and Cooper Rivers that form the harbor, and besides there is a lighthouse on Morris Island to help us steer our way into a safe harbor. Charles Town's blue-bloods will tell you that the Ashley and the Cooper Rivers are the only rivers in America named for one man—Lord Ashley Cooper—who was one of the Lord's proprietors who financed the first settlement at Albemarle Point in 1670 and that the two rivers merge in Charles Town Harbor to form the Atlantic Ocean. Charles Town folks are very proud people."

Captain Worley then told me to look to the right front that I would see "Long Island" just past Dewees and then a breech and another island named "Sullivan's Island." He told me that by me being a doctor that I may be interested to know that that is the place where they brought the slaves to be quarantined until certified for sale. He also told me that there was a leper colony on Folly. If a ship came to Charles Town with a plague or fever, Folly is the place they would moor the ship until the disease ran its course.

As we came into the harbor, I was given a guided tour from Captain Worley. We passed Cumming's Point at the north end of Morris Island on the left. The ship then turned to the left to head straight into the harbor. Captain Worley told me to look straight ahead to the outline of the city and focus on the tallest structure. He said that it was St. Philip's Church and at night there was a fire lit in the steeple to guide ships into the harbor. Then he told me to look to the right pointing to a Fort. He said that this fort was built by Gen. William Moultrie and is made mostly out of palm tree trunks and sand. If you fired a cannonball at it, the cannonball would just bounce off the walls. To the left was another fort commanded by Gen. Johnston. I could see the wharves of Charles Town just passed an island at the mouth of the Cooper River. Captain Worley said that we would pass the island owned by Mr. Pinckney and dock at Adger's Wharf. Mr. Adger and Mr. Laurens are good friends and we will off load the cobblestones there.

IN CHARLES TOWN FIRST TIME

As the sloop rolled up her sails and the ship slowly pulled in to port right between South Adger's Wharf and Vanderhorst Wharf, I could see that Charles Town was a bustling city of great beauty and charm. Mr. Laurens had told me that there were about fifty thousand people in South Carolina and most of them were in Charles Town. He predicted that within ten years, the city would triple in size. It was already the fourth largest city in America. He also told me that blacks far outnumbered the whites because of the slave trade and some folks were worried that there may be a slave uprising if King George did not send more troops. South Carolina was already getting up a militia to help control lawlessness.

I found Bacchus and Hendrick and saw that my belongings were piled up on the deck as I returned to my room. As we were walking down the gangplank, I waved good-bye to Captain Worley and I heard "Calling Dr. John de la Howe! Calling Dr. John de la Howe!"

I looked up and there on the street was a beautiful black carriage with red interior driven by two formally dressed Negroes. I answered "I am Doctor de la Howe, how may I help you?"

The fellow answered. "Please sur, we belongs to Mr. Laurens. He sent us to fetch you and take you to his-on house."

I looked at Hendrick and Bacchus and told them to place everything in the carriage and we would be off to visit Mr. Laurens. We drove west on South Adger's Wharf across East Bay Street where the Street became Tradd Street. Tradd Street, I am told it was named after Robert Tradd who was the first English child to be born in Charles Town. We proceeded another one-half block past Bedons Alley to Church Street. We took a right and went another half block to 94 Church Street. Out of the piazza door came Mr. Laurens. He invited me to come into his friend's home as he was expecting me.

We entered the door that led to the piazza and on to the front door of the house. We walked into a dressing room where a slave took our outer garments and hats. Mr. Laurens led me into a huge study and there by the fire was a portly but distinguished gentleman. "Allow me to present Mr. Thomas Bee." Mr. Bee, please allow me to make your acquaintance of Dr. John de la Howe, a surgeon whom I have contracted to care for our friends, the Huguenots when they come to town."

I bowed as did he. "Welcome to Charles Town and to my home, Dr. de la Howe. I have heard good things about you and I believe that you will be a great asset to our community. Please come and join us for supper."

I thanked him and asked him about my servants. Mr. Bee told me that they would be taken to the kitchen and then to the slave quarters behind the house. We would be pleased to have your assistant join us for our meal. I must say that I was greatly relieved that they accepted Hendrick as my assistant and not my servant.

We climbed the stairway to the second floor where a lavish table was prepared. People in Charles Town ate upstairs because of all the dust and horse droppings on the streets, and besides, there is usually a prevailing westerly wind this time of the year due to the land cooling around the waters. I noticed there was a balcony off the dining room and a curve in the wrought iron fence that people leaned against to speak to friends and neighbors on the street. I asked Mr. Bee if the curve was for adornment or did it have a practical purpose. He laughed and said that was to accommodate the women in their large hoop dresses so they could stand next to their men while catching up on the latest news and gossip. "All this comes from years of experience," he said.

We sat down to supper, and I noticed that we were having some sort of fowl. I presumed they were quail or squab, but they did not look like quail or pigeon. Mr. Bee saw my curious eye and told me that in honor of my visit, he had sent a couple of slaves into the marsh to hunt marsh hens. It is a brown bird about the size of a morning dove with a large breast and a unique taste when made with gravy and served on a bed of "Carolina Gold" brown rice. He explained that the locals have hunted the plover almost to extinction and now they are working on the marsh hens, but the marsh hens are so hard to get to that they will be preserved for a long time. He explained that you must pole a flat-bottomed boat through the marsh on a very high spring tide. The birds make their nests on the tops of the saw grass reeds and as the boat nears, they fly away, but they are very slow. Sometimes you can hit them with a pole but most of the time we use a shotgun.

After supper, Mr. Bee took me into the drawing room or music room to enjoy a pipe and a digestif. Mr. Bee passed me some brandy and a long stemmed pipe. He told me that Mr. Laurens had asked him to entertain tonight so he could talk to you more about your mission. Mr. Bee said that Mr. Laurens was a very influential member of the South Carolina society and that he was born in Charles Town, South Carolina, March 6, 1724; received his early education in Charles Town; went to England in 1744 to acquire a business education; upon his return to the United States in 1747 engaged in mercantile pursuits; served as lieutenant colonel in a campaign against the Cherokee Indians from 1757 to 1761. He served as a member of the commons house of assembly in 1757 and reelected to every session, with one exception, he declined appointment to King's Council in Carolina in 1764 and will do so again in 1768; and he has been invited to become a member of the American Philosophical Society, Philadelphia, Pennsylvania.

"So, you can see why he has such influence and power along with his great wealth. He is a modest man who does charitable works without recognition. He is helping the Huguenots get out of France because he has the means, and he is a Huguenot descendant, and he is determined to see his family and friends out of being tortured and prosecuted by the Catholic government ruling in France today. He will be here shortley, and he will tell you more now that you have committed to helping in this endeavor."

We sat in front of the fireplace smoking and sipping his well-aged and smooth brandy. When he needed wood for the fire, he would pull a narrow curtain strip that was the same color as the drapes and soon a slave would come to see what Mr. Bee needed. I could not help but notice that Mr. Bee always said please to his slaves and thank you when they were done and always called them by name. I wondered if the rest of the gentry did the same thing. I swore to myself that Bacchus and any other slave I may acquire would live as good a life as possible under the circumstances and that I would never break up a family if I had to sell any of them.

Mr. Laurens entered the room. "Please forgive me for my rudeness in making you wait. I had a messenger that came here with news of my ship *Friendship*, which is sailing out of Plymouth, England. The letter contains news of my friends Jean Louis Gibert and Pierre Moragne from the Parish of Saint Avid du Tizac. They and 168 other Huguenots made their way from France to Plymouth where I had a ship waiting to bring them to Charles Town. They left the first time in August of 1763 but were driven back to England by severe Atlantic storms. So you can see why I am concerned. They have suffered enough. This time they were resupplied and left England on the twenty-second of February and all is well. They are due to arrive here next month, in April, around the fourteenth if the sea god is nice to us. Thank you for your patience."

"Not at all," I replied. "I wish them Godspeed from now on." I wanted to ask him what he wished to speak to me about, but I thought he would tell me when he was ready. He walked over to the fireplace and picked out a long-stemmed clay pipe, loaded it with locally grown and cured tobacco, and lit it with a long slender stick from the fireplace. Mr. Bee poured him a libation and we all sat down.

It was getting dark and there was an occasional clickety-clack of a two horse and buggy passing or the clomp-clomp of a horse and rider. There were people walking on the street after supper talking about the day's events and greeting neighbors.

Mr. Laurens started, "I will not keep you waiting any longer. I know you would like to get on with our business, especially after your voyage, which I hope was satisfactory."

I replied, "Yes, in every way. Captain Worley was a true gentleman and perfect host. I feel that I have made my first friend in my new world; then I added, thank you for your generosity for giving me a manservant. I have named him Bacchus."

Mr. Laurens replied, "Ah, the god of festivities; he was around three thousand years ago and they are still celebrating him in Italy and Greece today. Good choice, I see you know your mythology. Your man Bacchus was born in Charles Town. His mother and father lived and worked on my plantation called "Mepkin" about twenty-five miles up the Cooper River. They were drowned when their boat capsized while seining for shrimp, fish, and crabs in the brackish waters of the rice paddies. He was anxious to see the big city so I brought him here. We go home occasionally but I am saving my three-thousand-acre Mepkin for retirement in a few years. I bought it for only eight thousand pounds from John Colleton in 1762, but his ancestors built it in 1681. I keep about thirty slaves on Mepkin and it pays for itself in rice and cotton. Bacchus is very intelligent and polite. He will make you a good servant."

"Now, the reason I needed to see you tonight. I have made arrangements for you to live in a large house at 11 Church Street. You go out the front piazza door and turn left and go to the third house before Church Street ends. There is a carriage house and the street is bricked. You will have to cross a bridge at Water Street. The mansion is furnished and you should be comfortable there. It belonged to one of my sea captains. He was lost at sea and his family moved back to Gloucester, Massachusetts to be near his relatives. You may move in tonight. I have left eight more slaves there who are accustomed to care for the head of the household. They are expecting you. From your home, you come back toward town for five blocks just past the Huguenot Church and almost across the street from the Dock Street Theater on the corner of Church Street and Dock Street is a building suited for your medical practice. What you did not bring with you, I will see that you have an account at the medical supply store."

"I think you will like the area in which you will be working. I need to warn you that there is a tavern behind you that is painted pink with a red light that caters to sailors, but just a block up the street is Saint Philip's Church where this parish got its name and records are kept there. You may want to visit them and enter your name on the Parish rolls. It is the oldest congregation in the city and has been there since 1680. It is an Episcopal church and well respected by the Community. Charles Town is called The Holy City because it has more churches than taverns, and there is a law that no building may ever be built taller than the highest church steeple."

"You will want to take advantage of the Dock Street Theater's productions. At age thirteen I saw the The "*Recruiting Officer*" there which was the first play produced in America. During horse racing season, there are many gatherings there and at the Planter's Hotel. They make a delightful punch called "Planter's

Punch." It has quite a kick and it is delicious. I am sure you will want to take advantage of Charles Town social events. We have dances and socials at the Customs House and private residences some of the wealthy rice planters call Summer Cottages in which they live during the summer to enjoy the sea breeze and avoid malaria. These 'cottages' are huge mansions and some parties go on for days."

"You are most generous and kind, sir. What have I done to deserve such fortune to befall upon me?" I asked.

Mr. Laurens replied, "It is what you are going to do for me. God has seen fit to endow me with a good mind for business and politics. In return, I have promised that I would use my money to tend to the cause of freedom for my Huguenot church family. I have witnessed the torture others have inflicted upon them. I have seen eyes put out with hot irons, women put on the rack and shamed like dogs, men skinned alive and worse, all to drive Satan out of them because they are not practicing Catholics. I have written to the Vatican about this, but the church stands firm and is determined to stamp out this threat to their religion. As I said, I now have the resources and clout to do something about it, and I intend to keep my promise to God no matter what it takes. Since you have given me your word as a gentleman that you will assist me in any way, and since you are from France and you know the persecution inflicted upon my relatives and friends. You were recommended to me by my detectives and many people who knew you in France and Hamelin. As an army surgeon and properly trained doctor with war experience, you have no equal, and after much searching and prayer, I know that you are the man for the job."

I was completely taken aback. I did not know how to respond. I heard myself say, "I pray that I may live up to your expectations, sir. Exactly what will be my duties other that keeping them healthy?"

"You will work with Mr. Gibert and Mr. Moragne when they get to Charles Town. You will plan to care for them and get to know them all. They will be put up in houses around town and will eventually, later this year, move two hundred miles up the Savannah River on the South Carolina side to a place designated by King George as Hillsborough. I have acquired over twenty-eight thousand acres in land grants to establish a township there. Rev. Gibert has plans to create a settlement named New Bordeaux. He will move there with about two hundred other Huguenots. They will bring grapevines from their homeland in France and also silkworms and other seed. Once established, they will plant other cash crops as the soil will bear. I have requested a four-hundred acre grant for you just across Long Cane Creek about a mile from New Bordeaux. There are hostile Indians there who are not happy that the white man is taking their land. You will be needed as a doctor, a leader, and I will get you a position as Justice of the Peace for Charles Town and Granville Districts. You may want to study up on the laws both there and here concerning property including slaves. I expect you to stay with the settlers as long as necessary. When they are settled and living independently, your responsibilities will cease, but by then you should be independently wealthy. You may repay me by using some of your wealth to help someone else."

"This is a daunting task. I will try my best to serve you and the Huguenots," I said.

"I know you will. That will be all for tonight, unless you have any questions."

I replied, "Not at this time. I must get home and get settled. You are a remarkable man sir, and I look forward to a long association with you."

"You are too kind, sir. If you do all that is expected, you will have earned every shilling. There are no coincidences, only divine appointments. Good night, go in peace and may God watch over you."

Hendrick, Bacchus, and I stepped into the carriage. It was dark now and the carriage had running candle lights lit for our short journey to my new home.

I arrived at 11 Church Street to a large white house. It is a Georgian structure that is two rooms wide and two rooms deep on each floor with a center hallway and a stairwell. As usual, the parlor was on the second floor to avoid the dust and noise of the street. I found out later that my house is what the locals call a "double house." Most of the houses in Charles Town are "single houses." These houses are built with the gabled end facing the street, and are one room wide and two rooms deep on each floor. The doorway leading to the street opens onto a porch or "piazza." The entrance to the house is in the center of the porch. Charles Town piazzas are always on the south or west of the house, to provide protection from the hot afternoon sun, and to provide cool, cross-ventilation from the prevailing southwesterly breezes when the windows and doors are left open.

As we came onto the piazza, I noticed by the candle chandelier that the roof of the porch was blue. I commented that it was a pretty color and Bacchus told me that most of the piazzas in Charles Town were painted blue to ward off evil spirits. He said, "Ain't no haints commin in dis heah place wid dat blue ruff."

I found out that there were many superstitions in town, especially practiced among the slave population. Why even the Congregational Church had been built round because it was thought evil spirits and demons hid in dark corners. The church is even called "The Circular Congregational Church." It was built in 1680 and has the oldest grave in the city.

I walked past the piazza door to the front door of the house and opened it. As I entered there were eight well-dressed servants to greet me. They lived in the slave quarters in back of the house where the kitchen was located. It was separate from the house the house so if it caught fire, the main house would not burn down. Between the slave quarters and the kitchen were whistle ways. They were usually brick or stone-lined paths. They were called "whistle ways" because some owners had their slaves whistle as they brought food to the supper table to show that they were not eating the food. The slaves ate in the kitchen. The house was furnished in beautiful walnut or oak furniture made right here in town. The wood was plentiful and Charles Town furniture was being shipped all over the world. Silk-lined sofas and huge rocking chairs near the fireplaces. *What a beautiful home*, I thought as I turned to the servants.

"What are your names?" I asked.

They looked at each other in shock. Masters hardly spoke to the slaves except to give orders.

Bacchus spoke up. "Hits awrite, Docter de la Howe won't do use no harm." Then he looked at me and said, "Days ben told dat youse gwanta gibum new names, suh. Day is anxus fer to see what youse gawnna nam'um."

"Let's see now, I have started a theme of mythology so I will name the men who will be working with me and leave the women and children with their present names. I think it would be confusing to change the children's names. The first three men will be Pluto, Cato, and Hercules. What are the other names Bacchus?"

Bacchus answered, "Deese two boys er named Carolina and Jack. Dis heah winch lady name Matilda and deese two girl cherin name Molly en Cecilia."

I said, "Welcome to my family. I am looking forward to a relationship that, I hope will last for many years." Again the slaves looked at each other in amazement. I said, "You all know your jobs and as long as you do it, I will not interfere. Now, please bring my bags to the master bedroom and Mr. Seles's things to his room and Bacchus, you will also have a room adjoining mine so that you may attend to me whenever I need you. Bacchus, you are to have charge of the help and make sure that they know proper protocol at parties and when I have dinner guests."

"Yes sur, Docter, I surely will." Now, let's go upstairs and git you settled for to go to bed."

Having said that, I continued upstairs followed by Bacchus and Hendrick. The bed was a beautifully hand carved four-poster bed with oval-shaped tips on the top ends of the posts. I asked Bacchus what these carvings represented.

He told me in his Gullah dialect, "See dees carvins, day is rice stawlks, and de ends of de shoot is de rice shucks. Dis heah be called a rice bed."

I noticed that the canopy was held in place by four knobs that looked like pineapples. Bacchus said, "Dees cones have tips on um en when youse has compny, en day dun stay too long, youse tun de cones upside down as a polite way of lettin' yo compny kno dat day dun stayed too long."

I laughed and told Bacchus that that was funny. He said, "No sur, dats de truf, anyhow, Dats how youse kin tel a rich man from a po man, a rich man has a canopy over his-on bed, en a po main has one under his-on bed."

It took a second for that to sink in and I smiled. Then I was concerned about the liberty Bacchus had taken by telling me this vulgar joke that is passed from slave to slave, but then I was happy that Bacchus was taking me at my word, and he is accepting me and I of him as one of the family. I am sure that Bacchus is feeling out his boundaries and watching my reaction. I am looking forward to a long and happy association with Bacchus. I am sure he would not display any such notion or actions in mixed company.

I let Bacchus know that I would bathe each night before I went to bed. I explained that as a doctor I deal with blood and disease every day, and I prefer to bathe and shave before eating supper and going to bed. I also told him that I may be entertaining also and that was another reason for me to cleanse myself and dress before supper. Bacchus assured me that he would have the tub filled with heated water when I got home. We always have plenty of water because Charles Town has about forty-five inches of rain per year, and we keep clean barrels under the copper down spouts to catch rainwater. The oldest water is used for bathing and cleaning and the freshest water is used for drinking and cooking. In dry months, some people will not bathe or they will go down to the salt water's edge and bathe and rinse off with fresh water. In really dry times, water is ferried from where the Cooper turns into the Santee River before it turns brackish and then into salt water as it flows down the Cooper River.

As Bacchus readied me for my first night in my new home, I got into the soft feather bed. The mattress was held off the floor by ropes used as slats. These ropes would slacken somewhat during the week so Bacchus would tighten them up when needed. Now I know from where the term "sleep tight" comes from. Bacchus covered me with a homemade patch quilt and asked me if I were comfortable. I said that I was fine and that I would see him in the morning. Bacchus lowered the chandelier and snuffed out the candles, and I blew out the bedside candle and said my evening devotions. Bacchus went into the other room where Hendrick was and helped him into bed. Then Bacchus closed my door and then closed his door, and I drifted off to sleep thankful for my good fortune and comfortable surroundings.

At daylight the next morning, Bacchus peeped into my bedroom to see if I were awake. I said, "Good morning, Bacchus."

He answered, "Mawning, sur," as he went to the closet which he had set up for me the night before. "Whut's yo pleasure fo to dress?"

I told him that I was going to start teaching him how to communicate. I asked him to try saying "Sir, how would you prefer to be dressed today." It would be necessary to ask me that every morning because there will be different occasions for different dress. Today, I will wear some of my best clothes to go down town to see my new office. You never get another chance to make a first impression and in today's society, a first impression is all important.

I doubt that I will have any patients, but I am sure that it will not be too long. If I am to accompany Mr. Gibert to the backcountry, it will take ten days to get there and I will have to stay until I am sure that their needs are taken care of, so I will probably need an assistant to work with me. Thank goodness for Hendrick.

Bacchus said, "Sir, how does you prefer to dress today?" I said that his language was better but we still need to work on it. I took a blue suit out of the closet. I put on a white frilly shirt and blue pantaloons with white stockings and black buckled shoes. The blue frock was covered in gold fleur-de-lis. I had a close brimmed hat and a white wig drawn to a curl in the rear.

I crossed the hallway to the dining room where the aroma of fresh cooked ham and bacon filled the room. I see that the slaves had already gone to the market and bought our daily supplies, cooked breakfast and had it waiting on me. Hendrick was already sitting at the table. I sat down, said a blessing, and took a fresh hot biscuit and spread butter on it and tasted it. I asked, "Who made these delicious biscuits, Bacchus?"

He smiled and said, "Matilda, sir. She done lernt from her mammy how ta cook." I noticed how he pronounced "Sir." It was perfect. He must have practiced during the night. I instructed him to omit the "done" and the word was "learned" to cook from her "mother."

He answered, "Yes sir. Kin I drives you to de office?" to which I answered "Yes, you may drive me to my office." He understood what I was getting at.

After breakfast, I excused myself and went out onto the front porch to wait for Bacchus to bring up the carriage. Hendrick was with me, Hendrick said, "What an exciting day. We are in a new home and a beautiful new town starting a new career. Are you as excited as I am?"

Looking out of the piazza slightly to the left, I could see the mouth of the Cooper River where it came into the harbor. Just before the river was a beautiful park with live oak trees and oyster shells all around. People were taking their morning constitution around the walls that protected the gardens from high tide. I later learned that this was called "White Point Gardens" because of all the bleached oyster shells. The garden is located where the peninsular of Charles Town came to a point at the conversion of the Cooper and Ashley rivers. The original settlers had built a wall to protect Charles Town from Indians and others who may tend to do harm to the city and with the advent of independence in the air, there is no telling what may befall the city.

Bacchus rode up to the stepping stone on the street and we stepped into the carriage. We made our way down Church Street for five blocks to the corner of Mulatto Alley and Church Street. On our way, I could see the steeple of St. Michael's soaring 186 feet above the ground with a 7-1/2-foot weather vane. The clock can be seen on four sides; facing north, south, east and west. There are eight bells being installed that will mimic the sound of Big Ben in London. The clock face has hour hands only, but I am sure that someday they will add minute hands. Saint Michael's was built because St. Philip's has too many parishioners, and St. Michael's is built on the site of the first St. Philip's Church at the corner of Meeting and Broad streets. Meeting Street got its name from the Meeting House at the Congregational Church. It is called a Congregational Church because they welcome people of all faiths there so they come together as a congregation.

We rode past Broad Street when I saw the Dock Street Theater on my left about a half block before the French Huguenot Church ahead on the right and dead ahead standing in the middle of the street was Saint Philip's Church. The carriage pulled up to a blue three-story building at #5 Saint Phillip Street. The street entrance has glass windows and a sign hanging outside that said "Doctor John de la Howe, Practice of Physick." I walked inside and saw chairs in a waiting area. Down the hall, there were rooms on each side of the hallway for treatment and past that was a room that used to be a dining room and a side door that led to Mulatto Alley. Outside the door I observed the house next to my office. It was a small three-story building with one room on each floor. This was the Pink House Mr. Laurens told me about. It had a red lantern over the door and smelled of old rum. I wondered how a client got out of the building if he was serviced on the top floor. The only escape is through the front door. He would have to climb over other clients engaged in whatever they were doing to get to the front door. I think that I will get some patients from this business.

Across the street to the right I saw a store with an anchor on it. I found out later from Mr. Laurens that it was called "The Pirate House." It was built about twenty years ago by a Huguenot merchant. It is made of Bermuda Stone. Mr. Laurens tells me that it is a place where pirates could trade with otherwise respectable citizens. In the early days, when the pirates aimed their privateering at the Spanish, the buccaneers and their free-spending were tolerated. However, the situation was changing because pirates were starting to turn their attention to the merchant ships of Charles Town. The most notorious pirate to prey on Charles Town was Stede Bonnet, the "Gentleman Pirate." In 1718, he and his crew were captured, hanged at White Point Gardens and buried below the low watermark in the marsh. Mr. Laurens said that his hanging went a long way to keeping pirates in line, but now things are getting bad again.

Mr. Laurens also told me that if you look at St. Philip's steeple, it is leaning a little to the right because of settling of the "pluff mud" upon which the church was built. Pluff mud is a result of millions of years of rotting vegetation and is so named by the slaves because when you throw a rock in it, it makes a "pluff" sound. It is all up and down the coast and at low tide has a very distinct odor.

Since the church steeple is distinguished by leaning to the right, ship captains will it use to steer their ships into the harbor. The church is also built on the highest point in the city. It is built on land that is eighteen feet above sea level. Mr. Laurens had also told me to be careful that my ears do not pop when I pass by the church.

Editor's note: On the next page is a 1764 map of the city of Charles Town. The square block in the center bottom of the map is the Customs House. One block to the right of the Customs House and one block up is where Dr. John de la Howe practiced medicine at the corner of Church Street and Mulatto Alley. Mulatto Alley is present day Chalmers Street. It is now a cobblestone which runs between Meeting Street and Church Streets one block north of Broad Street. The Customs House, which includes The Provost Dungeon, is at the foot of Broad Street. Broad Street is so named because it was the widest street in Charles Town. Two blocks to the left of the Customs house and one block up was the home of Dr. de la Howe. The area of the City where Dr. de la Howe worked was known as Ashley Landing.

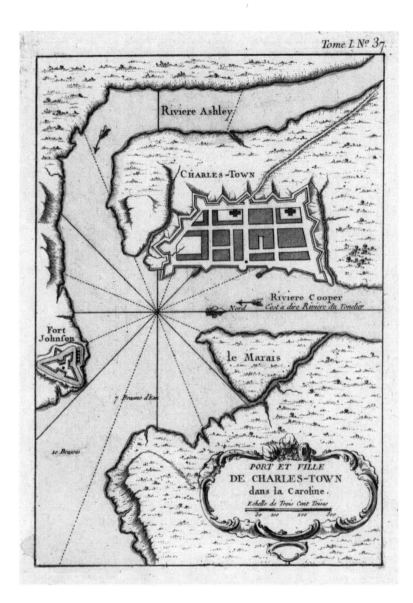

About that time, a wagon pulled up to the building. It was my supplies from the ship. Upon going back inside I found that Bacchus and Hendrick had begun to unpack my medical supplies.

Hendrick unpacked my small brass scales for dosing medicine and a pair of stilyards.

Hendrick then unpacked a small table to put them on and a round table for the brass scales and weights, three handsaws and two sieves, and a map of the Americas. They found my coffee roaster and a pewter chamber pot. They also found several bottles of oil and homemade salve, a tobacco box, some candle wicks, and four pounds of spice. Next were candle molds and a compass saw.

They then pulled out a couple of ink stands with ink bottles and feather pens. A walking cane that housed a sword, some linen sheets to cover the tables, a crosscut saw, and a froe. Bacchus asked me how I used a froe axe on a patient. I explained that the big saw was for cutting wood and the froe axe was used with a mallet to split the wood for use in the office. His mind was put at ease.

They unpacked a magnifying glass, lancets for bleeding and slicing abscesses, case scissors, boxes of knives and scalpels, a cleaver, red roots and a sieve, a box of files and other sharpening instruments, my old surveying instrument, several boxes of phials, and bottles of all shapes and colors.

Several boxes of gallipots which are bowls used to collect blood from bleeding and purging and to mix medicines. And there were many copper and tin canisters, copper kettles, boxes of medicines, and finally my beautiful and constant companions, my volumns of books. I have twenty volumes of Latin, sixty-eight volumes of French and Latin, seventy-nine volumes in English, and twenty-eight in German and French, and another whole trunk full of books and medical journals, all in different languages to put up on the shelves. There were other medical instruments that I will put in the back room for surgeries. I had special instruments designed to remove bullets and amputate limbs and all other medical necessities. I will have the best stocked medical practice in the city and certainly not many doctors will have the experience I have had because of the war.

Bacchus and Hendrick spent the rest of the day putting away instruments and stock while I arranged my big oak roll top desk. I started a list of the chemicals I would need and a list of charges for services rendered. That will assure there will be no confusion as to how much is due at the time of the service. I will let Hendrick handle the money so the clients will not become angry when I try to collect a bill.

Over the next few weeks, I grew accustomed to life in colonial Charles Town. Some folks are writing it as one word now—Charlestown. Mr. Laurens has spread the news about me and many of his friends have come to take advantage of my services. I am making a comfortable living and I often contemplate how much God has blessed me. Hendrick is working with me every day. He is very valuable to me because he sees that the infirmary is cleaned and the instruments are cleaned and laid out for the next day's adventures.

I am earning about £900 per year for my general practice, but when a ship comes into port I receive extra money from the government to treat those infirmed or to clear them of carrying contagious diseases. Most businessmen in the city will earn about £300 where a rice planter will pay each member of his family over £3000. Mr. Drayton, Mr. Middleton, Mr. Boone, Mr. Smythe, and several others have over a thousand slaves to work the rice paddies. I often make trips to the north, east, and west of Charlestown to the huge plantations to inspect or treat a slave for some illness. I am very well paid when I do this. Very often, I may spend a week at any one plantation. It is almost like visiting a city within itself. I admired the men who started with some land and built empires. I also admired the slaves that made their owners extremely wealthy of the sweat of their backs. I have heard of them getting beaten and whipped, but I haven't incurred much of this, only as a punishment for running away or learning to read or write or breaking some law. By in large, most owners keep their slaves healthy so they can make them money. They use them like tools or chattel. I often try to put myself in their place and I do not like what I feel. I know that it is legal and I am going to be appointed to be a Justice of the Peace and have to bring some of them to justice, but legal does not mean it is right. Now that the blacks outnumber the whites in this state, they have made the laws stricter. There are certain restrictions as to when a slave may appear on the street.

In 1739, there was a slave revolt in Stono, South Carolina just west of Charlestown. These rebels ransacked farms and an armory killing whites at random. The colonial militia put an end to the rebellion before they could get to Florida which is a free state.

Then in 1740, South Carolina passed the comprehensive "Negro Act," making it illegal for slaves to move abroad, assemble in groups, raise food, earn money, and learn to read English. Owners are permitted to kill rebellious slaves if necessary. That same year, Georgia and South Carolina attempt to invade Florida in retaliation for the territory's policy toward runaways. And in 1750, George II repeals the 1705 Virginia act by which slaves were deemed real estate. By 1758, Pennsylvania Quakers forbid their members from owning slaves or participating in the slave trade and now they can join the military with their master's permission.

The trend seems to be moving in their favor. I think, not in my lifetime, but eventually the slaves will be freed or sent back to Africa, but then those born over here would not survive in Africa and if they are freed they have neither property nor education, so what is the solution. For right now, I must abide by the laws that govern this society. I must weigh all the facts and try to come to an honorable decision. I still think that no one but God has the right to put another human being to death, but I will try each case on its own merit.

Today is Saturday April 14, 1764, and this is the day we have been anticipating for these past few weeks. The *Friendship* arrives after a seven-week voyage of hardships and danger, and I must be on the docks to greet them and inspect them for immigration.

On board were 112 males and 61 females. Mr. Laurens sent a messenger saying that they were here and I am to meet him at Adger's Wharf. I must certify that they are free of disease and then they will be quarantined for some time until they make the trip to the backcountry. I will join them after they get set up and settled to attend to their needs.

Since the season was far too advanced for the immigrants to get to their new homes and set up their farms and make a crop, the governor and council has decided to send them to Fort Littleton, near Beaufort, for four months where they could plant corn, potatoes, pumpkins, peas in order to survive the winter. In addition to what they could grow, they would be given a daily ration of a pound of flour and a quart of corn, and for their meat, a steer a week was promised. They were allowed to choose three of their number who would be provided with horses and a guide, to select land for their settlement.

I asked Hendrick to close the shop and go with me to the ship. I am sure I will need his help.

As I walked down the dock, there were curious onlookers standing on deck. They knew the routine. Then I spotted a very familiar face. It was Captain Charles Worley. He had been employed to bring the Huguenots to the new country. I came to the gangplank and Captain Worley greeted me with a big smile and said, "It is so nice to see you in good health my friend. I hope you are getting accustomed to life in the low-country."

I was glad to see a friendly face among those who would eventually become my neighbors, but for right now, they were strangers and patients. Mr. Laurens was already on board. Even though he was supposed to wait until the passengers were certified safe, he knew he was powerful enough not to worry about such things.

I then asked permission to come aboard which was granted by Captain Worley. No one could leave the ship until I certified the ship to be free of disease. Every passenger and crew member was now in my hands and I had complete authority. I started examining each of the 168 passengers. It took all day and up into the night. I checked for fever, skin markings, vomiting, and any other thing out of the ordinary. Everyone was still reeling from an epidemic of Yellow Fever that decimated Philadelphia. This way the Huguenot leaders could carry on with their plans and still not come into contact with anyone else. I made this very clear to all concerned. I let them know that I would check them daily and if all goes well in a month or so, I would let them go.

Mr. Laurens invited me to the captain's cabin along with Rev. Gibert and Pierre Moragne. After formal introductions and pleasantries, we all sat down with Mr. Laurens in the center of the room. We took pipes and tobacco and lit them, and a slave came in with some wine. Mr. Laurens reiterated about the land grant from King George and told us that King George is anxious for the new world to be settled by people beholding to him. He expects great wealth to come out of the Americas. The goods already shipped to England have been very profitable to the crown and he wants more.

Mr. Laurens pulled out a map of South Carolina to show us the routes available to Hillsborough.

Hillsborough Township is just below "Ft. Charlotte" on the map.

"Gentlemen, as you can see there are two ways of getting to our new township. You can take the Charlestown to Fort Moore trail, and find local trails forty miles further to Hillsborough. I would think that the Charlestown to Fort Charlotte would be the best route since it goes right past where Hillsborough will be located. New Bordeaux will be just a few miles south of Fort Charlotte. There will be a store in Ft. Charlotte where you can purchase supplies and obtain protection from the Indians in the area. I suspect that by May you will return with your guide, Patrick Calhoun, and in July you will be packed up and ready to travel with wagons to carry your baggage and tools. Most of you will leave from Charles Town. Governor Boone has gone back to England, but Governor Bull is very sympathetic to our cause and will send minute directions to Calhoun for purchasing provisions and surveying the town. Governor Bull is the one who named Hillsborough after The Earl of Hillsborough who was a member of the Board of Trade, and New Bordeaux he named for the city "from whence many of them came." By August, you will be settled in your new territory. "If Dr. de la Howe will approve this plan, we can get started."

I advised him that the plan would be satisfactory if Rev. Gibert would give me his word as a gentleman that no one from his party will ever leave the compound for any reason without my permission. Mr. Laurens told me he could do better than that; he said that he personally would give me his word and stand behind Rev. Gibert and Moragne. That is how much he thought of them.

Mr. Laurens told them to use their time wisely to get prepared for their trip. New Bordeaux was two hundred miles northwest of Charlestown and in good weather and traveling conditions, it would take a minimum of ten days. Once established, they would not be able to prevail upon Mr. Laurens for further assistance. They would be on their own. Once they got there, they would have to locate and lay out the township and assign lots for the immigrants to start building homes using the materials supplied by nature. There is a young man named Mr. Peter Gillibeau traveling with the Huguenots who is an expert carpenter and cabin builder so the Huguenots will have to draw upon his expertise to get the job done.

Upon establishing a plan for the town, they will have to each begin planting their crops. Mr. Laurens told them that he will try to get a "silk bounty" bill through the legislature to finance the production of silk in the upcountry.

He instructed, "Until then, keep growing the silk worms and soon they will pay off. Plant your vineyards and harvest your grapes. I hope your vines will produce wine like you had in Abbeville and Bordeaux because if you do, people will be knocking down your door to purchase the wine.

I know it will be a trying time, but at least you will not have people hunting you down to torture you because of your religion. Here in America, all religions are tolerated, even encouraged. I would like to invite you to come to the Huguenot Church on Church Street as soon as you are free of quarantine. When and if you come, be prepared to stay the day. Many Huguenots have settled on French Quarter Creek about twenty miles up the Cooper River, and they will come to church on the outgoing tide. Once they get to the church, they will preach until the next flood tide to take them home which makes for a very long service."

We sat talking and getting to know each other when Mr. Laurens told me that a friend of my family is coming to Charlestown soon. He said that a young man that I knew was in his employ and he would be here next month. I asked who he was speaking of, and Mr. Laurens told me it was John Lewis Gervais. I said that I knew his family back in Hameln in Hanover and that when I last saw him he was about fourteen or fifteen years of age. Mr. Laurens told me that he had grown up into a fine and ambitious young man from a wealthy family.

I told him that our families were close friends since the late 1600s. Mr. Laurens said that he is about twenty-two years old now and had close ties to King George I, who was a Hanoverian who ascended to the English throne in 1715. He had left Hameln and traveled to England and left Portsmouth in May and is due here on Thursday, June 28, 1764. Mr. Laurens said that Mr. Gervais is also a Huguenot, but he will not be joining the Hillsboro Company. He will be traveling with Mr. Theodore Russell, and they will enter into a business partnership with me. With my help, he has acquired 5,350 acres in the Granville District not too far from Hillsboro and has an option for another 5,000 acres if everything works out for him. He will have to maintain a close tie to Charlestown for many years but he indicated that he plans to build a plantation near the Hillsboro and name it "Herrenhousen."

"That is wonderful," I said. "I will have to visit him once we are all settled. I will come and welcome him to Charlestown if you will let me know when his ship gets into port. We will have a good visit to catch up on family news."

Leaving the company of the Hugenots and Mr. Laurens, I began my journey home. My relationship with all my newfound friends continued for months to come. The practice kept me busy, and meeting with both the local gentry and working class prepared me well for my judgeship. With every available opportunity taken to study the law, I now felt well versed on the subject. Bacchus was excelling in his English lessons, and Hendrick was of great assistance in helping me with my duties. Another month went by.

Finally, on Thursday June 28, 1764, Mr. Laurens sent word to me that Mr. Gervais would be docking today at the wharf. Hurrying to meet the ship, I was very happy a friend from home was coming to our new world.

As the ship eased alongside the dock, a handsome young man I knew as a boy emerged waving in my direction. He recognized me right away. "Dr. Jean, Dr. Jean, how good it is to see you. Please come aboard while I collect my things!" he yelled. I waited for the gangplank to be lowered and started up the plank when Jean ran to greet me. He gave me a big, strong hug and laughed. "How are you and how do you like Charles Town?" he asked.

"I am doing very well, thank you. How are you?"

"My father and mother send you warm greetings and said to tell you that they miss you very much. Come aboard and sit with me while I get my things."

"Will you dine with me tonight?" I asked.

"Most assuredly, we can help each other. You can tell me about Charles Town, and I can tell you about home. Mr. Laurens has granted me a few days to get settled and to spend time with you before I start my duties with him, but I have plans to move to the site of my plantation and establish it right away. I hope you will visit me there."

"I will be coming to the New Bordeaux settlement from time to time and will be looking forward to a visit with you," I told John Lewis. "It will be a pleasure to introduce you to my assistant, Hendrick, and my man Baccuhus. We will have dinner and afterward take a stroll to White Point Gardens then down East Bay Street and back to Church Street. I am sure this will provide an excellent opportunity to introduce you to many of my neighbors, friends, and clients along the way."

After a three-day visit with me and touring the city, John Lewis said, "The time has come that I must direct my attention toward my business with Mr. Laurens."

"I quite understand," I replied. "I bid you a fond farewell, and I will see you as our busy schedules permit."

Monday morning, the ninth of July, as I enjoyed breakfast in the dining room Bacchus appeared. With worry in his voice he said, "Mr. Hendrick look lack he be ailin this mawnin. You best check on um.

Not overly concerned I went to Hendrick's room and found him lying in bed looking feverish. "Hendrick," I asked, "are you not feeling well?"

"No, Doctor Jean, I am experiencing fever, chills and a general achiness over my whole body. I tended some people on a ship from Philadelphia about ten days ago which I suspected of having yellow fever. I now seem to be experiencing the same symptoms."

The conventional treatment consisted largely of supportive therapy with bland diet, cool fluids, rest, and perhaps mild stimulants or a dose of Peruvian bark. Often, a grain of calomel, with or without a grain of the vegetable laxative jalap, this is what I prescribed. I explained that if the fever got better for two or three days and then relapsed that we were in danger. In severe perhaps typical cases, hemorrhagic phenomena are prominent, especially nosebleeds, ecchymoses (bruising), and gingival and gastrointestinal bleeding. (Another common name for the yellow fever at this time was the "black vomit.") Jaundice is usually present during the second phase of the disease. That's where "Yellow Fever" comes from. Myocarditis (inflammation of the heart muscle) with shock is a particularly lethal complication, but other organ failure syndromes contribute to the mortality, which varies greatly from one epidemic to another.

After a few days, Hendrick appeared to get better and I was praying that this disease had run its course, however, he turned yellow and started vomiting blood. I knew that we were in trouble. I remembered reading a manuscript written in 1744 by Dr. John Mitchell of Urbana, Virginia, detailing his experiences with yellow fever from 1737 to 1742. Dr. Mitchell's account included autopsy reports. Mitchell was greatly impressed by the gastrointestinal hemorrhage present in the fatal cases, which he attributed to vascular spasms. He recommended purging and bloodletting as an effective treatment. I immediately adopted these therapeutic suggestions with some moderation, but I feel that it is too late to save my friend.

I preferred frequent and small, to large bleedings in the beginning, but toward the height and close of the disease, I saw no inconvenience from the loss of a pint and even twenty ounces of blood at a time. I drew from Hendrick seventy and eighty ounces in five days, and sometimes a much larger quantity. In the end, we both knew what the outcome would be. Hendrick thanked me for our friendship and told me that he was sorry that he did not get a chance to pay me the money and charity that I afforded him. He told me to take his meager belongings asked to see a priest. With a smile I let him know that he had paid me back with something more precious that gold. How can you put a price on true loyalty and friendship? I was holding his hand on Friday, the thirteenth of July 1764 when he went to his reward. My heart was broken.

I said a prayer on his behalf and I thanked God for his companionship and praised God because now his suffering was over. I was sure that I would see him someday on the other side.

The next day, I went to the register of St. Andrews Parish and informed them that Hendrick had passed away and for them to please issue a notice in their next edition coming out Sunday the fifteenth so all of his friends and mine would know what happened.

I returned home that Sunday after bidding my friend farewell and wept over the loss of my friend. I arose Monday morning, and I realized that I had patients to attend to. I went to the office and hung a sign saying that the office would be closed for ten days due to a death in the family. I really did not intend to close the office for ten days, but I knew the incubation period for the fever is about six days and if, at the end of ten days I had no symptoms, I knew that I would be disease free. I informed no one what had happened. I feared widespread panic and since this was an isolated case and the ship that carried the fever was gone, I thought it best to wait and see. I made sure that I stayed at home over the next ten days and read and mourned. I also instructed Bacchus to inform any visitors that I was indisposed and to come back in a week. At the time, no one knew how the disease spread or what caused the fever only that over almost 80 percent of the patients died. I kept a close watch on my servants and let only Bacchus into the house for the next week. Eventually, I could see that Hendrick was an isolated case. Thank God, and that soon all would return to normal.

On Monday, July 30th I returned to my practice. There were well-wishers all along the drive to my office. Hendrick had made many friends and helped me treat many clients. He was liked and admired by everyone he touched and he touched everyone he knew. He will be missed.

I took Bacchus with me to clean the office and to gather up Hendricks's belongings, what little there was. I gave Hendricks's clothes to the slaves in my house to divide between them as they saw fit.

ANN AND FAIRBANKS

It is now a year since the passing of Hendrick. It is the summer of 1765 and my life was carrying on, and the Huguenots are getting settled in their new home in Hillsborough Township. I suspect that I will have to go to visit sometimes. I heard the tinkle of the front door bell. In came a statuesque lady apparently of quality. She was not stunning, but she was very pretty and maybe a couple of years younger than me.

"May I see Dr. de la Howe?" she asked.

"I am Dr. John de la Howe," I said and bowed. "Welcome to my establishment."

She said, "My name is Mrs. Ann Walker Boyd. I live on Fairbanks Plantation on Daniel's Island and I must get help for my slave, Marcus, before the tide turns so I may get home. My sister has a home in town, but I really need to get home tonight with my load of supplies."

"I am pleased to make your acquaintance, my lady. I shall do all within my power to help you." I noticed that she carried herself very well and seemed to be quite intelligent and sure of herself. She had a nice body from what I could see that was not concealed under that bustle.

"My slave Marcus has been hurt. He was getting out of the carriage to open my door when the carriage rolled forward and ran over his foot. He is one of my field hands and he mans the helm when we sail to Charles Town. I will need him well for the harvest coming up."

"Let me take a look." I asked Bacchus to help Marcus out of the carriage and into the side door in one of the treatment rooms. I asked Bacchus to have Marcus take off his shoe. Mrs. Boyd told me that she was glad to catch me in because her home was four miles up the Cooper and two miles further up the Wando River from Charlestown, and they needed to get back before the tide changed and the slave was needed to stow the food. I asked her if Marcus was to do the paddling, and she replied the she had other arrangements for that.

I asked her to have a seat in the waiting room not knowing if she had a weak constitution or not. I entered the room and Marcus and Bacchus were giggling and talking. I found out that Bacchus sat Marcus down and as Mrs. Boyd and I were talking, Bacchus went and got the froe axe and told the poor slave that I was going to chop his foot off, but right in the middle, Bacchus broke down laughing and Marcus was so relieved that he started laughing too. Bacchus had washed the foot and had it drying on a towel by the time I got there. I told Bacchus that it couldn't be that bad for them to be laughing over the matter. Bacchus told me that his fellow slaves had a special bond amongst them, and they did not have much of a chance to socialize much less laugh occasionally. Bacchus said that Marcus will go back to the plantation and tell the others what happened with the froe and everyone will laugh, and this slave will be popular for a long time. For years, the story will circulate among the slaves on the island, and they will ask him why he used his foot as a chock for the carriage in the first place.

I examined the foot and observed that it was cut fairly deep because the steel rim of the wheel caught the side of the foot. I knew that I would have to sew the wound closed to stop the bleeding. I asked Marcus if he needed any pain relief, and he did not know what I was talking about. I told him that I had some powder made from the opium poppy that caused the pain to go away for a while. He said that he would try it so he could get back to work sooner. I mixed up some opiates with some water and had him drink it. As I let him sit for about a half hour so the opium would take effect, I joined Mrs. Boyd in the parlor and explained that I would have to stitch the wound and that it would take another hour before I was through. She asked me if my man Bacchus could drive her to her sister's house after we were through. I assured her that I would do anything to help her in her present crisis.

Back in the treatment room I doused the wound with sulfur powder, got a curved needle and sewed the wound closed. I wrapped the foot, and Bacchus helped Marcus into the carriage. Since I did not trust the narcotics to wear off anytime soon, I was concerned that Mrs. Boyd might wind up in the middle of the ocean if she let Marcus steer the boat. I advised her accordingly with the recommendation that she not try to return home tonight. Mrs. Boyd asked me how much she owed me, and I said the price would be to allow me and Bacchus to escort her to her sister's house.

"I really could not impose," she said. I told her that she was my last patient for the day, and I would be pleased to drive her home. She finally agreed.

I sent Bacchus to hitch up the carriage. I would drive her carriage and Bacchus would drive mine to her sister's house on Meeting Street only two blocks from mine. As we were driving, I asked her if I could send a message to her husband so he would not be worried. She said that her husband had passed away a few months ago. She said that he was sick in June of 1764. Not knowing if she would be able to run Fairbanks he placed an ad in the paper without her knowledge. She took out a copy and showed it to me. I read,

> To be Lett, by the year or on lease, the plantation on Daniel's Island lately belonging to Capt. Thomas Walker, deceased, being in a most delightful situation, bluff upon

> Wando-River only 6 miles from Charles Town, and very
> convenient for the market; on it are a very good dwelling
> house, with all necessary out houses, a good flock of cattle,
> and a great number of soville and China orange trees with
> quinoa, apple, peach, and other fruit trees.

She explained, "He also advertised for a lease of his other plantation near Cainhoy of 520 acres. It was listed by my husband Robert and he and his business partner, Mr. Edward Martin. He died soon after that and I have refused all offers, and I will never sell it or lease it," she said.

I apologized and asked her to please forgive me for bringing it up. She said that it was not uncomfortable for her to talk about it. She told me that I could get a general idea of what the plantation was like by the AD in the gazette.

I mentioned that I had not traveled up the Wando River as of yet and was looking forward to doing so in the future. Perhaps it would also serve as an opportunity to see her plantation. She smiled and said that it just so happens that having a social this weekend with her neighbors; the Lesesne's who owns the plantation to the south of Fairbanks and that I would be welcome to attend. I would have a chance to meet her family and Elizabeth, her two-year-old daughter and her pride and joy. She said that she has a sailing sloop that belonged to her father waiting at the North Adger's wharf and that I could sail to the island with her and her older sister Elizabeth and her husband Isaac Lesesne Jr. Ann's sister Elizabeth was her daughter's namesake. I thought that this would be a good thing because townsfolk would see that we were properly chaperoned, and there was a strange feeling taking place in my heart. I asked her what time and she told me that they would sail at 8:00 a.m. I agreed to meet her at that time. I tried to hide my excitement, but I feel that she sensed my new found enthusiasm and lust for life. I thanked her for her invitation and told her that I would love to attend.

As we drove down Meeting Street, we passed the home of Mr. James Simmons at 37 Meeting Street. He was standing in the front yard and waved and said, "Hello there Dr. de la Howe, how are you this fine day?" He bowed to Mrs. Boyd and said, "Hello, Ann. How is you beautiful daughter?" Ann nodded her head and waved thinking it unladylike to raise her voice while riding in her carriage. The beautiful house had piazzas on each side of the house and Mr. Simmons had them closed in for privacy. The locals call the house "The Bosom House" because of the protruding round facades enclosing the piazzas.

I am aware that Ann knows this, but I would not dare bring it to light. It would be considered rude and crass.

I waved and said, "Good day, sir," as we rode on to Ann's sister's house.

Ann asked me if I knew the local legend about the "Bosom House?"

I was shocked as she gently but confidently smiled as I said that I did not know of any such legend. She told me that the locals swear that Stede Bonnet buried treasure in the backyard of the house before he was hung and Mr. Simmons has found holes dug in his yard overnight. I told Ann that some people will always believe that where there is smoke, there is fire. If there is a rumor, there must be something to it. How do these rumors get started anyway? She told me that Charles Town was a very old and proud city that reveled in its superstitions. Every one of any statue has its own ghost in their house. It adds charm and position to the gentry and it gives them something to talk about. Ann asked me "Do you really believe pirates would bury treasure and not divide it and spend it?"

I agreed with her but said that people will always think of scenarios where the pirates have no choice but to bury treasure and it is just waiting there to be found. "It gives them hope," I said. About that time we reached the house.

I parked the carriage in front of the house and Bacchus helped her slave Marcus to the slave quarters. As I extended my arm as a support to help her out of the carriage to the buggy stepping stone, Ann asked me if I would stay for dinner, to which I replied that I would not dare impose on her sister and her family by having a surprise guest for dinner. As she got out of the carriage, she took my arm and I politely escorted her to her front door. I thanked her for the invitation, bowed like a gentleman should and she curtseyed. I got into my carriage and told Bacchus to drive on. As we pulled away I had the strongest urge to look back. I did and as I did, I saw that she was looking at me. She waved as did I and I knew that we shared a special bond.

As I was eating dinner, I thought of how forward and maybe rude it must seem to Ann that I agreed to see her this weekend. We live in such a polite and proper society. Most ladies would not address a man unless they have been properly introduced and presented by a trusted friend, but then I realized that we were two mature adults with more experience than most and it did not seem improper to me to seek her company under the circumstances. I was looking forward to our gathering tomorrow.

I should have asked her if I needed to bring any of my sevants to help, but then I figured that she had probably planned this for weeks, and I am sure that she has slaves if she owns a plantation. I also knew that the plantation owners in the area did not get into town so much for social gatherings. The plantation owners have many social gatherings, tea party, dances, and other events as a means to catch up on all the news and local gossip and to meet suitable suitors for their daughters and proper young ladies for their sons.

I called Bacchus into the room from his room. I advised him that we were going to Daniel's Island up the Wando River tomorrow morning and that we would probably be gone until Sunday evening. I let him know that I would require both traveling and formal attire for this trip. I suspect there will be waltzing and chamber music, and I planned to tour the plantation with Ann. Bacchus smiled and said, "Yes sur, Ise er, I am glad to see you takin an interest in da ladies. You bin too busy wid der doctorin and da war befo dat and all, to git busy wid da courtin."

I saw a twinkle in his eye. I knew he knew me better than any man alive, and he knew something was in the air. I complemented him on his better English. I knew without a proper education and his Gullah up-bringing that he would always speak with the "dis (this), dat (that), dees (these), and does (those) as most Charlestonians who have been nursed by their black mammies do speak in this town. It is an accepted practice and an endearing one to the locals. When traveling to other cities, you can always tell a native Charlestonian by his accent. They will speak to each other this way unless they are making a proper speech or in the Halls of Parliament where they will speak very clearly. They know how, but choose not to when in casual conversation.

Bacchus repeated, "Yes sur, I'm gonna fix you sometin spcial. Who knows that I might have two to care fo soon."

I reminded him of the old adage about putting the horse before the cart, but he just grinned that knowing smile and left the room.

I called the house servant, Cato in and inquired as to Matilda's whereabouts. Cato answered, "En da kichen suh."

I rose from the table and told Cato that he may clear the table, and I walked out the back door down the whistle way into a brick building where all the cooking was done. Matilda was sitting at the table eating with the other slaves who were not busy chopping wood or taking care of the cooking fire that was busy almost twenty-four hours a day or the others who busied themselves with caring for the house and grounds. I left the assignment of chores up to Bacchus. She rose up from the table, folded her hands together, and rested them in front of her and bowed her head. She looked frightened as if I had caught her in something but I quickly put her mind at ease.

"Hello, Matilda I enjoyed the dinner you prepared tonight. Thank you for doing such a splendid job." I told her that I was going away for the weekend and that I would like her to prepare lunch for the short cruise up river tomorrow.

She curtsied and said, "Yes suh."

I noticed that Hercules, whose country name was Sam, seemed to always be in her company. Matilda is young and very pretty, and Sam was strapping, well built, and ruggedly handsome. Could I have the first romance among my slaves? It seemed to me that romance was affecting everyone. Hercules would have to come to me to get permission to court and marry, or as they put it, "Jump the broom," together. I would depend upon Bacchus to guide me in such matters.

"Good mawnin, Doctor," Bacchus said as he pulled the drapes open to let the daylight in that filled the room. I stretched and yawned, and Bacchus said that he had everything packed and ready to go and that I needed to get up and have breakfast because I needed to be at the dock by 8:00 a.m. Acknowledging that he was right as usual and I got up and got dressed. As I sat down to eat I asked about the fresh fruit that was placed on the table. Cato told me that Bacchus had gotten up before dawn and took Matilda and the boys to the market and returned before I got up.

We lived together as one big family, but in the back of our minds, there was that knowledge of that fine distinction of class between master and slave. Neither they nor I could never forget that. I often wondered how I would feel if I were captured and taken to Africa and sold to an African family as a slave. I took very little comfort knowing that other African tribes would raid a village and enslave others of their own kind and sell them to white men. If white men did not buy them, there would be no trade. Many countries and some states have outlawed the trade of slaves or they have bills on the books that they will vote on soon. I do not see this happening in South Carolina any time soon. There is just too much money to be made off the backs of slaves, and those with the most money wield the most power. It suffices me now to be content to live the life God has predestined for me and just to be thankful for the blessings bestowed upon me.

I was about finished with my breakfast when Matilda entered the room with a sweetgrass basket that she had made. The sweetgrass is imported from Africa because it will not grow here in the marsh. The basket was filled with fried chicken, pork chops, fresh fruit, and bread and linen napkins, silverware and everything to make me and Bacchus comfortable in our crossing. I thanked her for her effort and went outside. Bacchus had the carriage waiting with Plato to drive the carriage home from the pier. I stepped into the carriage with Pluto's help, he climbed on the driver's seat with Bacchus and we were off for the weekend.

We arrived at the pier and there was a beautiful black single mast sloop. Ann was already on board and said, "Good Morning Doctor, how are you today? Come aboard and stow your things. We will be at Fairbanks in about two hours or so depending on the wind and tides."

I smiled and I was happy to notice that she was just as pretty and amiable in the morning as she was when I last left her.

I crossed over the plank and stepped down the stairs to the deck of the boat. Bacchus and Pluto handed the basket of food and trunks of clothes to the slaves on board and then

Bacchus climbed aboard and sat near the bow to be available if I needed him.

Ann introduced me to her older sister Elizabeth and her husband Isaac Lesesne Jr. He bowed and she curtseyed. I bowed and told them that I was happy to make their acquaintance.

Ann shouted out, "Heave ho! the bow and stern lines." She took the helm and then she said, "Lower the mainsail."

I was pleasantly surprised to think that a lady would be steering the sloop much less act as its captain. Elizabeth told me that their father was a sea captain and so was Ann's former husband. They were raised on the water all their lives. Their father Thomas Walker and his brother John had purchased the 245-acre plantation in 1732 and had worked it since then. Since the only practical way to Charles Town was by water, they both learned to sail at an early age. They would sail down the Wando to Cainhoy or up the Cooper River to other plantations to attend outings such as the one they are having this weekend. The brothers worked the plantation which did well. Thomas was a mariner and John a planter. Thomas got the idea to become a chandler of the marine industry and John took care of the planting. When they were clearing land, Thomas noted the huge Spanish moss covered live oak trees which abounded on the plantations. She told me that her father knew about manufacturing masts from the English oaks but that he was impressed at the quality and strength of the live oaks. He manufactured a mast of live oak and found it superior, so he started manufacturing spars and masts off the wood from the cleared fields. He built a good clientele. She said that they had nine slaves working in the sawmill and the fields of indigo, as well as growing vegetables to eat.

Isaac then said that his father was already on the island when the Walkers moved there. His father, Isaac Sr., died in 1736 and bequeathed Elizabeth and Ann's father "one mourning gold ring" as a memento of their lasting friendship. He inherited the land from his father. He said that he and Elizabeth had fallen in love and had married in 1743. He said that they had a four-year-old son, Thomas, who was waiting for them at home along with Ann's daughter Elizabeth. They will be anxious to see what we brought them from the mainland.

Isaac told me that his wife Elizabeth maintained a house in Charlestown because she liked the city life and seldom visited the plantation. He described Elizabeth and Ann as polar opposites. Ann dearly loved the island life and he doubted that she would ever live anywhere else. Ann was born in Fairbanks and married Captain Boyd in 1761. She had his child the next year as he was out to sea, and the ship was lost with all hands. She remained at Fairbanks and seemed to withdraw until now. I am glad to see her getting out and socializing again. I inquired if he was aware his name in France would be *Le Sesne* which means "The Swan." He acknowledged and said that his ancestors must have been swan herders at some time. We laughed and said it would be like herding cats. They would have earned their names.

As he was talking, I watched Ann guiding the sloop; she was very comfortable in her position and I saw how happy she was sailing. She would occasionally look at me and smile. I walked over to her and told her that I was impressed by her ability to captain a ship. She laughed and said that it was as natural to her as walking. She was wearing what appeared to me as a pirate's wardrobe with trousers and a frilly shirt and buckled shoes. She had a scarf protecting her hairdo because she knew that she would not have time to redo it before the party. From my vantage point, I could see for the first time her striking figure. *What a beautiful woman.* I am a doctor, and I see all sorts of females from thin to fat and everything in between, but there was something about Ann that made her special. Her personality and her looks combined to really stir deep emotions within me, and I knew that I wanted to get closer to her; however, I mustn't be too hasty. There are proper protocols in our society.

It was a beautiful day as the harbor was fairly calm and the sea breeze was fresh. There were ships all over the harbor waiting a place to dock to take wares back to England. There were bags of rice on the docks along with bales of cotton, indigo, and lumber which had grown scarce in England, and all sorts of other goods waiting to be loaded and shipped. Ann was very skillful in navigating around these ships until we reached the mouth of the Wando River where the shipping lanes turned left to go up the Cooper and we turned right to go up the Wando.

I told Ann that I had packed a lunch if she was hungry but she explained there was no time for lunch. Ann told me to look ahead to the port and I could see her dock. The dock was a fairly large dock that could accommodate a large ship if that ship needed to install a new mast. Most of the time, the ship would pick up the mast or spar and take it to a shipyard, but in an emergency, it could be done right there. We passed some shallow sand bars, but Ann knew exactly how deep the water was at every part and guided us into the slip with confidence. There were slaves on the dock to off-load the supplies.

It was about noon and Ann suggested that we take a walk and eat the lunch I had prepared. I marveled that if I had known how much skill she had as a captain, that I would not have suggested that she wait until morning to take her wounded slave home.

"But then," she said, "I would have not had a chance to ask you to come with me."

Similing I realized her purpose for staying overnight in Charles Town. We walked down the dock to dry land.

Ann asked Elizabeth to check on her daughter Elizabeth and their son Thomas and that she would be back in time to get ready for the party. I requested that Bacchus take our things to the main house and unpack for the weekend. We walked off the pier onto the sandy water front and on to where the soil turned dark. This loamy soil was rich and I could tell that it was good for planting. I thought that the soil would be very sandy, but due to millions of years of vegetation layering the ground it was very deep in natural fertilizer. I was most impressed at the natural beauty of the island. Live oaks with long clumps of Spanish moss, pine trees, palmettos, lots of scrub oaks and other vegetation and just about every kind of hard wood you can imagine. I commented on the beauty of the live oaks, and Ann told me that there was a live oak tree on Johns Island just before you cross onto Wadmalaw Island that was owned by the Angel family that was three thousand years old. It had branches larger that most trees. She said that locals would cross the Ashley River like going to Savannah, the Wapoo River onto James Island, then cross the Stono River onto Johns Island and it was just off the main road. She said that we could get very close by sail boat if he wanted to go sometime. It is a site to behold. She also told me that Spanish Moss was not a parasite. It gets its nutriments from the air and rain and does not feed off the tree it is growing on.

"I imagine living on an island across the harbor would be difficult, particularity for obtaining supplies", I wondered aloud.

"Living on the island is wonderful! We have all we need on the island. We grow most all of our staples and we have cattle and a abundance of wildlife. There are raccoons, opossums, wild turkeys, fowl, and the ocean provides us with all the fish, shrimp, crabs, oysters and turtles we desire. Even fresh water can be found in amazing places. Salves will often quench their thirst by taking fish that has been filleted and cubed, placing it in a cloth and squeezing fresh water from it. Deer are so plentiful they almost become a nuisance at times. If a man lived on Daniel's Island , or anywhere in Charles Town for that matter, and starved he would be one sorry and lazy man indeed."

You are very well adapted to your surroundings," I said with a smile.

As we walked across a hand constructed bridge she looked down toward the mud and asked, "See those small holes in the mud? They are called key holes and if you dig them up you will find a clam. The little crabs running around on the sand and mud are called fiddler crabs. The ones with the giant claw are males. They are called fiddler crabs because when he meets another male or tries to impress a lady crab he will raise the big claw up and down like he is playing a fiddle."

"My, what a handsome fellow," I smiled as I picked one up for examination. "We humans sometimes play for our ladies also."

Ann laughed and said that they kept the beaches clean and they made good bait for sheepshead and spottail bass. I asked her what "sheepshead" are. She told me that they are fishes that feed among the rock on bivalves, barnacles, crabs and other shellfish. They get to about thirty inches and have rows of front teeth that crush their prey. Her eyes twinkled as she told me that when you fish for them, you must jerk the line just before they bite to catch them. They are so skillful at getting the fiddler off the hook that you will seldom feel them bite.

"I am sure I will learn more about island life as time goes by. Since most of my days are spent dealing with the work of a doctor I had not realized how much I was missing. There are not many doctors in Charles Town, therefore there isn't much spare time available to me. This time I am spending with you is delightful as well as educational," I told her as I let the poor fiddler crab go back to his burrow.

Ann explained, "The slaves come to the water's edge or up the creek just past the landing and seine for fish and shrimp. Others will catch blue crabs and collect oysters at low tide and that night we will have an oyster roast and gumbo boil. It is quite good."

I told her that I would have to bring my slave girl cook with me next time so she could learn some of the dishes.

Ann said that we should return in order to get ready for the party. As we crossed the little bridge, this time she held my hand until we got across and even a few yards further. Then she wrapped her arm around my elbow, and we walked arm-in-arm back to the plantation house.

There were several other boats of all sizes and shapes coming to the dock. Some came under sail and some river scows with several slave oarsmen. Most of them had on their country clothes and would head straight for the plantation house to prepare for the party.

As we walked into the house, a slave greeted us at the door and told Ann that Ms. 'lizabeth was in the parlor playing with some other children. I walked into the study room with her and there were several men standing around talking politics and business. All the gentlemen stopped talking and rose when Ann entered the room. Ann told the men to continue enjoying themselves and introduced me to the gentlemen. She then asked to be excused and went to the nursery, and I heard, "Mommy, mommy, you're home." Ann closed the door and went into the nursery.

I enjoyed talking to the gentlemen, most of whom were planters and some merchants from the city and surrounding areas. Most of the conversation was about King George and his tariffs and how the winds of America's independence might help our economy and stimulate us as a people. They were very upset with King George's Stamp Act. Britain was deeply in debt because of the Seven Years' War so Parliament passed a Stamp Act so that every piece of paper or document had to have a government stamp on it to make it legal. Newspapers, deeds, and even playing cards had to have the Stamp Act tax paid. The colonists were extremely upset because we were paying taxes without being represented in the government. The saying was "No taxation without representation." Most of the colonists believed that this would lead to our declaring our independence from England. There were about half for independence and half for the status quo which made for some lively discussion as more and more drinks were served.

After a while, Ann sneaked the door open and waved for me to come into the nursery. As I entered I immediately noticed a darling little girl in the middle of the room, playing with several other children.

Pointing toward the little girl Ann said, "That is my daughter Elizabeth and the little boy is my sister's son Thomas. Later I would like for you to meet Sarah Walker Lesesne. Sarah is my uncle John Walker's daughter. She married Isaac's brother Henry James in 1741, but she was widowed in 1752. She inherited her uncle's share of Fairbanks before my father died two years ago and father left the plantation to me. It is in litigation as we speak. It will be mine in a couple of years. Sarah, like Elizabeth, does not seem to care anything about running the plantation. I think that if it weren't for me, Fairbanks would shrivel up and die, but as long as I am alive, I will fight with all my strength to maintain my Fairbanks. I know it is small compared to some of the larger plantations, but it is just right for me. I have always loved Fairbanks and I always will. Now if you will excuse Elizabeth and me, we need to get ready for the ball." Ann reaches over and cuffs my arm with her hand and gave it a gentle squeeze and smiled. With that, she carried Elizabeth upstairs. The stairway divided half way up and one stairway went to the right for women and another went to the left for men.

Upstairs Bacchus was waiting with hot water. I bathed the dirt off me from today's outing with the fiddler crab, shaved and told Bacchus to get out my favorite indigo-colored suit with indigo pants and a white frilly shirt with lace cuffs. I put on a beautiful wig, white stockings and black shoes with gold buckles. I told Bacchus there was magic in the air.

He grinned—that toothy grin of his—and said that he was going outside to visit the other slaves who were also having a get together down the slave cabin row. Bacchus said that he wanted to find and talk to Marcus, the slave whose foot was run over by the carriage, and see if he was bragging about his expose yesterday. I told him that I would see him in the morning. Bacchus asked me if I wanted him here when the party was over to prepare me for bed and I told him not to bother and to have a good time.

I returned to the study where the men were smoking cigars and pipes, sipping their home made wine or whisky and chatting as they were solving all the world's situations. I joined them but my thoughts were of Ann. I knew that I was smitten.

Soon a well-dressed Negro came into the room and announced, "Dinner is served." I went into the dining room and there was a long oaken hand-carved table with several wide leaves in it. On the table were all sorts of food from shrimp to gumbo to steak to foul and desserts. We stood behind our chosen chair and waited for Ann to come into the room. The gentlemen knew that she was the host and that there would be no man to seat us, so they politely waited until Ann came into the room and stood behind her chair at the head of the table. The men then helped the ladies find their seats and then Ann sat down and then the gentlemen. Ann asked an attending preacher to ask the blessing, and we all waited for Ann to pass the first plate of food to the right. Then the feast began.

As we were finishing the meal, a quartet started playing chamber music. Some of the couples started to dance and I escorted Ann into the ball room and sat next to her at her right. Many ladies and gentlemen came by and greeted Ann and some engaged in small talk. Ann was always courteous and always presented me to those who did not know me. I had my usual hypochondriacs asking me all sorts of questions hoping for a cure, but I was polite and told them to come by my infirmary and I would diagnose their problems. As I was talking to one such person, I felt a tap on my shoulder. It was Ann.

She said, "Let me rescue you. You haven't asked me to dance, so I felt that I must ask you first. May I have this dance?"

I noticed that she was wearing a beautiful indigo-colored dress that showed off her ample bosoms and slender waist. She had on a wig with her hair in a beehive with beautiful mother-of-pearl combs in it. She was breathtaking. I smiled and told her that brilliant minds think alike. She did not understand until I pointed out that we were both wearing indigo and we matched.

I extended my left arm and she placed her right hand on mine, and we waltzed and we did the minuet. Being from France, I was doing the minuet since I was a child. I noticed the ensemble of musicians was playing a catchy but beautiful tune which I had not heard before. I asked one of the musicians and he told me it was a song from a twenty-year-old court musician in Salzburg named Wolfgang Mozart. I said that it was shear genius and I hoped to hear more of him.

Ann and I danced as much as we could. She was busy being the perfect host and trying to see me as much as possible. She only excused herself once to put little Elizabeth to bed and she came right back to me. We danced until about midnight when she said that she needed to attend to her guest and put the women to bed. She told me to stay up as long as I liked and socialize with the men. Most of the men were going to bed and only those who were heavily drinking were staying up. I decided that since Ann left, there was no enjoyment left for the evening so I retired to bed. The room was full of snoring men who would get up and leave in the morning. I thought it a fair trade to get a chance to get to know Ann, so I closed my eyes and my thoughts turned to Ann.

I woke up and most of the men had gone home. Downstairs Ann was in the nursery playing with Elizabeth. As I entered the room she said, "Good morning, Dr. Then she turned to her daughter and said, "Elizabeth, say good morning to my friend Dr. John." Elizabeth said in her childish voice something that resembled, "Morning, Dr. John." Ann asked me if I had breakfast.

I have not, would you be agreeable to joining me?" I asked. cooks were used to these socials and guests eating at all times of the day.

The cooks had large kettles over the fire that contained grits and the slave would keep it watered as it dried. The cook had ham and bacon and sausage and cooked eggs to order. There was sorghum syrup and biscuits and gravy and fish. I asked Ann if some folks actually ate fish for breakfast, and she said that "grits and grunt" was a favorite. I asked her if they grunted when they ate it. She laughed and told me that there were many species of grunt fish. They are of the snapper family but without teeth. They make a pig-like grunting sound when caught and in the wild they come up to each other and kiss with their lips. The most common grunt fish here is Whiting, Porgy, Spot, and Croker. The Porgy, Spot, and Croker are also called "Pan Fish." The slaves filet the fish if it is big enough. If it is not, they will fry it whole and serve it with grits and biscuits. Shrimp and grits is another favorite. It is good eating.

"I think I shall try some "grits n grunt" this morning. I noticed how fine the grit meal was ground and I asked her how they got the meal so fine? She said that they had a very smooth stone that reground the first grindings which makes the grits smooth and cooked with gravy is delicious. I agreed.

She apologized and said that she would not be able to accompany me to the city because they were about to start the indigo harvest and processing. I revealed that I was familiar with indigo from the way they grew it in France. She explained that one of the reasons for the party was so the other nearby planters could bring over their workers and everyone could all harvest quicker. This movement continues from plantation to plantation in this manner and everyone benefits.

She said, "We usually go to church on Sunday and we take or allow our slaves to go if they want to, but during harvest, we have a short time to reap that we work seven days a week. Indigo is the second leading cash and export crop in South Carolina behind only rice. I purchased the seed from Eliza Lucas Pinckney, a lady who owns a plantation on the Wappoo River. She had developed the plants and grew her first crop for seeds. We found that our soil is greatly suited for growing indigo. It makes a beautiful royal blue dye used in the clothing industry. We call it blue gold."

Ann accompanied us as Bacchus and I walked to the boat for the return trip to Charlestown, I looked in the adjoining fields and saw rows of slaves. Some were cutting the plants, some were bunching, some were drying, and some were bringing bundles into the shed to be cured like tobacco. They were rhythmically singing and working together. Some plantations process the dye, but it is usually shipped to England or other parts of America to be processed.

Ann hugged me and kissed me on the cheek and I stepped into the boat. She said that she had a good time and for me to come back when I could. Bacchus handed our gear to the slaves in the boat and we set sail for Charlestown. I watched Ann on the dock waving as we turned left into the Cooper River. Bacchus was talking to the slave whom I had sewn up his foot. They were laughing about him getting off working in the fields and when he got to Charlestown he was going to kiss that horse in the mouth. I heard Bacchus ask him if he ever kissed a horse in the mouth before, to which he replied, "No, but I always wanted to." They laughed and laughed and I had a hard time pretending that I did not hear them. I could hear the bells of Saint Philip's Church as we crossed the harbor. It was a beautiful day and I knew that my life would never be the same. I also knew that I would be very busy and I did not know when I would see Ann. Maybe when she visited her sister Elizabeth or maybe we would have a social. I was trying to reckon when I could see her again. I knew that I had feelings for her but I also knew that she had her life on her beloved Fairbanks and I had mine as a doctor. I hoped that someday I would care about a place as she cared about Fairbanks. I smiled as I thought of us wading in the creek and the fiddler crab and the fun we had at the dance. It was a new experience for me, one that I enjoyed, but I wondered if it would get mundane for me as the years passed. I am not an outdoors sort of fellow. I am a big city doctor and I need to remember that. We shall see.

BACK IN CHARLES TOWN

Another year has passed and it is now the summer of 1766. I will turn forty-nine years old this year and Ann turns forty. Ann and I have been able to see each other occasionally. She will send me a message when a boat comes from Daniel's Island to the city for supplies to meet her at her sister's house for supper or we may see a play at the Dock Street Theater or attend a social together. Town's people are getting accustomed to seeing us together and many are asking when we will get married. Ann and I have spoken of our feelings for each other but we have avoided the subject of marriage. I am so busy and she will never move from Fairbanks, and it seems we are at a stalemate, even though we have love for each other. I miss her very much and I am going to earnestly talk to her soon about marriage and see if it is too soon after the loss of her husband or whether I am ready to make concessions to spend time on Fairbanks as she would have to do to spend time with me in Charlestown.

I think that you could call me a bonafide Charlestonian now since last year's notice in the minutes of Saint Philip's Parish for 1765, when my name was published with a list of doctors practicing "Physick" in the parish.

Another beautiful day, it is Tuesday morning on July 1, 1766, and I am going to work. As I come outside my front door, I see a ghastly site. One of my carriage horses has been stabbed and cut. I attend to the horse but it soon died. What kind of coward would do such a thing? Were they trying to get to me? Bacchus has related to me rumors of me having an affair with my pretty winch slave girl Matilda, but I am completely innocent. I would not bring shame on Ann or my reputation by doing this nor would I as a gentleman. I am completely baffled. I will find out who did this and bring them to justice. I will send for the constable, and I will place an ad in the newspaper. I will not rest until I find out why someone would do this.

I arrived at the office and there were no patients waiting. I retrieved a piece of paper and wrote,

> Fifty Pounds Reward! Whereas in the night of the first or second of this month, some malevolent person did with a sharp cutting instrument, inflict a wound on a horse, the property of the subscriber, (and by marks of blood is supposed to be done before the house of his mansion in Church Street,) whereby the animal died within a few hours after. He hereby offers the above reward of fifty pounds currency to any person that will give such information or may bring the offender to justice, payable on conviction.
>
> John de la Howe

The article came out in the *South Carolina Gazette* on July 7 but I never got any clues. The constable told me it was probably street violence of which there had been a rash of lately and that he doubted that anyone will ever come forward.

I received a note from Ann expressing her condolences for the incident. She said that was another good reason for living on an island, everyone knew everyone's business and no one could have gotten away with such a dastardly deed. I don't know if she is making a general statement or hinting that I ought to move to Daniel's Island and live in Fairbanks with her and manage her plantation. I am definitely neither a farmer nor an overseer. I am a Doctor of Physick, properly trained and legitimate. I treat sick people and that is all I have ever done. My father and my grandfather were doctors. That is all I have ever done and it is hard for me to visualize doing anything else. There are so many "faith healers" and other "voodoo-type" doctors here. It seems that anyone who has a backwoods cure for anything may hang out a sign that proclaims him or her to be a doctor. A formally trained doctor must build a reputation in order to practice medicine. I have a good clientele built now and I am making a good income. Why should I sacrifice all this to live on an island? I love Ann and Elizabeth, but I would tire of island living very quickly.

Ann is coming to Charles Town today to spend the day with me this Saturday, and we are attending a charity ball at the Customs House tonight. We have a Huguenot sponsored club in Charles Town called "The Two-Bit Club" where the members agree to meet at a fellow Huguenot's tavern or some other place and contribute 15 pence (two bits). Back in 1737, for a few years, the money went to support his flagging business. Now the funds go to support local charities. Edward Rutledge, Arthur Middleton, and Thomas Heyward along with John Rutledge, Charles Pinckney, and Charles Cotesworth Pinckney have been laying the foundation to start a college in Charles Town that will teach Liberal Arts to our children. They are talking about a college that will teach both gentlemen and ladies. These are rich and powerful men, and I am sure that they will soon have their college and then the "Two-Bit" charity will support the college with scholarship money.

I still wondered how they came up with "bit." The British "pound" came from a system that based its value on a pound of silver. There are 20 shillings in a pound and 12 pence in a shilling and 240 pennies in a pound. I was told that if you took a Spanish gold-milled dollar and cut it into 8 pieces like a pie, each piece is called a "bit" of the whole coin. So, two bits would be a quarter of the dollar or equal to 15 pence of our money. Oh, well I have more important things to worry about, but it is fun to figure these things out.

Ann sent me a message that she had arrived at the public dock and that I she was going to her sister's house to visit and get ready for the social. My heart started pounding a little, and I realized that I wanted to be near her. I finished up with my last patient, and he was paying the bill when Bacchus come into the room and announced that he had the carriage ready to take me home and get ready for the ball. I thought to myself how much Bacchus meant to me and how often I wished that there was not that barrier between slave and slave owner. But, there was that social barrier and I would have to live with it.

I requested that Bacchus drive me to King Street instead of going straight home. On the corner of King and Broad streets, I stopped at a jeweler who had busied himself for the last month making me an engagement ring. It was gold mixed with platinum to make it white with a large marquis diamond setting. I am sure she is used to the nicer things in life and I do want to show her how much I care for her; however I do not want to be too garish. I love this setting because the engagement ring and the wedding ring interlocked within each other. It is a symbol of how I feel towards Ann, and I pray that we will have a happy married life if she accepts my proposal. We will work out the details of our living arrangement after she accepts my proposal. I have already sent word to Isaac Lesesne, her older brother-in-law, telling him of my plans and he and Elizabeth have given me their blessing.

We arrived home about 6:00 p.m., and it was still daylight outside. It was late summer and the days were longer. I told Bacchus that the days were longer because when things got hot, they expanded with the heat, so summer days were longer than the winter days. Bacchus smiled and told me that he had one better than that. He said that he was plowing corn with a mule one day and it was so hot that the corn started popping. The mule thought it was snowing and froze to death. I laughed from the backseat of the buggy and I know folks must have thought I was crazy. I was starting to realize how intelligent Bacchus really was. Since Hendrick had died, Bacchus has helped me in my practice. I do not have him attending people for fear of offending them by a slave touching a white person. Since the slave uprising in 1739, the laws have been made stricter for slaves because they outnumber the whites almost two to one in the city. A slave is not even allowed on the street unless accompanied by his master, and when a slave purchases something in the store or sells something at the Old Slave Market, the money will be laid on the counter as is the change so their hands will not touch. Being a doctor, I have learned that their bodies are exactly like ours and the same cures that work for us will also work for them. The only difference is the pigment in their skin, but I would never publically profess this because I would lose all of my business. Bacchus is even learning to read and cipher numbers on a daily basis, but I dare not formally teach him. If he asks me a question, I always try to answer it to the best of my ability. The more he knows, the better he will be able to run my household. There is much that goes on behind the scenes of which slave owners are not aware.

We arrive home and I go in for my bath. Cato, Pluto, and the boys; Carolina and Jack are preparing my bath, and Hercules is in the kitchen with Matilda. He is chopping wood and taking out the ashes, sharpening knives, taking her shopping and anything else he can think of to be near Matilda. It is too bad that we cannot have a double wedding.

As I was bathing, Bacchus asked me which suit I would like to wear this evening. I told him that it had to be special because this was going to be a special night. Bacchus smiled and asked me if I would keep him when Ann and I got married. I assured Bacchus that he would always have a home with me as long as either one of us lived and that I would never send him away. I realized that I did not think of him as a slave but more as a servant or a manservant in my employ. He was a constant companion and as good of a friend as I had in this place. I was feeling brotherly love for Bacchus, and I think he feels the same about me.

We picked out a red and gold coat with indigo pantaloons and white stockings and my black buckled shoes. I wore my usual wig which most men wore because they would shave their head to keep from getting head lice, but I was a doctor and had no such trouble. Bacchus shaved me with my straight razor which he would sharpen and hone on glass. I splashed on a dab of bay rum and scented powder, and I was ready for the ball.

Bacchus drove me to Elizabeth's house to pick up Ann. She came out onto the porch with an indigo dress with gold patterns and a frilly blouse that was low-cut. She had on a wig done up in large curls and lots of jewelry and around her neck were strands of pearls which her husband had purchased in foreign ports. She was gorgeous. She smiled when she saw how pleased I was and she spun around to model her evening wares for me. It was beautiful, but she did not have to worry about me. I was smitten.

Her man Marcus and I helped Ann into the carriage, and I got in on the other side and Marcus was folding her dress into the carriage. Ann told me that she was looking forward to tonight's festivities. Everyone will be there. I had prearranged for Bacchus to drive to White Point Gardens where, overlooking the Ashley River and Charles Town Harbor amongst the live oaks and Spanish moss, I asked Ann's hand in marriage. I wanted Ann to know that I was aware Spanish moss was emblematic of a weeping lady, but it was my hope that she would be weeping with a joyous heart over the prospect our joining together in marriage.

She said, "You honor me, sir. There will be no weeping of any kind tonight, just happiness; of course I will marry you Dr. de la Howe."

I placed the ring on her finger and kissed her. Bacchus slapped Marcus on the back and they laughed. We got back in the carriage and Bacchus said, "Well, go on den, mule!"

I wanted Ann to be able to announce our engagement to all of her friends and neighbors and show off her ring tonight at the party. In the back of my mind were some thoughts of how we were going to arrange our lives. Would she be an absentee landlord at Fairbanks or would she expect me to run the plantation for her? We would worry about these things later, but right now, I just wanted to enjoy the moment.

It was twilight when we pulled to the rear of the Customs House. It was actually the front facing the harbor, but since it was opposite Broad and East Bay Streets it seemed like the rear. The building probably has two fronts. I helped Ann down and Bacchus and Marcus drove off to wherever they would wait for the party to be over. I am sure that they had an entrance somewhere where the servers would sneak them some food.

As we walked to the entrance on East Bay Street Ann said, "How about an April wedding?" She said that it would be planting time at Fairbanks and things would be fairly slow, and we could come back here and have our wedding.

To which I replied, "That sounds like an excellent plan to me". Now she had a time frame to tell her friends so that they could clear their calendars for her special event.

We came to the entrance and there was a divided stairway so the ladies could walk up the right side and the gentlemen could walk up the left side, so the gentlemen would not be tempted to look at a lady's ankles, which would be vulgar at the time.

As we approached, we could hear the orchestra playing chamber music, waltzes, and minuets. There was already a good crowd and Ann started socializing as soon as we entered the wide doors. I could hear the squeals of young ladies as Ann would show then the ring, and they would talk of how she would plan the wedding. She was not sure whether to have the wedding at Fairbanks or at Saint Philip's Church where we both were members. We would decide that together at a later date.

Between Ann showing off her ring and telling others of our plans, we danced and socialized and had a great time. Ann was very sure of herself. She was fairly tomboyish, but she knew when to be a lady also. I suppose that you need to be somewhat of a tomboy to survive on a plantation in which the men have passed on and left the work to the girls. She was both an owner and an overseer. As I watched her, I admired her to think that she managed a 245-acre plantation and nine slaves and raised her daughter in that environment. I wondered how I would fit in with all that was going on. All I knew at that moment is that I wanted to be near her and love her.

Bacchus was still smiling as he pulled the carriage up to the stepping block. Marcus came running to help Ann into the carriage. I got in and Bacchus said, "Where we gwain?" I told him that we would take Mrs. Boyd home and then we would go home. We were entering a period of engagement, and the townspeople would be watching for any morsel of gossip they could find. We needed to be extremely careful and proper in our actions.

We arrived at Isaac and Elizabeth's house on Meeting Street and I walked Ann to the door. She told me that she wished that her daughter Elizabeth was awake so she could tell her the news. She decided she would tell her soon in her own way. She gave me a hug and a good night kiss and told me that she loved me and that everything will be all right. She must have an inkling of what has been on my mind. It hit me that I would be the child's stepfather. Would she call me "Father" or "Doctor," or what? This is another thing we will have to discuss as we spend more time together. It will feel strange to me to turn fifty years old and become a husband and a father all in one swoop. I am apprehensive but confident. Marcus got her wrap, her umbrella and her shawl and followed her into the house. I got into the carriage and Bacchus took me home.

In 1761, "The Bounty Act" was a direct result of the French and Indian War (1756–1759 in the colonies) and the Cherokee War (1760) in South Carolina. This act provided cash money to anyone who brought settlers to the up-country area of South Carolina to serve as a deterrent against future Indian attacks on the colony. This is the act which Mr. Laurens and the Huguenots took advantage. This act was due to expire in 1767 and as a result, there were thousands trying to take advantage and there were boatloads of immigrants that kept me busy. As the Huguenots were on my mind, I think I need to make a trip to the backcountry to see them and make sure they are all well. I do not know if they have a real doctor amongst them or not. There are some very influential people settling in the area. The Calhouns have moved from the low country, John Lewis Gervais, and several other families. There are new towns springing up all over and the country is growing. I should plan a visit soon. I will see Mr. Laurens about this.

As the time for our wedding approached, I was busy treating immigrants and billing the State of South Carolina for my services. I still had my house on Church Street, and Ann spent most of her time at Fairbanks. I would go to the island from time to time, but usually only on a Saturday. Ann said that I could have full use of her sloop, but I did not want to take advantage and besides there was always a boat from one of the plantations up river that would give me a ferry to Fairbanks. Almost everyone knew Ann, her father, and her husband. Especially those who owned plantations on the Cooper or Wando, they all worked together at planting and harvesting season.

MY WEDDING

The day is finally here. It is Thursday, April 23, 1767. Ann and I are to become husband and wife today. I will marry a whole family with a child and in-laws. I am not marring an individual, I am marrying a family. I am dressed in my finest as I head for Saint Philip's Church. Ann is probably already there with her family. Little Elizabeth will be her flower girl and ring bearer, and her sister Elizabeth and her cousin Sarah will act as her maids of honor. John Lewis Gervais is in town conducting business with Henry Laurens, and John has accepted my invitation to stand with me as did Mr. Laurens and Captain Charles "Chuck" Worley, whom I consider to be my best friend. There are three aisles in the church and a balcony for slaves, but the middle aisle is the only practical one to use for weddings. Bacchus and my other slaves will be there. They are like family to me, but I would not let on. Ann's slaves are in the balcony also and the mammy's are crying joyful tears. The rector is the Rev. Robert Smith who will perform the service. I will wait at the pulpit, which is a raised round box overlooking the audience who sits in numbered square closed-in pews. The more you give the church, the closer your family sits to the preacher's pulpit. Ann will come down the center aisle with

Isaac Lesesne to give her away. Little Elizabeth will be the ring bearer and will stand with Ann.

I tried not to make this into a large affair, but Ann has other plans. I will suffer her to do what she pleases and we will be just as married as anyone else. Ann asked that we spend the honeymoon at Fairbanks, but I told her that I still had patients to see on Friday and that we would spend Thursday night at my house and leave Friday afternoon to go to Fairbanks. She was satisfied with that. I am fifty years old, and Ann has been through this before so there are no unrealistic outlooks on our nuptials. We know what we want and what to expect out of our union. Love and companionship will do for now. It was a lovely service. The Rev. Robert Smith did a fine job. I hope Ann will have fond memories of this day for the rest of her life.

By 1751, the English colony of Charleston, South Carolina had outgrown the church of St. Philip's. The Colonial Assembly divided the parish and built St. Michael's with a large steeple to contain a ring of bells and a clock. The ring of eight bells with a tenor—the largest bell that weighed1945 lbs.—was cast in 1764 by Lester and Pack of London. The bells have specific names and musical tones.

Bell #	Weight	Musical Note	Name	Cast
Treble	509 lbs	E-flat	Seraphim	1764
Two	594 lbs	D	Cherubim	1764
Three	722 lbs	C	Thrones	1764
Four	768 lbs	B-Flat	Dominions	1764
Five	927 lbs	A-Flat	Virtues	1764
Six	1058 lbs	G	Raphael	1764
Seven	1359 lbs	F	Gabriel	1764
Tenor	1943 lbs	E-Flat	Michael	1764

They built St. Michael's Church on the corner of Broad Street and Meeting Street which was the original site of St. Philip's which is now at the end of Church Street. I know that Ann has told me several times that she hoped to be buried in St. Michael's Church yard where her parents are interred when it was her time to pass on. With the state capital, the post office, and city hall on the other three corners, this intersection is called "the Corners of Four Laws" since it has the national, state, city, and church governments represented. I am told they are not represented in this manner anywhere else in America.

We exited the church onto Church Street amongst a crowd of friends, patients, and acquaintances. Bacchus and Marcus were waiting on us in the carriage which was draped in white linen and someone (Bacchus, I am sure) tied some old shoes on the buggy bumper. The slaves hold to old traditions that shoes are to represent a fruitful marriage, but since I am to inherent a five-year-old, I have no such plans for children of my own. With the winds of war and the rigors of my job, I feel like it would be unfair to me, Ann and the child if we had any. Most of the upper class of Charlestonians have Mammy slaves or a white Nanny to raise their children. If I am too busy to spend time with my family, I will not bring a child into this world at this stage of my life. I also see a broom tied onto the carriage. This custom came from England and Scotland that when a couple would elope, they would "jump the broom," or over a branch of flowering broom (shrub) or a besom made of broom shrub. To picture a besom, think of a witches' broom. When the slaves perform their own ceremonies on the plantations, they will "jump the broom."

We get into the carriage and as our friends throw locally grown rice called "Carolina Gold" at us, we drive off to my and now our home.

We got out of the carriage and proceeded into the house. There, Matilda had a lunch prepared. I noticed Ann looking at Matilda as she scurried about, and I did not like what I saw.

Ann said, "Do you always permit slaves in the house?"

I said that I did not give it much thought. Ann told me that she has heard rumors of my relationship with my slaves and especially pretty little Matilda. I wondered if Ann was really concerned or just thinking of her own reputation. I replied that I was from France and most Frenchmen did not own slaves and that I was not privileged to the ways of this society, and I treated my slaves as I saw fit and that she could do the same with hers. "Let's please not argue our first day as husband and wife, especially about such trivial things."

She said that she would drop it for now but that she intended to run the household, and she asked me if I had any problem with that. I said that I did not, but I wondered in my mind what was going on. Had she heard something that I did not know about? Was she trying to establish her dominance so early in our relationship? I will not worry about that right now. This is supposed to be the happiest day of my life so far, but I have an eerie feeling. I asked Bacchus to have Matilda to go to the kitchen and remain there or in the slave quarters out of sight of Ms. Ann for a while. Bacchus left the room as Ann, Marcus, and Elizabeth came in. Marcus stood by the door and I helped Ann into her seat after Ann seated Elizabeth. We ate dinner served by the house servants and not Matilda. I usually tell Matilda how much I enjoyed her cooking but tonight I did not dare. I have a feeling that Ann might think there is something to the rumors of me and Matilda. Once someone believes such a thing, it is almost impossible to change their minds. I am hoping that Ann is brave enough to withstand the innuendos and maybe now that we are married, the rumors will stop. I pay no attention to such things. I know that I am innocent and so far, no one has confronted me with any questions about my integrity. Maybe if I scolded my slaves or beat them in public, such rumors would not exist; however, I will never mistreat any one much less the people with whom I live every day. They cannot be family by law, but they are an intrinsic part of my life.

SETTLING DOWN

Ann inquired if I would like to take a stroll after supper. I responded I would find a stroll with her most pleasurable. We finished our meal and sat and sipped wine. Elizabeth's mammy took her into Hendrick's old room to prepare her for bed. I heard mammy singing her to sleep as Ann closed the door and came in and sat down.

I looked at Ann and told her that she was very beautiful and that I was so proud of her at the wedding today. She smiled and said that she was glad that I was pleased. Then she said, "Let's go for that walk."

We went out of the front door and turned right, walked one block to White Point Gardens. There was a band stand about a hundred yards from the sea wall or battery. Sometimes, on Sunday afternoons, quartets, or other music groups would play chamber music for the locals. Live oaks with Spanish moss, wildlife, and fresh sea breezes filled the air. We sat on a bench facing the Ashley River and held hands. Ann said that she was sorry about the scene at the house, but that was the first time she saw Matilda. Ann told me that she was surprised by her beauty and charm and that the rumors came flooding back into her mind. She never believed the rumors, but just the appearance of a rich doctor living with a beautiful handmaiden, even a Negro, is cause for jealousy and gossip. Charles Town is a very cliquish society, and the women with their servants have little to do but to socialize and gossip. To a less powerful man or one that people do not have to depend upon to treat their illnesses and for someone whom they depend to save their children in epidemics would have been destroyed long ago. Fortunately, you are such a man and everyone is watching to see how we manage our affairs with you in town and me at Fairbanks. Ann told me that she promised to try to live with me as much as possible, but she did not want to give up Fairbanks.

I assured her that she did not have to give up anything and that her income from Fairbanks should be put in savings for Little Elizabeth. Elizabeth should always have Fairbanks in her future, and I hoped that she loved Fairbanks as much as her mother. I have no expectations of her part in our marriage except to love me and be my confidant and my companion. I think that it is as the preacher says that we should become one flesh and work together to face the world.

We walked back toward the house. I was apprehensive but anxious about my wedding night. I know that I am a doctor and as such, I have seen it all but now I was going to have to separate my profession from my personal feelings and try to love a body instead of examining it. I knew that I would have no trouble with that as far as Ann is concerned. I loved Ann with all my heart and tonight I would try my best to show her.

We got home and Bacchus had my bath ready. He did not say a word during my bath, but he had that knowing twinkle in his eye. He had several kinds of scented oil for my bath for me to pick out. I wanted tonight to be special. I entered my bedroom and Ann was waiting for me. She smiled and closed the door.

The next morning, we slept late and no one disturbed us. We got up and opened the curtains. Bacchus had readied breakfast in the dining room of fresh fruit, shrimp, and grits as a tribute to Ann. She was delighted and I hoped that she and Bacchus will grow close, but she was very standoffish as far as slaves are concerned. She was raised by a hard-nosed sea captain who stood no nonsense from plantation slaves. They were properties for him and his brother to work on their plantation. They were no more to them than tools or mules used to plow. You took care of them because they made you your money, but other than that, they were a separate culture in which you did not mix.

I was thinking that if I am going to move to Jacksonborough, I need to make plans now so I went to the newspaper—the *South Carolina & American General Gazette*—and wrote out an advertisement that came out on June 5, 1767, which read:

> The subscriber begs those indebted to him to excuse this public method of intreating them for immediate payment; his intending shortly to depart this province, and the absolute necessity this induces of previously satisfying his creditors, impatient of ulterior delay, do not allow him the choice of a more dilatory way.
>
> To put any accounts into other hands and to have them recovered in a more disagree-table [*sic*] way shall be a violence on his own mind; but unavoidable in as far as they shall not be paid by the fifteenth of July next. Those who have accounts against him as yet not given in, are desired to do it by that time.
>
> John de la Howe

I realized that Ann could be a bit possessive and might be jealous and because of the rumors and by us just beginning our married life, I think it would be best for all concerned if I had a housekeeper to help me in my business and to chaperone during examinations of young ladies. I do not think that Ann would appreciate her husband examining ladies of any sort without a lady nurse present just in case any question comes up or any more rumors are started. I waited until time for the next publication, and I wrote out this ad which came out in the July 17, 1767, issue of the gazette,

> The subscriber disappointed in what he expected from his former advertisements, gives this *last notice* that all accounts unpaid by the last day of July, shall without distinction shall be put in suit; which, however disagreeable it may be to him, cannot be avoided.
>
> He also again and again gives this public notice, that he will not be accountable for any debts whatsoever, unless contracted by himself personally, or by a written order from under his hand. John de la Howe

> ### WANTED
>
> An industrious housekeeper, chiefly to wait on young ladies and look after negros; a character will be required.
>
> Enquire of the printer

I noticed an advertisement in that same newspaper that ran from July 2 through 17, 1767, the gazette advertisement read,

> Rebecca Woodin,
>
> Removed from Meeting Street into a healthful and convenient house of Mr. Dandridge's on White-Point, at the foot of Dr. Murray's bridge, next to Mr. Morris the painter.
>
> Continues to teach young ladies, in the different branches of polite education—viz., reading English and French, writing and arithmetic, needle work, music and dancing by proper masters. And takes this method to return thanks for past favors, as well as to request a continuance of the public's encouragement and recommendations, flattering herself that she shall be able to give satisfaction to all who place their children under her care.
>
> N.B. She has room for House and Day Boarders.

Thomas Woodin,

Carver and cabinet-maker, teaches drawing in all its branches, at the same place; And has to sell, on the most reasonable terms, some curious mahogany work—viz., desks, and book cases with glass doors, ladies' divesting tables with all the necessary apparatus, Chinese bamboo tea tables, kitchen stands, etc., all London made.

I thought what a remarkable woman that must be to run a boarding school and be able to teach young people in all those subjects. I think I may go to look at Mr. Woodin's furniture and get a glimpse of what a woman of this stature looks like. She sounds intriguing, but I would be ill-advised to try to satisfy my curiosity for the present.

For the next year, we lived together as much as we could. She was away for much of the time during harvest season at Fairbanks, and I was very busy with my practice because of the "Bounty Acts" expiring. I was tending many immigrants for the state. Thanks to Mr. Laurens.

England has passed "The Townsend Act" and it has the colonies up in arms. The act taxes just about everything that we export, and we still have no voice in their parliament. Lord Townsend proposes to tax tea, paper, wine, glass, oil, and any other thing we manufacture or grow. Charles Town and Boston have already had a "tea party" where we boarded ships bound for England and threw the tea overboard in defiance of the new law. I fear war for independence is inevitable. There are a good many in the City of Charles Town who are loyal to the king; however, they are wealthy merchants who do not want to change the status quo. By in large, the country folk and the plantation owners are all for independence. I am neutral. I can exist in either economy, and I pray that I will never see such a damnable thing as war again.

I received a note from Mr. Laurens asking me if I would consider a trip to New Bordeaux to have a clinic for the Huguenots. I would take a large quantity of medicines and instruments and stay as long as needed to care for the settlers. Mr. Laurens told me that he would finance my trip and that he would pay for the treatment of the Huguenots. I was to keep a record of treatment and medicines that I dispensed and bring him the bill. *What a generous man.* Here he is blessing people whom he will never meet, and most of the patients will never know who has blessed them. He is one gentleman who practices what he preaches. He told me once that it is much harder to live a sermon than to preach one. I think of man's inhumanity to man in war and then I think of men like Mr. Laurens. It is an enigma that I will have to think about.

DISCOVERING PON PON
AND LETHE

It is a two-hundred-mile trip and we can make about twenty miles on a good day. I have some friends who live in Pon Pon on the Edisto River about twenty miles south of Charles Town. Originally, it was the Indian settlement of Pon Pon, the town of Jacksonborough took its name for John Jackson who was granted land along the Edisto River in 1701 and around 1735, it became a settlement. Mr. Isaac Hayne was married in 1765 in my parish, and I attended his wedding with Mr. Laurens. He lost both parents when very young, and was raised by his stepmother Mary Bee and her second husband James Donnom. From his father he inherited Hayne Hall, a 900-acre plantation in St. Bartholomew Parish, and twenty-three slaves. Hayne increased his holdings. In addition to Hayne Hall, owned Sycamore Plantation (600 acres) and Pearhill Plantation (700 acres), two settled plantations in St. Bartholomew; 5,875 acres scattered throughout the Carolina backcountry; 1,000 acres on the Turtle River in Georgia; town lots in Beaufort and Charleston; and one-half interest in iron works in York District. He was a member of the Bethel Presbyterian Church at Pon Pon and of the Charleston Library Society. He will make a good friend and a powerful ally. All this and he is only twenty-three years old.

The Edisto River is the most beautiful river that I have ever seen. It has "black" water. It is fresh water that runs to the sea but millions of years of compressed vegetation which gives the water a dark color. The river is teeming with fish and alligators, and the soil is perfect for farming, rice, and indigo production.

If I am to travel to New Bordeaux very often, I may look at some property in Jacksonborough. It is only a day's trek to Charles Town and will save me some time in my travels to the backcountry. I am also thinking that if war comes to America, I do not want to be caught in Charles Town.

I will take all of my men slaves for protection and company during the trip. There are some inns along the way, but mostly we will find a good spot to camp for the night.

What a trip! I passed by Pon Pon and spent the first night. We left there and took the trail into Walterboro and on up to Ft. Moore. Then we took the Ft. Moore to Ft. Charlotte trail into Hillsborough and to New Bordeaux. I did not make any arrangements because there is no mail service here yet but a few months ago, John Lewis Gervais, on one of his trips home from Charles Town, told everyone when I was likely to arrive. One of my slaves rode ahead to find Rev. Gibert to let him know that I was on the way and to provide lodging for me and six Negro slaves. Upon arriving at Hillsborough, a group of townspeople met us at the Indian fish dam on the Little River creek named Long Canes Creek. They were Rev. Gibert, Mr. Moragne, and a fellow named Rev. Pierre Boutiton. Rev. Boutiton told us to follow him to his home less than a mile away to a plateau that overlooked to Long Canes Creek. He lived on a 175-acre plantation adjoining other farms in the area. He ran a store for the locals and had wares shipped in every month. Rev. Boutiton is now sixty-one years old and he is the son-in-law of Rev. Jean Louis Gibert. Rev. Gibert was to be the leader of the Huguenot settlement, but he decided he could best serve the Huguenots by staying in Charles Town and lobbing for their welfare. Rev. Boutiton became the leader of the first settlers to the area. Rev. Boutiton has lined paths and fruit trees and six dwellings on his place. He had the store, an overseer's house, a kitchen situated right on the road for welcoming visitors, and three slave houses. He asked me to set up operations there because he had plenty of room and the slaves could double up. During the first night, we had supper together and made plans for me to see the settlers whom needed my services the most. After that, we would check others for diseases and finally see anyone else who had concerns. Pierre Moragne is now thirty-two years old and has made quite a name for himself. I enjoyed his company very much.

I worked a whole week tending the sick and ailing, and giving medicine and advice to others such as those ladies who were with child and children to make sure they were strong and healthy. Eventually, they would be needed to work the farms and plantations.

The difference between plantations and backcountry farms, as I see it, was economies of scale. Small backcountry farms had a small labor force and concentrated on subsistence farming, which means that most crops were produced for personal use; any surplus was used to trade for goods not produced on the farm. The economy of the plantations was based on a massive labor force and the ability to produce large quantities of cash crops. Most plantations used slave workers and concentrated on one major crop like cotton or rice and maybe one or two other crops like indigo, tobacco, or sugar cane.

I certified that there were no diseases with which to be concerned. After a week of hard work, I had time to somewhat explore the countryside. I fell in love with the area. Never had I seen such beauty. It was the fall of the year and the hardwoods were all the colors of the rainbow. The harvest was coming in and there was an air of excitement and thanksgiving. Rev. Boutiton took me on a tour of his property and told me that he was getting old and soon would move to the nearest city to retire. This was still the backcountry and one had to work to make it in this society. He offered the plantation to me at a very fair price and I asked him if he would give me an option for a year to see what happens in Charles Town. He agreed and I knew in my heart that this was the place I would live, develop, and grow old. I hate to make any decisions without the input of Ann so we will talk when I return.

I finished seeing all the patients that cared to be seen, and I spent the last day with Rev. Gibert and Mr. Moragne. We caught up on all that was going on with them. They had silkworms and trees started, grape vines that were cared for all the way from France near Abbeville who's residence have made some of the best wine in the world. Peter Gibert showed me a 1760 map of the layout of Hillsborough. It was a twenty-eight-thousand-acre square with New Bordeaux right in the middle. New Bordeaux was laid out in a square of 198 lots of a half-acre each; above it, on both sides of Long Canes Creek, a vineyard plot of forty-four, each four-acre lots. Below the town, were a common of 195 acres and a glebe of three hundred acres reserved for an Anglican minister. The farming fields and the vineyard were just to the north of the village. Just to the south and on the border of New Bordeaux was an Indian-built fish dam and across the river from the fish dam and New Bordeaux was Mr. Boutiton's 175-acre farm and store. It was a perfect place for me to live if anything happens in Charles Town like war with England or just to get away from it all. I am due a great deal of money from the state soon for treating the state's indentured servant immigrants, and I am thinking strongly about purchasing this property and the surrounding property to build my own plantation. I am pleased that Rev. Boutiton, persuaded by Rev. Gibert and I am sure Mr. Laurens had some input and gave me a year to consider the matter. I know they would like having a physician living in the area.

I thought of the hardships, the moral fiber, and intestinal fortitude of these frontiersmen and women. Mr. Pierre Moragne was kind enough to allow me to read some of his diary to try to understand what they went through. He wrote that in February 1765, after completion of the barracks, "I have begun to labor on my own land, on my own half-acre, and afterwards on my own four acres. The thirteenth of June, I finished planting corn and beans on all of the land which I had been able to prepare; being then very feeble, having only a little corn to eat, and being placed under the necessity of grinding it at an iron mill. Though we have not a sufficiency, yet, with the aid of God, we may always have enough to keep us from starving." I see that these are remarkable people determined to be living in a free society, one without religious persecution. All they had to do was to renounce their religion and they would have been well off; however, I deem that they would rather starve and die than give up their beliefs.

On the way back to Charles Town, I stopped over again at Pon Pon which is now called Jacksonborough. I visited with my friends and spent the night. The town is being laid out into lots and progress is all around me. I went for a ride into the laid out section of Jacksonborough. I met with Mr. Roger Peter Handasyde Hatrley who had his house for sale and I took an option on it. I paid him £1,760 cash money and mortgaged my nine slaves, all my plate household furniture, books and medicines, one chair, two tracts of land; one of four hundred acres on the Wateree and one on the Savannah Rivers, plus all of my real estate for £880 to be paid before October 26, 1770. That is how sure I am that I will have the money soon.

I value land more than any other possession. When we go to war with England, what will be our standard? Will it be gold or silver, or will be still use the pound or go to the dollar standard? Who knows? But land is forever. Once the deed is recorded in the official books, it is yours until you decide to sell it or give it away. The land has always been here and it never changes. It is in limited supply and as others buy up the land and it becomes scarce, it also appreciates in value. I have never owned land that the value went down and every piece of land I have ever owned has made me money. As long as I can afford it, land will be my future. I will invest in all the land I can get my hands on.

As soon as I return to Charles Town, I am going to see Mr. Laurens about the land grant he mentioned. I will try to get the four-hundred acre grant next to Rev. Boutiton's farm. I am looking forward to the coming year of 1768. It will be a year of life changing decisions that will affect me and my new family for the rest of our lives.

IN CHARLES TOWN (AGAIN)

It is a cold (for Charles Town) and windy day in January of 1768. I have been notified that I must report to the public treasurer, who had brought before the colonial government vouchers for payment of "public creditors" to me for medicines and attendance of Irish Protestants. These were shiploads of indentured servants imported under the Bounty Act of 1761 which expired the last day of 1767. After I received the check from the treasurer, I made a deposit at the bank and on the way I stopped to see Mr. Laurens to see about the progress of the land grant that he was handling for me through Mr. Jacob Valk who is a local prominent attorney who also works closely with Mr. Laurens. Jacob told me that the grant was coming along nicely and that they expected conformation around the middle of March. He also told me that the land would be situated along side of Rev. Boutiton's property in Long Canes just as I had requested, needless to say that I was overjoyed. I asked Mr. Valk to start proceedings for me to purchase Mr. Boutiton's property on Long Canes Creek. That will give me almost six hundred acres to start my plantation. I plan to become a planter and harvest indigo as my major crop. I already have slaves to work the land while I am in Charles Town practicing medicine. That way, I will have an income while getting established in the backcountry. I also told Mr. Laurens that I had need of about five more workers the next time one of his ships arrrrived. I informed him that they did not have to be of the Gullah tribe because I was going to be the first to try to grow Indigo in the backcountry the French way.

I have an opportunity to receive another four-hundred-acre grant on the Wateree River which is north of Mr. Lauren's Mepkin Plantation up the Cooper River. The Cooper branches about fifty miles upstream; the Santee goes to the left and the Wateree goes to the right. From Ann's plantation, we would just have to sail up river to get to this property. I heard about it from a patient who told me that they are trying to settle that region of South Carolina. If I get caught in Charles Town in the war and if they take over Fairbanks, we can always sail upriver to a plantation around Manning. If for some reason I do not use the property, I can always sell it. That property will be an investment and a hedge against any problems that may come because of or during conflict.

For the next few months, Ann and I have been dividing our time between Fairbanks and Church Street. I don't think that either of us will ever give up our independence and find a mutual place in which to live. I have been thinking about moving to Jacksonborough for several reasons. I would hope that Ann and I could make a go of it there. We would be close enough to the city to commute on the weekends, but it would be far enough from Fairbanks for Ann not to go home every weekend. It would really give our marriage a chance. Jacksonborough would be a good place to raise Elizabeth. It is in the country on the Edisto River where there is good fishing and plenty of good water to drink. We would live in a planned city with good schools and we would be away from the war when it comes. Another reason and probably the most important to me is the fact that I can come home from Charles Town and rest a night before traveling to my plantation at New Bordeaux. I will have slaves at all three places and running them will not be such a chore. I fully believe in investing my money and not just letting it sit, and besides I have seen what happens when war comes to town. People with influence have their property taken away as prizes of war and given to those who helped the winning side. I am all for America gaining her independence, but I am not sure that she has the power needed to accomplish this mission. The war is still years away, but now would be the time to prepare and try to fix it so I will retain my wealth.

All of 1768, Ann and I are working on loving each other and living together as husband and wife. There are still rumors of discord that abound by the Charles Town's gossips. I am afraid that it is taking its toll on Ann. There are rumors that I am making plans to leave Charles Town and my practice and walk. To "walk" is a term that is used when a couple had a bad relationship and fights all the time. When a man has had enough of discord, he simply walks out of her life and goes God knows where and starts over again. Those who walk are seldom found or ever heard of again. It is a terrible thing to do, but divorce is just out of the question unless the wife has been unfaithful and even then the church controls who can and cannot get a divorce. It just is not done.

Ann and I have been working hard on a loving relationship and we both are trying to make our marriage work. We have talked about Matilda, and Ann has asked me to get her out of our house on Church Street. Also, people are constantly asking me if I am still going to leave Charles Town. I may move to Jacksonborough, but I will maintain my practice here. There are just not enough patients in Saint Bartholomew's parish for me to make the kind of money that I am accustomed to, so on August 15, 1768, I wrote this ad and it came out in the South Carolina Gazette.

> John de la Howe offers a valuable trusty Negro wench,
> a good plain cook, and qualified for keeping a single

man's house. The subscriber, who has no use for her, not intending to leave this province, the town or even the house he livith in (as some malicious persons, amongst other things equally false, have spread about to answer their own purposes) will give one or two years credit, the purchaser paying interest, and giving approved security.

This will let everyone know that I am staying in town and I am hoping that I can lease out Matilda just to get her away from our family. I really do not want to sell her because I may need her at one of my other properties, and she already knows my likes and dislikes, and besides, she and Hercules (Sam) have a relationship and it would be rude and mean of me to break them up. If they were to "jump the broom" together and have children, it would add to their value to me. I do not like to think of it that way, but it is another argument to keep her in my possession. If something does not happen in the near future, I can always send her to live and work on my backcountry plantation. The people there would not be so unforgiving towards her and will have no knowledge of the rumors. The only trouble I would have is getting Ann to agree to move two hundred miles away from Fairbanks.

By October, Ann has consented to live with me in Jacksonborough. She will hire an overseer to run Fairbanks on Daniel's Island and besides with the Lesesne's owning the adjacent plantation; there will be plenty of family and slaves to keep the plantation profitable.

With the money that I received from mortgaging my property, I will purchase a house and there we will make a home and ride out the coming unpleasantness. If Ann and I will ever make it, the time that we spend here will determine our future.

Today is Thursday, October 26, 1769. The property in Jacksonborough became officially mine. Things at Fairbanks have been busy. It is harvesting time for the cotton and indigo. Ann has had her usual yearly ball and other plantation owners have come and brought their workers to participate in the harvest and then they will go to the next plantation and do it all again. There is just no other way to get the harvest in on time. By doing this, the plantation owners get to socialize and talk politics and get their crops in the barn ready for export. Ann is still suffering me to keep Matilda, but she sees the condemning way the other women look at her while talking and the men who smile when they are gathered smoking and passing gossip. I will take Matilda to Jacksonborough with us until I can take her to my backcountry plantation.

I will be moving to Jacksonborough soon. Things are heating up over the cause for Independence for America. Earlier this year, Samuel Adams and James Otis circulated a letter denouncing the king for the Townshend Act and sent it to each state assembly. John Hancock's ship *Lydia* was boarded and taken away because he is a rebel and is a member of "The Sons of Liberty" organization. Last May, a British warship arrived in Boston Harbor to protect threatened custom officials there. In July, the Massachusetts assembly was suspended for refusing to obey the crown and resend the circular that Adams and Otis wrote and by October, British troops had occupied Boston.

At socials and at my practice, people ask me of my opinion about whether we should go to war to claim our independence. I tell them that I have been to war and it is not a pleasant place to be. I hoped that we could settle our differences without a physical war, but I agree with John Adams who once wrote, "But what do we mean by the American Revolution? Do we mean the American war? The revolution was effected before the war commenced. The revolution was in the minds and hearts of the people." I am afraid that the tide of war is upon us and that we are in for a great turmoil for the next ten years. I am going to do all I can to have a minimum impact on it all.

I instructed Bacchus to gather up most of my belongings and have Marcus gather Miss Ann's things and Elizabeth's toys and other things and get enough wagons to take us to Jacksonborough.

I wanted to be living in Jacksonborough by Christmas. I will be commuting to Charles Town and staying during the week here at my Church Street address and working at my office near St. Philip's Church. Bacchus will remain with me wherever I go, and we will get another cook to take Matilda's place. Maybe now the rumors will stop. It is no one's business what I did with her. As far as anyone is concerned, she was sold by that ad I took in the gazette.

Today, Mr. Laurens came by my house and had with him six slaves that I asked him and John Lewis to find for me. They were born on Mepkin and worked for Mr. Laurens. Mr. Laurens asked me to accept them as a gift for caring for his friends and family at New Bordeaux. They will work here in Charles Town for a while and then we will go to my backcountry plantation. I must to come up with a name for the plantation. He had in the wagon newly arrived slaves from West Africa. He had six slaves—three young men, a boy of about seven, one woman, and one young girl. I named them Pompy, James, Brister, Charles Town who will be called Tam-O in the country, Felice, and Becky. I will keep Felice, Becky, Pompy, and Bacchus with me here in Charles Town and take the others to New Bordeaux. Ann will have Marcus and her maid slave with her in Jacksonborough and the seven of her other slaves on Fairbanks, and I will have eleven at New Bordeaux.

I was sitting by the fire one night when an epiphany hit me. I have struggled all of my adult life with war and the devastation it brings. I want to live in a place far away from any conflict and try to forget the past that haunts me with images that I cannot forget. I have flashbacks and nightmares of the fighting and cruelty of men on both sides. They think war allows them to become animals with no conscious. "Please God, let me forget and be at peace."

"Lethe!" That is what I will name my plantation. Lethe, it is the name I have been looking for, what a great name. It comes from Greek mythology. It is the personification of oblivion. Lethe was the daughter of Eris, the Greek goddess of chaos, strife, and discord. That is precisely what my life has been so far and it is going to get worse. One of the rivers that flows through Hades is named for Lethe and from which the souls of the dead had to drink to forget their past lives spent on earth. She is the Spirit of forgetfulness and that is exactly what I feel toward all this talk of war. I have been through seven years of war in France, and I want never again to work in those circumstances. I would love to drink of the waters of Lethe to be able to forget the agony and suffering of my fellow man. I became a doctor to comfort and heal the sick, not to put them back together after battle so they could go back and kill and maim and harm others. The first sentence in my Hippocratic Oath is "To do no harm." I would do harm in perpetuating war, but I have to heal the sick. How do you know what is right or wrong? I know another war is coming and I dread the future. I just want to be away from the war as far as I can get. I don't care who is right or wrong. No one is right in war. I will not take sides. I can survive in any scenario, whether the Americans win or the British. Just leave me out of it.

Events of destruction are all around us. An eleven-year-old boy named Christopher Seider was killed when a man named Ebenezer Richardson fired a gun trying to disperse a mob protesting the tax on tea in Boston. Later, another mob was fired upon by British troops who were sent there to protect British loyalists. Then a piece of ice struck Private Hugh Montgomery, who then slipped on the icy ground. He regained his footing and fired the first shot. The remaining British soldiers then unleashed a deadly volley. Eleven men were struck; three died instantly. One man would die within the hour, the other several days later. No shots were fired at the soldiers. The mob dispersed only when the governor promised an investigation.

This year of 1770 is the year that the College of Charles Town received its charter. It is the first municipal college in America and the first coed college. Mr. Rutledge and the other rich plantation owners will now have a place to send their children. Maybe, in a few years, Little Elizabeth will want to go there. Right now, she will live with Ann and me at Jacksonborough. I am fifty-three years old and Ann is forty-three and Elizabeth is now almost eight years old. Bacchus is about thirty-five to forty as close as we can tell with no records of slaves being born at Mepkin. We will get a private tutor for Elizabeth when we get to Jacksonborough.

For the next four years, I worked in Charles Town and lived in Jacksonborough. Bacchus stays with me wherever I go. Ann and Elizabeth seem to like Jacksonborough; however, they both go to Fairbanks as often as time will allow, especially at planting and harvesting time. They also visited Ann's sister, Elizabeth, in the city. We all love our weekend respites at Fairbanks Plantation. Marcus will meet us at the dock and we will sail across the harbor to Daniel's Island to enjoy a party and music and watching the slaves cutting indigo and harvesting other crops. Isaac tends to the lumber business and the Ship's Store is bringing in a steady income for Ann and Elizabeth. I love to go to the island and fish and watch fiddler crabs and use them to fish over the oyster banks and try to outsmart the Sheepshead. You really do have to yank your line just before they bite to hook them.

During the week, I would see patients at my office on Church Street, and Ann and I would go to local balls and theater productions. Sometimes we would all get into the carriage and go for a Sunday ride visiting neighboring plantations, but having to commute from Jacksonborough to Charles Town every week, the carriage rides get old.

I have an opportunity to go Lethe once in a while. I have been aggressively adding to my property there. I have purchased four hundred acres from Mr. Henry Marque who was the storekeeper of a store that was in the fork near French Mill. The locals sometimes called Long Canes Creek and Little River, French Mill Creek. His property joins mine and during a flu epidemic, I treated his whole family for weeks. In lieu of payment, he offered me his land and store, which I gladly accepted. Then Mr. Francis Hero and Mrs. Mary Webber, upon deciding to leave Long Canes and return to the city, have offered me their land. Mr. Hero sold me his one-hundred-fifty-acre tract next to Lethe in exchange for two hundred acres that I had been given in payment of medical services further up the road near Ninety Six. Mary Webber sold me another hundred acres next to Lethe. She was concerned about living there all alone since her husband passed away last year. She will be moving to Union, South Carolina very soon. My neighbors, Peter Gaillard and Daniel David, are in declining health and their farms have not been producing enough money to live on, so they are selling me their hundred acres each and moving to Charles Town. This brings my total land at Lethe to 1200 acres. I will accumulate even more as time goes by, but right now, this is enough to start a low-country plantation in the backcountry. I will start clearing the rest of the fields and plant indigo. One slave can take care of two acres of indigo a day, so with fifteen slaves, I should have enough to grow cash crops and take them to market. I can send it by barge down the Savannah or by wagon train leaving Ninety Six, a bustling crossroads community. Some mistakenly believe it was ninety-six miles from the nearest Cherokee settlement named Keowee. Others think it is because early maps of the region was measured in "chains" and by that method, Ninety Six was located ninety-six links from Lexington and ninety-six links from the Savannah River. No one really knows from where the name comes. Ninety Six is the county seat for Granville County, probably the largest county in size and population in the backcountry of South Carolina.

I am beginning to see why Ann loves her Fairbanks plantation. She was raised there and spent most of her life there. Her environment and her life on Fairbanks have shaped her life and her personality as much as she influenced it. She was raised on a working plantation at the forks of two mighty rivers. She needed to be tough growing up because her lifestyle demanded it. Although she had the finer things in life and was taught how to be a proper young lady, she also learned sailing, farming, and overseeing. She became accustomed to working right alongside of a field slave and then would dress for a ball in the evening. In this same way, I fell in love with Lethe the first time I slept on her soil—the rolling hills, massive virgin forest, and rich soil. There is something about the up-country and especially Lethe. I have carved out a 130-acre homesite to which I have added buildings and outbuildings. I now have over twenty such buildings. Most of the cabins and quarters have root cellars and we even have built a spring house in which to store milk and vegetables and to cure indigo and tobacco. In addition to the six original houses there, I have built an ornate wall at the road entrance to Lethe and welcome house just beyond the wall where visitors may leave their carriages and horses to be cared for while they wait. I had the slaves dam up a creek which runs down the south slope of the property. The dam has caused a pond to back up and the pond spills into a ditch that goes down the north side of the property across the road so that the greeter's house and the other three cabins alongside the wall has fresh running water at all times for the animals. The house next door to the greeter's house following the man-made spring is a slave house with a large well in the yard. He tends to the livestock. The next house on the road past the welcoming house is the kitchen. Here, we eat community meals. I have hired a white woman as my chief cook and woman slave overseer. Her name is Anna Cook; I thought it was serendipitous to have a cook named Cook.

I thought that by having a locally known woman to run my household, it may squelch any rumors that may have followed me from Charles Town. No one took me up on my offer to sell Matilda, and there may be those here in New Bordeaux who may have heard if not spread the same old rumors.

I have built a large kitchen for Anna. She will be in charge of meals and guests welcoming which includes patients, and running the household. I am going to run an advertisement in the *Charles Town Gazette* for an overseer to run the plantation because Lethe needs to be self-supporting. Right now, we are running out of money because there are not enough patients who can pay cash money for services rendered. The construction of Lethe has left me without the reserves that I think I will need to support the plantation until we start exporting indigo. One of the troubles I have is that the slaves that I have are primarily of the domestic nature and that are not used to working in the fields which was fine in Charles Town and Jacksonborough; however, here at Lethe, I will need field hands who are familiar with planting and harvesting. I was thinking about bringing some from Fairbanks, but Ann and I have not seen each other in a good while. She does not understand why I cannot run Fairbanks and be content there. She will never understand why I need a respite from all the fighting going on and Daniel's Island is less than a one half day's journey from the city. Here, I am a comfortable distance from the war and no one has to know where I am or what I am doing.

I left all sorts of pipes and tobacco along with wine with Anna in the greeting rooms of the kitchen, especially Madeira wine which is extremely popular now. She has the women slaves and two other slaves that live next door to her as I have mentioned who would be available to help a sick person into bed until I could come and examine him. I will do the treating in my house and the convalescing in the kitchen which will also be used as an infirmary.

If you walk out of the back door of the kitchen about twenty steps, you will come to my house. I am building a magnificent house for the backcountry. It will be about forty feet square with all the necessary outbuildings. The living room and the treatment room will have fireplaces, and I will have about ten rooms with a large cellar where I will distill wine and whisky for the vineyards that border my property. Wine is so important to our health. We put it into all of our water drinks to kill whatever may contaminate our water. Jesus's first miracle was to turn water into wine because it was so important to the wedding guests and it will be so in my house.

My house will be built in the old French way of *Porteaux en terra*. This means "posts in the ground." You lay out a building and dig holes in the ground for tree stump poles as high as you need them. Then you fill in the gaps with mud or concrete and lay boards over the poles inside for walls. This type of architecture will accomplish several things for me. It will let everyone know of my heritage since it is of French origin and it is good for this kind of environment, meaning the post do not have to be all the same size. The boards inside will be nailed up using hand wrought nails, and I will have glass in the windows and carpet on the floor. It will be a showcase in the up-country. It will be most elaborately built and expensively and tastefully appointed. The furniture will be brought from Charles Town and will be made of walnut, cherry, and mahogany. We will drink from wineglasses and porcelain cups and eat from nankeen china using silver flatware. I will have avenues of trees, flanked by fruit orchards brought from Fairbanks. Nearer the river, I will have vineyards and trees and shrubs of exotic and native growth and paved walkways throughout so that I may walk and contemplate and reflect upon nature's beauty. I will be doing a good deal of entertaining here and I wish to welcome my friends and make them feel at home.

My grounds and barnyard will consist of cows, horses, sheep, pigs, and pea foul, a rarity in the upcountry. I will be one of the few physicians in the Granville District and I hope to develop a profitable medical practice.

Come out of my front door and turn right on the paved path and we pass a shed. The path turns left past the cutting house and we come back to the road that goes to the creek, and across the creek is the Huguenot worship site. We venture down the road about seven hundred feet till we come to the store that Rev.

Boutiton built. It furnishes the locals with hardware and feed and seed and pretty much anything else they might need to run a farm or a household. From there, we would turn right and go north. The next house is a large structure that was the home of Rev. Boutiton and my first home when I started coming here. I am saving this home to be the overseer's home. I am hoping to run an ad in the gazette when I get back to Charles Town for an overseer to manage the plantation for me and leave me to the practice of medicine until the plantation becomes self-supporting.

We go past the Boutiton house to another slave house and turn right to follow the creek. After about fifty yards, we come to a creek that divides and forms an upside-down Y and over the top of the Y, I have constructed a spring house where we will store milk and perishables in the coolness of the spring. We will also cure indigo and tobacco in this house. We continue past the spring house past another slave house on till we come to a house with a porch built over another spring. Across from this house is the ornate wall that is the first thing you see when you enter the property. We turn right, go past two slave houses and the greeter's house and we are back where we started.

And there is always Ann and Elizabeth in the back of my mind that maybe someday they will choose to join me in the backcountry and grow old with me. She desires to be with me, but she cannot stand the thought of living in the wilderness and it is probably too much to ask of her. She was raised in the Charles Town aristocracy society, and I really do not expect her to leave all of that to come and live here in the woods. Her plantation is her security and her lifestyle, and I hope she will find solace and happiness there with Elizabeth.

I am satisfied that Lethe will become my home; however, I have obligations in Charles Town that I must close out my accounts there and give my patients a chance to find other physicians. I will have to return for a while to get all this done.

BACK IN CHARLES TOWN (AGAIN)

Bacchus and I arrived back in Charles Town in May 1774. It was good to see that my slaves have kept the place on Church Street in good order. After resting from my trip, I go by the *South Carolina Gazette* and I write out an AD to run for three months.

> The subscriber being under a necessity of closing his concerns, hath put all his affairs in the hands of Mr. Jacob Valk, with full power to have them settled, and with further instructions to commit those to the care of an attorney at law, in which his own application proves ineffectual, whereof he hopes everyone concerned will take notice.
>
> John de la Howe

For the next few weeks, many patients and neighbors came by to see what was happening. There were many concerns as to my health and well-being. Many others thought that Ann had left me, and I was moving because of an affair with Matilda, but these were few and I paid then no attention. They are the kind of people that will always be quick to condemn regardless of the circumstances. They will always believe the worse and love to spread it around. I think it must be something in their constitution that likes to bring rich and powerful men down to their level which in turn, as they think, brings them up to a level to which they would not otherwise obtain. My God tells me that I must forgive them and love them, but that is so hard to do. I am trying my best just to ignore them. I will be so glad when I can move to Lethe and live there. I love Charles Town. Its beauty and grace is unsurpassed and the people are the friendliest of any place I have been, but there are always those few.

Mr. Laurens came by one day and asked about his friends and neighbors in Hillsborough. I apprized him of the fact that New Bordeaux was becoming a ghost town. Most of the inhabitants are moving away and intermarrying with the Irish and German settlers who were already there for a hundred years before them. Rev. Gibert, young Mr. Moragne and his family were still there as were several other families, but it did not look good for the future of New Bordeaux, especially with the war coming soon.

Mr. Laurens said, "Yes, I was afraid of that. I have done my duty by bringing them here and given them a new start, what they do with it is their business. I have been appointed to the newly formed South Carolina Assembly which has delegated me as a representative to the Second Continental Congress. I will submit your application to become Justice of the Peace in Long Canes and eventually a judge for all of Granville District. This will be voted on in August and the list will appear in January 1775. I assume that you will be back at Lethe at that time."

I thanked Mr. Laurens for his confidence in me and let him know I would consider it a welcomed change from the rigors of practicing medicine in Charles Town. I declared that I would never give up the practice, but that I would no longer make house calls when I returned. I also thanked him for the use of the house on Church Street and assured him that I would leave it as I found it. It was a great place to live but now I would be a Plantation Owner and country doctor.

I wonder if I should try to see Ann. Elizabeth is about twelve years old now, and she is turning out to be just like her mother.

She is very confident in herself and is both tomboyish and a proper young lady at the same time. I wonder if she is to that age when she is taking a young man down to the creek and showing him fiddler crabs and teaching him how to catch sheepshead? I know that she and Ann are still having "harvesting and planting" socials. I would like to see her, but I had rather not if it causes her stress and embarrassment.

By August, my attorney Mr. Jacob Valk told me that there has not been anyone come to see him in a month about settling up with me. My books were clear and by my records, no one owed me anything. I asked Mr. Valk to handle the sale of my property in Jacksonborough and to please allow me to retain his services as needed as my representative in Charles Town for any legal matters that may come up. This would save me a month's traveling time to not have to come back for some trivial matter.

I again packed up my things, and Bacchus, my six house slaves, and I left Charles Town for Jacksonborough. We will spend the night there and longer if necessary to close my affairs and move on to Lethe. I left a note with Mr. Valk addressed to Ann at Fairbanks and asked him to see to it that she got it. She would be coming into town to see her sister Elizabeth and he could see her then. In the note I thanked her for the love and happy times we shared. I wished her happiness and good health, and that I would always remain her loyal servant. She should not hesitate to call on me if I could ever be of assistance to her in any manner.

While in Jacksonborough, I visited the home of Isaac Hayne who had become a colonel in the South Carolina Militia. He had several of his neighbors over for supper and we were having our digestif and smoking our long-stemmed clay pipes talking politics as usual. I could not help but to admire Mr. Hayne. He was only thirty years old and already a very successful rice planter and businessman. He, like me, did not want to choose sides in this war. Last year, I treated his family for smallpox, from which his wife may never recover. While he was in Charles Town, he was forced to take allegiance to the British as were many other citizens. When the fighting breaks out, he said that he would join the Americans in the fight for independence but only if he was forced to choose. Most of the guests were of the same opinion.

The next morning, as Bacchus and the other slaves were loading up the wagons and preparing horses and my carriage, I took a stroll down to the Edisto River to enjoy its beauty once more before leaving this place. I would have enjoyed living here if I had not found Lethe. Never have I seen such a beautiful river with such abounding wildlife. I will really miss this part of my life and I have no regrets about the time that I have spent here. Pleasant memories of Ann and Elizabeth came back to me as I watched the flowing dark waters of the river as it heads to the sea. I will make it a point to come by here if and when I visit Charles Town. There are better and more direct routes to take to New Bordeaux, but what little you go out of the way is certainly worth the effort.

During our trip, Bacchus and I talked of our lives at Lethe and we made plans for its operation. I asked Bacchus if he would consent to become an overseer until I hired one to oversee the farm operations. Bacchus said that he was my man servant and that is all he knows. He said that taking care of me was his responsibility, and he did not want to work the rest of the slaves. I asked that he give the matter his consideration. None of the people would be mistreated in any way if he were the overseer and I would teach him what he needed to know about running a plantation.

"Bacchus, there is no one that I trust more than you to undertake this responsibility", I said. "If at any time you find that you are having difficulty with the duties I will welcome you back into the house to resume your normal position without question."

Bacchus asked me to let him think about it for a while if I did not need an answer right away.

"I will await your decision", I replied.

I told Bacchus that I needed someone to run the store also. I needed someone who could read and write and cipher numbers to give change and take in money. Bacchus said that he didn't know anybody like that. Certainly, no slave could do that. I knew that no slave would ever admit to being able to read or write and cipher because it was strictly against the law. When a law is made for Charles Town, the legislators do not realize how it affects the backcountry or they didn't care. Think of the advantages of having literate slaves, but then if they were literate, they would realize their predicament and would not stand for it very long. It is another argument for the after dinner drinkers and the pipe smokers to settle.

I needed to tell the locals in Charles Town and Jacksonborough that I would be leaving Charles Town for good, that I would be in New Bordeaux, and that I would no longer be available to make house calls as they are used to. I also needed to tell them why to avoid any further rumors.

I wrote down an AD for the gazette which read,

> The declining years and constitution of the subscriber obliged him to decline the laborious part of practice, for which reasons he hath determined upon retiring to his plantation near New Bordeaux in Hillsborough, Township, where he will continue the practice only by giving advice and medicines to those who will consult him at the said place. As the distance, he proposes to move to induce an absolute necessity of satisfying previously his creditors; he requests those indebted by bond, note, or book debt to enable him to do his departure by settling with him before that time, as the same reason of defiance will not allow of ulterior application.
>
> John de la Howe

This ad ran in the December 1774 newspaper in Charles Town and all over the state. People will know that I am in good health, but I am also over fifty-seven years old and most people of means have retired by my age.

I heard that Ann and the Lesesne's were having a big Christmas Ball at Fairbanks. I went to Elizabeth's house and spoke to Isaac Junior and Elizabeth to find out if it would cause any problems if I were to attend. Isaac said, "Of course not, John. You are a part of our family. You are my brother-in-law and you are welcome in our home and at Fairbanks at anytime. We are just sorry about the circumstances that have arisen in your marriage. We understand both sides and we hoped that you could come to some middle ground. We do not blame you or Ann. However, Ann is blood kin and we have to stand by her and support her."

I said, "I completely understand. I am happy that she has her family to support her. We knew this marriage would be difficult from the start. Me with my medical practice and her with Little Elizabeth and Fairbanks, it seems now that it was doomed from the start. It was unfair of me to ask her to leave her comfortable life in the low country in exchange for the uncertainty of the wilderness. I would like to see her once more and tell her good-bye."

Isaac said, "You may cross the harbor with us in the morning and spend Christmas Eve at Fairbanks and Marcus will bring you back in the morning."

I thanked him and told him that I would see him at first light.

Bacchus woke me up while it was still dark. I dressed and ate breakfast and told Hercules and Cato to be sure to have the luggage and medicine wagons ready to go the day after Christmas. Bacchus pulled the carriage up to the stepping block and we went to the pier. There were twenty-two wharfs in Charles Town now. Mr. Laurens and Mr. Gadsden owned the two largest wharfs located at the far southeast of the Charles Town Wall. Fairbanks' sloop was docked at Mr. Lauren's wharf. Marcus was there to sail the boat, and I met Isaac and Elizabeth who were waiting onboard.

As I got into the boat, I was thinking that this would be the last time I would cross the harbor and sail to Fairbanks. The crossing was rough and cold. There were twenty-knot winds and three-foot swells in choppy waters. The others did not seem too concerned about the rough seas, but I was wondering how long a body could last in the frigid waters if something did happen.

My fears were not well founded because we passed over the six-mile waters without incident. Marcus was a good sailor and he took the boat at an angle to the wind so the ride would be as smooth as possible without too much spray.

I looked at Bacchus and he had turned from black to green. He was so sea sick I felt sorry for him. He said to me, "Furst I thought I wuz gwain die, en den Ise fraid I wazzn't gwain die. Why is I sick, doctor?"

"No one really knows, Bacchus. It has to do with your middle ear bones and your balance. People with really good balance will usually get sick in rough seas, but I can comfort you that you will not die. Come up on deck and go to the stern where the ship moves the least and breathe deeply until we get to the river. The only advice I can give you is that if you get sick, check the wind direction before you heave."

After about an hour of tossing and tumbling, we reached Fairbanks Plantation Dock. There were several other boats from the different plantations already there for the festivities. Bacchus and I walked down the dock straight to the house. Most of the people were in the dining room having breakfast. I sat down and told Bacchus to bring me some shrimp, grits, sausage, eggs, and toast. And I also told him that he could leave and socialize with the slaves.

Ann came into the room with Elizabeth. I was shocked to see that Elizabeth has turned into a beautiful and proper young lady in her teen years. Ann looked beautiful. I had hoped that she dressed up because of me, but then how would she know that I would be there? She saw me and I was apprehensive as to how she would receive me. She smiled and ran over to me, hugged me, and kissed me. Elizabeth curtsied and hugged my neck.

Ann said, "Welcome, I am so glad you could come. I miss you when we are apart. How are you?"

"I am very well, " I replied. "I hope that we may spend some time together and talk before I return to Charles Town later in the day."

She said, "Too bad. You are going to miss a great party, but you always were on the move busying yourself with your life. I hear you purchased a plantation in the backcountry. Do you think you will be happy as a farmer?"

I said, "I don't know but we will find out. I will never give up my medical practice. If the plantation does not support itself, I will always have my practice to fall back on."

Ann finished eating and told me that we should retire to the study. She closed the double oaken doors and asked me to have a seat. I sat down and I started nervously speaking.

"Ann, I never stopped loving you. I hope by me coming here today that we may part under pleasant circumstances. I understand your feelings for Fairbanks and I would not ask you to give it up. I want you to know that you are welcome to accompany me to Lethe and live with me there, but if you decide to stay, I will wish you happiness and I will understand."

"John, you are nearly sixty and I am fifty years old. I think we both know what we want in life. I love you also, but I cannot give up my way of life here on Daniel's Island. Fairbanks is my life, and for for my sake and Elizabeth's, I cannot see us living in a cabin a hundred miles from nowhere. I will always love you and you will always be my husband, but please don't expect me to go with you. I have Elizabeth in a boarding school in Charles Town and she is becoming a lady in her own right. Where would she go to school in Hillsborough?"

"I completely understand. I don't know what the lure of Lethe is, but I must get out of Charles Town and try to ride out the war as far as possible from it. I was just getting to the place that I would not remember those circumstances every day. I see in my head young men with half of their bodies missing or their faces blown off and even worse. This was an everyday way of life. I am sworn to treat anyone who may need my assistance and for me to be loyal to one government and not to another is against my every fiber. I will not choose sides if I can stay away from it."

"I know that you are not a coward, John and having lived with you for eight years, I know that you are a man of intelligence and feelings. You could not do the things you face every day if you did not have intestinal fortitude and tenacity. I admire you and I wish you well. Let me walk you to the dock."

We walked from the house to the dock. It was a blustery day. Bacchus followed and ran to get on the boat and help me into the boat. I put my arms around Ann, kissed her and said, "Goodbye, Ann. Please let me know how you are in the future and if you ever need me, you know where I will be."

As I walked to the gangplank, I looked under the dock and there were the fiddler crabs, lifting their big claws almost like saying "good-bye" to me. I smiled and got into the boat.

The trip back to Lauren's pier was another rough crossing. As the spray wet me and the cold began to bite, I thought of Ann and what might have been. Bacchus told me to come into the cabin, but I wanted to watch Fairbanks as long as I could. I was numb to the salt spray, the wind, and the cold. I really was not heartbroken, but I was disappointed to think that our marriage did not work out. I blamed myself more than Ann, but what good would it do to lay blame? We could debate who is right or wrong for years but that would not bring us back together.

1775

Today is Friday, January 6, 1775. Today I was officially notified by the *South Carolina Gazette* that I had been nominated and elected by the General Assembly that I was to be a Justice of the Peace in the Long Canes community. The lieutenant governor was given my name by Mr. Laurens and he brought it up before the assembly. It does not pay much but it is another source of income and since I am well known in the community as a physician, it will be a good fit. I cannot believe how much the community of New Bordeaux has diminished. People have married women who have inherited farms and moved out of the area. Others grew their crops but it was barely enough to live on. I wonder how this will affect my practice. I hope that my savings, the medical practice, and the plantation will provide enough income to feed the seventeen souls that will be living at Lethe.

The trip back to Lethe was a long and cold one. Thank goodness for the slaves. They kept me warm with fires and fed me well. When I stopped at an inn for the night, I always made sure that my slaves were lodged in a stable or barn so they would not have to sleep in the cold. It is important that we all maintain our health as much work lies ahead of us.

As we passed by Fort Moore which is located across the Savannah River and a little south of Augusta, and about two days from Lethe, I wrote a note to the *South Carolina Gazette* to be delivered by the next mail courier to Charles Town. It is an ad for an overseer to run Lethe while I continued my medical practice and judgeship. I instructed the newspaper to run the ad for three months starting in February. I also instructed the paper to see Mr. Valk for payment. I wrote,

> "Wanted to go upon shares. An overseer well acquainted with the management of Negroes, having a few of his own, and willing to make indigo in the French way, upon a healthy plantation in the backcountry, whose fitness of Soil and Water for the intent, are not exceeded by any spot in this Province; a sample of indigo made on said Plantation may be seen, and the terms known by applying to Mr. Rutledge in Beardsford Alley in Charlestown, or at Lethe near New Bordeaux, to John de la Howe. Who being represented as having left off practice, gives public notice, that he hath not, nor ever will decline practice, in the way of giving Advice and medicines, having a fresh and ample Supply of those, but that finding himself unequal to the same fatigues formally, he hath declined the visiting of patients except on particular occasions when he shall expect a previous fee."

I hope people will realize that, by this advertisement, I will not make any more house calls except to the French Huguenots, as a gesture of appreciation for what Mr. Laurens has done for me. Thereby I expect my medical practice to be limited to Lethe, making my plantation a constant resort for the stranger invalid and the affected.

We arrived at Lethe late in the afternoon and I see that the slaves that I left at Lethe have finished my house under the supervision of Mr. Guillibeau. The place looks lovely. Right behind the kitchen and in front of my house, they have erected a beautiful garden structure with a seat for relaxing and a beautiful sundial. There is the strange sound of pea foul that rings out. I am sure the neighbors are wondering what in the world is making that sound. I am sure they will get used to it. The fruit trees from Fairbanks have been planted and I hope they will at least bloom this spring if not bear fruit.

I asked Bacchus was to unload my things in the kitchen/infirmary room and take my medicine and doctoring tools to my house and in the morning we would decide where to place everything like we did at my office in Charlestown. I thought of Hedrick and how much he would have loved to come to Lethe and live out the rest of his life helping me in my practice. He would have been a great help with the overseeing of the workforce here at Lethe.

Bacchus was to have all the slaves in the kitchen area in an hour. I entered the kitchen and spoke to Ms. Cook. I asked her if it would be an imposition for her and the slave women to cook a quick dinner for me and the others who traveled with me from Charles Town. She said that she would be glad to. She had plenty of beef stew left in the big pot over the fire and plenty of pone and some fresh collards she had Matilda pick today. She sent Matilda to the spring house to get a mess of collards and washed them in the spring and put them in a pot with lard and fatback and cooked then over the open fire. Anna said that supper will be ready in an hour. I informed her that I would be having a meeting in the infirmary tonight and I would like her to attend.

I introduced her to Felice and Becky. Anna had been working with Matilda and now the girls, Molly and Cecelia, were old enough to work in the kitchen or wherever she deemed necessary. Anna was to keep the kitchen and the medical supplies as I or she needed them. She would send Bacchus with other slaves to Fort Charlotte for supplies. Ft. Charlotte was about ten miles up the Savannah from Lethe. You could get there and back in one day if you left early enough and knew what you needed and where to get it. We also get supplies from the store which for now, Ms. Cook will have to run until I get an overseer. I may train Bacchus to run the store.

She said that she would be at the meeting and asked to be excused so she could finish dinner. She told Felice and Becky to follow her, and they could start drawing water and learning their way around the kitchen.

After supper I joined everyone gathered in the infirmary room at the backside of the kitchen. They all stood as I entered the room. I informed them that I had advertised for an overseer in the Charles Town newspaper. I hoped that we would find one soon because we need to plant indigo. Now was the time to plant but we may not have a full crop this year. I explained, "An acre of good land may produce about eighty pounds weight of good indigo, and one slave may manage two acres and upwards, and raise provisions besides, and have all the winter months to saw lumber and be otherwise employed in. But as much of the land hitherto used for indigo is improper, I am persuaded that not above thirty pounds weight of good indigo per acre can be expected from the land at present cultivated. Perhaps we are not conversant enough in this commodity, either in the culture of the plant or in the method of managing or manufacturing it, but we will do the best we can."

I went on the say, "This is now, and forever will be our home. We will each have to do our part if we are to survive. I plan to keep you all as a family unit, but if we do not support ourselves, I will be forced to sell you and concentrate on my medical practice. I have enough money for about two years until we become self-sufficient. For the time being, Bacchus will act as the overseer and you must mind him as you mind me. If Bacchus is off with me on a trip, then Hercules will run the farm and make the decisions. If he comes across a problem and I am not here, he will report to Ms. Cook who will make the decisions until I return. There are nine slave houses not counting the store. I will leave it up to Bacchus to decide who will live in which house. Ms. Cook may decide to keep the women and girls in the kitchen house or not. Families will stay together and I will never sell any of you if it remains in my power to keep you. I know that you are my property, but we will have to work together and live together and carve out a home that we can enjoy as much as possible. You know what is needed and expected of you. Do any of you have any questions?"

"Excuse me sur." It was Hercules whose country name was Sam. Sam was his given name at birth and the one used by the other slaves. I used it also while on Lethe.

I said, "What is it Sam?" knowing what he wanted. He and Matilda have been in love since the early days in Charles Town and now that we were all together again, he wanted permission to "jump the broom" and marry Matilda.

"Well, sur, Ize in love wid Matilda, en she feels da same and I wuz wondrin iffen wez cout git married."

"Of course, Sam. How would you like to handle the ceremony? Do you want the slaves to throw you a party or would you like Rev. Gibert to perform the wedding vows?"

"Weeze tuck up a cabin down by the creck, da one wid da poach. We'd lack ta git married dare en since youse da Justis o'da Peace, we figgered you coult paform da weddin legal like and den we jump da broom."

I looked at Matilda and asked her if she was in agreement. She smiled and said, "Yessir, I is."

I was very glad that they felt comfortable enough to ask me to marry them. I was happy to tell Anna that we had a wedding to prepare for. There were not that many slaves in the backcountry. Some folks had one or two, but by in large they just cost too much. The farms were producing just enough to live on and people were moving out of the area. They are moving to the cities and towns to get work or marrying women who have been here for years and have inherited other farms in which they could work.

I suggested that if they would wait until Sunday the ceremony could be held at their house. That would afford them time to move their things into the house and be set up by the time they were married. I asked them if Sunday, January 15, would be all right with them. They said it would.

The rest of the slaves were informed that we would work six days a week and rest on the Sabbath. There would be no unnecessary work done on Sunday at Lethe. Medical emergencies and cooking excluded.

I will perform the wedding ceremony on Sam and Matilda's porch, and Bacchus will be in charge of the broom jumping ceremony. I have told Sam and Bacchus that they could have guests from other plantations and farms in the area, but they said they have not been here long enough to get to know any of them. I suggested that this would be an excellent opportunity to get to know them.

I sent a note to Rev. Gibert, John Lewis Gervais, Patrick Calhoun, and Richard Rapley who was the largest slave owner in the district with fifty-seven slaves. I told them to please invite anyone whom they wished. We would enjoy a meal and an evening of fun and games. This event will be a good way of me giving my new neighbors a look at Lethe, and we may become better acquainted.

Today is Sunday, January 15, 1775; Sam will marry Matilda. On Lethe Plantation, these vows will remain sacred and the families will stay together as long as I live. Their names will be entered on the ledgers and I will issue a legally stamped document certifying that they are indeed a properly married couple. Being a Justice of the Peace, I have studied the laws concerning slave marriages.

Slave marriages have neither legal standing nor protection from the abuses and restrictions imposed on them by slave owners. Slave husbands and wives, without legal recourse, could be separated or sold at their master's will. Couples who resided on different plantations were allowed to visit only with the consent of their owners. Slaves often married without the benefit of clergy, sometimes the marriage ceremony in most cases consisted of the couple simply getting the master's permission and moving into a cabin together. That will not be the case at Lethe.

Formal marriage ceremonies for slave couples were generally reserved for house servants. In such cases, slave owners would have a white minister or a black plantation preacher perform the ceremony, and a large feast and dance in the "quarters" would follow honoring the slave couple. The ceremony could include the slave marriage ritual of "jumping the broom," which required slave couples to jump over a broomstick. The custom of jumping the broom could vary from plantation to plantation. On some farms, the slave bride and groom would place separate brooms on the floor in front of each other. The couple would then step across the brooms at the same time joining hands to signal that they were truly married. On other farms, each slave partner was required to jump backward over a broom held a foot from the ground. If either partner failed to clear the broom successfully, the other partner would be declared the one who would rule or boss the household. If both partners cleared the broom without touching it, then there would be no "bossin'."

Most people agree that the act of jumping the broom was a "binding force" in the slave couple's relationship and made them feel "more married."

At noon, I walked down the path with Rev. Gibert and John Lewis Gervais to the cabin where the ceremony will take place. I saw Sam and his friends over to one side. I believe someone has brought a jug of homemade hard spirits. They are laughing and kidding Sam about the honeymoon tonight. Matilda was inside the house being careful not to let Sam see her before the ceremony. Molly, Cecelia, and Becky were there to attend her. Anna was in the kitchen. She had prepared most of the meal, drinks, and pipes the night before and she left her duties to watch the wedding.

I called everyone together and performed a marriage ceremony that would have made the Saint Michael's bishop proud. After I pronounced them husband and wife, they came off the porch into the front yard where Bacchus and some other slaves have cleared out an area and had two brooms lying on the ground. Sam and Matilda held hands and jumped over the brooms and everyone cheered. Then Bacchus held a broom about a foot off the ground and Sam jumped over it backwards. Matilda came forward and lifted her skirt and jumped over her broom backwards and Bacchus announced, "Da won't be no 'bossin' in dis hear house, jist love and lots o babies."

The white men returned to the kitchen. We left the couple receiving congratulations and some homemade gifts of pottery and dough bowls and such. We heard a great deal of laughter as we departed. I thought it best to leave them to their own company and let Sam and Matilda get on with their own life.

When we got to the reception room of the kitchen, the men were gathering to smoke and drink their aperitifs and talk politics and other things on their minds before dinner. Bacchus had had the slaves to barbeque a pig and a cow the day and night before, and they were taking off roasted oysters from the fire. The way they learned to roast oysters came from the low country. They would build a big fire and let it burn to glowing embers. The oysters would be placed on a large sheet of metal or grate and covered with wet burlap bags. When an oyster reaches the temperature of 140 degrees, it opens and the oyster is ready to be shucked. I always wondered if the term shuckin' oysters came from shucking parties like shucking corn or did the slaves name it because when you would open an oyster, the knife would slip or the oyster, whose shell is sharper than any knife, would slip cutting the opener causing him to holler out "shucks." We bought oysters that had been kept in barrels of sea water and shipped to Ft. Charlotte from Charlestown or Savannah. Of course they were expensive to ship, but for special occasions it was a dish well received.

Anna had side dishes of creamed corn and corn on the cob, slaw, baked beans, and seasonal greens. Anna had fruit bowls and several different kinds of desert. All the women gathered in the kitchen to either help or talk. It was turning out to be a great afternoon.

After lunch the men gathered in the reception room for digestif drinks. I had a keg of Madeira wine that I brought from Charlestown with me. I am setting up three stills in my cellar for making wine and whisky, but it is not producing yet. I thought they would enjoy Madeira because they are used to French wines. Madeira comes from Madeira, Italy and it is delightful.

During our social, Rev. Gibert brought a man to me to be formally introduced. His name was Jean Louis du Mensnil de St. Pierre. St. Pierre's primary venture was grape growing in New Bordeaux. He came here in 1768. On Thursday, August 8, 1771, it was reported, "Yesterday, embarked and sailed for England, in order to go from thence to France, and procure persons experienced in the culture of wine and silk, Mesnil de St. Pierre, Esq. Later, the Ship *Carolina Packet* brought thirty thousand plants of vines producing the true Champagne and Burgundy grapes, procured by the Assiduity of Mr. Mesnil de St. Pierre for the French settlement at Long Canes called New Bourdeaux who has received great encouragement in London to perfect his scheme of making wines in that part of this province and obtained from the Society of Arts a gold medal."

Mr. Mesnil de St. Pierre was now second in command behind Rev. Gibert, but he is so strong willed that most think that he is the real leader. He is also involved in establishing a militia of patriot forces. The militia will be named the Long Cane Militia and it will seek out and disband English loyalists by any means necessary. He would be second in command in the militia also.

Of course with Mr. Pierre there, the conservation turned to the American Revolution. Mr. Pierre asked me about my intentions concerning the revolution. He said, "South Carolina is in the process of raising an army to do battle with the English and the Loyalists. The Americans have already held the first Continental Congress to draft papers to declare our independence. Judge Drayton of Charlestown has come to the backcountry to gain support for our cause. The Cherokees are siding with the English, and England has offered freedom to any slave who will join their forces. We need all the support we can get sir. How say you?"

I enlightened Mr. Pierre of my desire to remain neutral in the upcoming conflict. I have seen war at its worse and I came here to get away from war. The English have a mighty army and navy. We have no navy or army nor do we have the industrial might to sustain a prolonged war. If we go to war, we would have a hard time of it.

Mr. Pierre got red in the face. He stopped short of calling me a coward for not siding with the Americans. He made mention of rumors he heard about my character which would explain a great deal. He just could not understand that I wished to remain neutral. In the presence of my company, this insult would not be overlooked. I stood up and as I did, Rev. Gibert stepped in front of me and stood between me and Mr. Pierre.

Rev. Gibert said, "Gentlemen, please. Let us not get into an argument over what has not happened yet. If we fight, we fight for freedom and the right to have our own say and our individual opinions. The conflict will not start here nor will it be resolved here. Let us act like neighbors and change the subject to something we can all agree, like how the planting is going this year."

Mr. Pierre bowed and asked for my pardon. He apologized for having disrupted my dinner party and bringing up such arguments in my own home. He asked to be excused and he left. I heard later that one of my guests and my neighbor, Pierre Engevine, went to Mr. Pierre's home and asked him to explain himself as far as the accusations against me were concerned. Mr. Pierre repeated his feelings about me. Mr. Engevine felt it a duty to protect my honor and challenged Mr. Pierre to a duel. They named their seconds and met at Ft. Charlotte to settle their differences. I understand that the duel was fought with pistols and that no blood was spilled. Both men stepped off the ten paces, turned and fired over each other's head. Both men were satisfied with the outcome. This became the first duel fought in the backcountry of South Carolina.

I was so relieved to hear that neither man was injured. There are enough rumors that spread without more speculation as to what caused the duel. Both men has since come to me and apologized for letting our argument getting out of hand. They assured me that the matter was settled and there would be no further talk or actions taken.

As far as I am concerned, I accepted his apology; however, I feel that I have not heard the end of this matter. I do not understand how a man can live a life as a Huguenot, persecuted as they were, came to America to escape that persecution only to turn into a war hawk after being here only a few years. I wonder what he is basing his anger upon.

One of Mr. Rapley's slaves had learned to play the violin or fiddle as they called it. We listened to some old country songs and some old hymns, and we talked and socialized into the late afternoon. I invited those who wished to spend the night so they could drive home in the morning, but being Monday and a workday they all decided to go home that afternoon. Rev. Gibert needed to have church services at the worship site across from Lethe. I could stand on my plateau overlooking the river and see them standing or sitting on logs and the ground during Huguenot worship services. In the spring, there will be baptisms in the creek with much rejoicing.

As each guest sent their slave to ready their carriage and wagons to return home, things quieted down and soon everyone had left the gathering. I thought of how different this party was compared to Ann's more formal balls. Here, the men came in their country clothes and brought their workers in their homespun clothes. At Fairbanks, the party would go on sometimes for a week until the planting is done or the harvesting was in the barn. We had an afternoon of barbequing and socializing before the guests had to get back to their farms and plantations. Except for the actions of Mr. Pierre, it was a good day.

For the next few months, we finished building all the structures at Lethe. We made a slaughter house and a loom house along with barns and outbuildings for storage and necessities of nature. I learned that a full moon on an outhouse door meant it was for men, and a half moon or a crescent moon meant it was for ladies. There was a privy for each house and two for the infirmary/kitchen. I had four sheds which held tools and other things such as shot for the guns and powder and horseshoes and other such things. I had built the basic house which was about thirty feet square with a porch and onto that structure we kept adding rooms as we needed them. I had all my books in the library as well as my medical books for reference. There were fireplaces in the living room and the treatment room. I keep these going day and night because I never know when a patient may show up with an injury or having a baby or what laymen may call an emergency. When someone requires a stay in the infirmary, Anna and the girls act as nurses under my supervision to take care of those who have infections or high fevers and things like that.

This year, I have added to my land at Lethe. On Wednesday, the fourth of January, I purchased a hundred acres from Henry Webber on Rocky Creek below Cuffey Town in the Ninety-Six District. On Friday, July 28, I purchased 150 acres from Maria Farrestau Gaban in Hillsborough. On Tuesday, September 12, I purchased 300 acres from Pierre Engevine in Hillsborough and that Friday, September 25, I purchased 100 acres from Callas Bordayeau of Hillsborough.

This brings my total land holdings to 2,250 acres of which 1750 acres compose Lethe. I still have my 400 acres on the Wateree and the 100 acres on Rocky Creek was given to me as a payment for physician's fee. It is about 10 miles southeast of Lethe. I purchased 100 acres from Mary Webber two years ago on Long Canes Creek next to Lethe and now Henry Webber is selling me 100 acres on Rocky Creek. I do not know if they are any relations.

The revolution began on Wednesday, April 19, 1775 with the skirmish at Lexington, Massachusetts. The Colonists are calling it "the shot heard around the world." The Declaration of Independence has not been signed yet, but it has gone to each state's assembly for ratification.

When the news of the Battle of Lexington broke out, the locals took up arms to seek out the loyalists, and the loyalists seek out the rebels to fight each other. It was almost like a civil war.

The Continental Congress, of which Mr. Laurens is a member, met in Philadelphia and appointed Gen. George Washington as commander of the Continental Army.

Since the Battle of Lexington, we have had the Battle of Concord and the Battle of Bunker Hill.

Early in the war, many skirmishes were fought between loyalists and rebels with no interference or participation by the British military. Victories for the loyalist in these battles were often short-lived because the loyalist could not sustain victory without maintaining control over the territory gained and its inhabitants. If the rebels were defeated, the defeated rebels would resort to gorilla-type warfare tactics of sniping, destruction of personal property, and threats to families to intimidate loyalists. A loyalist victory was followed by an immediate need for the victors to escape with their families and knapsacks to seek a safe haven within an area under British control, only to be abandoned when the British forces got orders to move to another location. Except for a few isolated instances, Britain never attempted to consolidate these loyalists into groups.

On November 19, 1775, patriot forces of the Long Cane Militia fought loyalists in the First Battle of Ninety Six resulting in the death of James Birmingham, the first South Carolinian and southerner of the war. As a result of this battle, Col. Richard Richardson led a large party of Whigs into the upcountry to arrest loyalists and to assert the power of the revolutionary General Committee over the entire colony.

In June, the British attempted to break out from the cramped confines of their coastal perimeter resulting in the Battle of Bunker Hill (the battle was actually fought on nearby Breed's Hill). Technically, it was a British victory but they suffered heavily, losing one-third of their force in storming the hastily constructed lines of the rebels.

Throughout the colonies, rebel units began to take up arms. In Virginia, British governor Lord Dunmore offered freedom to slaves who would fight for Britain. From one thousand to two thousand blacks joined him and in December, the patriots defeated a force led by Dunmore at Great Bridge, south of Norfolk. It must have impressed General Washington because on December 31, 1775, he issued an edict for the recruiting officers to recruit free black men into the militia, and when he did, over five thousand black men enlisted.

Now it all begins. With the civil strife, I do not see how I can remain neutral. I will wait and see and if I am called upon for medical treatment, I will not ask if it is British or American.

The town of New Bordeaux is almost nonexistent now. A few of the old established families are still here, but it has taken a toll on my medical practice. I have extended myself to build Lethe and now New Bordeaux and most of Hillsborough have left and with the advent of war, I may have to make some temporary plans to go back to Charlestown and resume my practice there, only until I can save enough money to keep Lethe supplied and in operation. The plantation is not making as much money as I hoped it would. Bacchus is doing his best. We have the land but not enough of it is cleared right now for the indigo crop to be profitable.

On November of last year, I thought it was ironic that Mr. Jean Louis du Mensnil de St. Pierre, second in command of the Long Canes Militia which fought the first battle of the war brought wounded soldiers by Lethe to be treated. It took me a week to treat the wounded and when I asked for payment, Mr. St. Pierre told me to make a record of the medicines I used and make him a bill for services rendered, and he would give it to his commanding officer to request payment. He was angry that I even mentioned payment. I think he thought it was my civic duty to treat rebel troops. I doubt that I will ever see any of that money, but I will maintain my records.

I thought it also ironic that such a hot-head would cause the first official battle of the revolution in South Carolina. I have to admire his bravery and conviction and my God tells me that I must love my enemies and forgive them. I wish him well in his endeavors. I just pray that he does not come after me. Now that I have treated his wounded and he owes me, I do not think he will be around to visit very much. I would like to know how his vineyards are doing and if he finally planted his thirty thousand plants of vines producing the true champagne and Burgundy grapes. The grapes of the vineyards planted by the New Bordeaux settlers are good grapes from Abbeville and other grape-producing areas of France, but they are for non-specialized wine. If Mr. St. Pierre will ever stop fighting the war and settle down, I would like to purchase some of his seeds or cuttings to experiment with my vines to see what we can produce.

I always maintain at least thirty gallons of wine aging in my cellar. I love the art of winemaking and being a doctor, I love the chemistry of winemaking. I think all children should learn the art not only for their own consumption and guests but also something to fall back on if they become unemployed. If you can grow grapes, you can produce wine and you can always find a market for wine.

In the January 4, 1776 issue of the *South Carolina Gazette*, I had an ad come out as JP for Long Canes. It read,

> John Foster of Pareimon Branch, informs me of a light gray filly, with four black hooves, being swayed and neglected and keeping with his bones; is about two years old and hath no particular mark nor brand visible. The owner must prove his property within the time limited by law.
>
> John de la Howe

In the April 10 issue, I was appointed Justice of the Peace for the whole Ninety-Six District. This widens my territory considerably.

I have been trying to clear land and make Lethe profitable, but the South Carolina Militia keeps bringing wounded men to me to be patched up. It is not as bad as it was in the Seven Years' War yet but it is getting there. On Friday and Saturday of this week, which was August 2 and 3, the militia brought me over a hundred wounded men. The South Carolina Militia is a rebel contingent. The casualties whom I treated were casualties from a campaign of rebels against the Cherokee Patriots north of New Bordeaux in the Keowee–Seneca region. I worked for two days without rest. Bacchus and Ms. Cook helped me but they too were overwhelmed. We had the infirmary filled with mangled bodies, and we set up another infirmary in my house and then in the greeter's house and the three houses that run by the ditch next to the wall. Even then, we were crowded with men in the halls lying on the floor with blankets over and under them. The stench of rotting flesh is horrible. It is an all too familiar one. I wish that there really was a Lethe river here. The worst thing about all this is that this is just the beginning.

I had my workers dig a fissure on the hill to the south of my property away from all the cottages to bury the human remains, bodies, and soiled linen which has acted as bandages or cleanup supplies.

I am trying to tell Pluto, country name (Ben), Cato (Boze), Hercules (Sam), Pompy, James, and Brister what to do each morning about planting indigo, but I am afraid that instead of an individual handling two acres a day, I will be fortunate to get a half or less production out of my fields. We just cannot clear the forest fast enough to plant a large crop. My desire is that we would never have to cut a tree down, but we have to build log cottages, firewood, and tools such as work benches for horseshoeing or milking or even shining shoes. Nothing of the tree is wasted. We use birch leaves to stuff mattresses and pine straw to line flower beds. Pine straw is a natural deterrent for grass and weeds. We salt meat and fish to preserve it. We get salt fairly cheap because along the coastline, there are people who have gated a large flat surface of tidal ground. When the tide is in the flow, the field is filled with sea water, and then when the tide ebbs, they close the gates trapping the water. After a few weeks, the water evaporates and there is pure sea salt left to be scooped up and put into barrels. This is another good thing about living in South Carolina. Thank goodness we are growing our own food, and we have plenty of livestock so we will not go hungry.

Lethe is not at all what I wanted or planned for but it is the circumstances into which I have been fated to endure, so let me make the most of it.

I read in the January 8, 1777, issue of the gazette a most interesting advertisement. It states,

> Rebecca Woodin proposes opening a boarding school for young ladies, January 19, 1778, at Mr. Wish's large and commodious house in Mazyck Street, lately occupied by Lieutenant Bush, where they will be instructed in the different branches of polite education, such as needlework,

musick, French, drawing and dancing, as proper matters will favor her with their attendance. As her utmost abilities will be exerted in the tuition of the young ladies, she therefore hopes to give satisfaction to those who may be pleased to entrust her with their children.

Ms. Woodin, in extreme sorrow, that, from the direness of every necessity of life, she is obligated to raise the prices first proposed to those ladies and gentlemen, who have already engaged their children to the following terms, VZ. House boarders, 400. Day boarders 200. Day scholars 50. Per annum, exclusive of entrance.

Wanted to hire, a Negro wench, who can be well recommended as a good cook and washer, and of good disposition.

I don't know what it was, but I found this advertisement most intriguing. First of all, she must be very intelligent to teach all those languages and etiquette. Surley she had been raised a very proper young lady by knowing the rules of etiquette so well that she is able to teach it. She advertises for a Negro wench who can cook and this fits Matilda perfectly. Matilda is young, pretty, and very amicable and if I were to lease her to Ms. Wooden, it might dispel the vicious lies circulating about her and me. Of course, I have to figure Sam into the picture, but if I leased her Matilda and gave her Sam, the problem would be solved.

In March of 1777, Mr. Pierre LeRoy who had changed his name to Mr. Peter Michael King, which I thought was clever since LeRoy was French for royalty, he changed his name to King to prevent persecution in France. He approached me because he was going to sell his land grant of 200 acres that joined Lethe. I was delighted to purchase the land because most of it has been cleared for farming. This brings my land holdings to 2,050 acres.

I had a talk with my head of household Anna Cook. I said, "The plantation is not producing enough to sustain the seventeen lives that are here for now. With the combination of the war and the demise of New Bordeaux, coupled with not enough land at

Lethe being cleared for farming, I am running out of money. I have enough for a couple of more years, but that is pushing it too close for me. When we treat wounded soldiers, I write two receipts for each soldier. I have the soldier in charge sign both of them, and I send one copy with him to give to his commanding officer for payment. Since America has no treasurer, the states will have to burden this responsibility and with so many battles being fought here in South Carolina, I do not know when or even if I may receive payment. In fact, South Carolina has had more battles than any other colony during the revolution. You need not worry about such things as the finances of Lethe, I will always provide and you can trust me about that; however, to solve the immediate problem, I think that I will return to Charlestown and take up my practice there. The city will be bustling with military and civilians since it is the major port on the eastern seaboard. Many of my former patients will use my services and I will be in a better position to treat the wounded."

"I have written Mr. Laurens and informed him of my intentions and he has agreed. He told me that I would be a great help for the cause and that he had an empty house on Tradd Street because one of his colonels was killed at the Battle of Bunker Hill, and that he would be glad to lease it to me at no charge if I would agree to treat American wounded."

"I answered that letter and told Mr. Laurens that I would be honored to treat American wounded, but if a wounded British, Indian, or slave came to me for treatment, that I would be obligated to treat them as I would anyone else. I also informed him that I would make arrangements to cease my affairs here, for a while, and bring a few slaves and I would be there in late spring or early winter. I have not since heard from him and I know how busy he is, so I am going to take it for granted that he will expect me in May or June as soon as I can arrange things here."

I called for a meeting of all the slaves and Anna in the infirmary. I explained the situation to them and told them not to worry about anything because I would always take care of them; however, in order for me to do that, I needed to return to Charlestown and sell my services for ready cash.

I called the names Bacchus, Sam, Matilda, Cecelia, Phyllis, Jack and Tam-O. I said, "You will accompany me to Charlestown so get your things ready for the move. We will make the trip as soon as we all are ready. Do not fret, this is a temporary move. Our home is here at Lethe and we will return, but it may be a year or it may be ten years, but we will come home to Lethe I promise."

"Matilda and Sam, I read an article in the *South Carolina Gazette* for Ms. Rebecca Woodin needing a Negro wench to help her in running a boarding school for girls and a day school that also included boys. I would like to offer her you and Sam as a couple to help her in her endeavors. You will be treated fairly and she would relieve me of the responsibility of feeding and clothing you until we return. Matilda, you are an excellent cook and housekeeper, and Sam can help you in the kitchen by collecting wood for cooking and keeping the house warm. He could go with you and Ms. Rebecca to the market and he could do household repairs as well as provide a taxi service to the day students. Would this arrangement be agreeable with you and Sam?"

Sam looked at Matilda almost in disbelief that I, would even consider asking a slave married couple if they were agreeable to anything much less being leased out to another person. Matilda smiled that toothy grin of hers and nodded her head.

Sam turned to me and said, "Yessur Doctor, Weeze glat to hep wid tha fambly a needin' us. Thanky fo lettin'us stays toggeter. Kin wese cum heah back ta Lethe adder da war?"

I said, "You will always be a part of the Lethe family. If Ms. Wooden still needs another cook when we are ready to leave, I will find a replacement for you and Matilda. I remember my promise to all of you about splitting your family and I will remain true to my word. This will allow the two of you to remain together while we go through this difficult period but we must make our move now while time is still ours."

"Bacchus, I continued, "You have been by my side as a friend and confidant for the past thirteen years. I have always endeavored to treat you with the utmost respect and honor much to the chagrin of other slave owners, some who are both friends and family. I am also taking you with me. I thought about leaving you here at Lethe to manage the estate, but I prefer to have you at my side. Not because you are my manservant but I need someone in whom I trust and have complete confidance in to assistment me as I go about my duties in Charles Town.

"Phyllis, you will go with me and run the household. You will cook and manage the kitchen. You will see that we are supplied with food and whatever else we may need in our daily lives. I know you can neither read nor write so you will tell Bacchus what you need and he will make note of it. I know that Bacchus has been studying behind my back and has learned to read and write. Bacchus, keep this confidential and let no one know. It is illegal and by me being a judge, it would be taken badly by the townspeople. It could mean death to us both if it were to get out."

"Cecelia, you will go with us and help me in my practice during the day as will Bacchus. You will be needed to help treat the wounded and dispose of the dead as well as keeping my office and instruments in clean condition. You will make sure that all blood is washed off the floor and the walls and dispose of severed limbs. There is a dump at the west end of the city in the marsh near the Ashley River. I will give you and Bacchus a pass and soon the guards will know you by sight. Cecelia, you too have been with me from the first day in Charlestown in 1764, thirteen years ago, and you know the city and you know what I do. Now we will be much busier than before and I know that you will be a valuable asset in my practice. Bacchus will do Hendrick's job and you will assist Bacchus. There will be times when we are not at work, so you may help Phyllis with the kitchen and household chores. Are you agreeable with this arrangement?"

Cecelia said, "Yesssur, I is. Yo bin goot ta me all dis time en now I be goot to yo en does yo a goot job. Weeze got ta stik togedder en dese haud times."

I said, "Thank you Cecelia, I know I can count on you." Then I looked at Tam-O and Jack.

"Tam-O, you are almost seventeen now and it is time you learned something of city life. You will go with us to Charlestown and help around the house with the cleaning chores, cutting firewood, and running errands. I do not need your permission because you are still a boy and you will do as I say. You have a good speaking voice and you speak plainly and well, and you have a nice and friendly attitude. I think you would be good material to teach for future generations from whom to learn at Lethe. While we are in Charlestown, you will be called Charles Town. I know that your given name is Tammany and the other slaves call you by your country name Tam-O but while in the city we will call you Charles Town. Do you see any problem with this?"

Tam-O shook his head and said, "No Sur. I be wantin ta go."

I said, "Jack, you being the youngest will help with the house work and laundry and anything else Bacchus or Phyllis tells you to do. There will be a time when all the others are busy and that is where you will come in. I expect you to go with Phyllis or Bacchus or Sam or Tam-O to get a load of firewood or to market or to help around the grounds. It is very important that you learn how to wash the linen that I use in my medical practice. They must be washed in lye soap and hung in the sunshine to dry. Phyllis and Cecelia will teach you all you need to know. I expect you and Tam-O to work together and learn so you will earn your keep. Do you understand?"

Jack answered, "Yes sur, will I be workin fo Tam-O?"

I said, "No you will work together. Time may come for a decision to be made, and if you are not comfortable making one and neither I nor Bacchus is present, we will go by age as to who makes the decisions."

"The rest of you will be given your orders to remain here at Lethe and run the plantation. I do not have an overseer, but I have asked Rev. Gibert and Mr. Moragne and others to look in on you from time to time to see if there is anything you need and to let me know if there are any problems. Most of you have been with me since I came to Charlestown over thirteen years ago, and you have all seemed satisfied with our living arrangements. I have never heard of even a hint of any of you running away. If you run away, by law you will be hunted down and punished. I do not wish to see this happen. Those who hunt you down will do horrible things to you. I have seen them cripple fellows and even cut a foot off. They may whip you with a bull whip that rips the flesh every time it hits you. Some of the white trash in the country will chain you up and force you to work for them. Many of them do not value human life. I have see them hang runaways to a grist mill wheel outside and let you hang there while the rock goes round and round and you go with it. I have even heard of hanging being used because it is believed to be a deterrent to others who consider running away. I do not wish to see harm come to any of you. That's just the way is presently. We all need to live as best as we can in our circumstances. I want your word with your hand on the Bible that you will not try to run while I am gone or any other time. I do not need to be worried about such matters while I am in Charlestown."

I had taken my Bible off my shelf from my office and held it out. I said, "If you believe me on my word that we will return to Lethe and that we will have a good life here and you swear by Almighty God that you will not run away, then come forward and profess your intentions as a testament in front of these witnesses. This pledge goes both ways. By pledging your allegiance to me, I therefore pledge my allegiance to you. I will take care of you as long as I live and I promise never to sell you as long as our labors can provide for you.

The first one was Bacchus. I advised Bacchus that his pledge was unnecessary as I had every confidence that we would continue our lives side by side, but he said that he wanted to be the first to pledge his word to me on the Bible that he will never leave me for any reason. I know that neither he nor any other slave could read because this Bible was printed in Latin. I also knew that Bacchus believed in God and he has accepted Jesus as his Lord and Savior, so I knew that when he promised God, he was serious. I did not want to take this blessing away from him so I proceeded.

I instructed Bacchus to place his right hand on the Bible and he could make a statement or I could make one for him and he could repeat it. He asked me to make one for him and the others and each one would come forward and agree or they could make a statement by themselves. Bacchus looked at the other slaves and raised his right hand and told them that this was the right hand. He placed it on the Bible and I asked him to raise his left hand toward heaven. I told all the rest of the slaves to do the same when it came time to place their hands on the Bible and all they had to say was "I do." Then I said, "Bacchus, repeat after me."

"I, Bacchus, do solemnly swear by Almighty God that I will never make any attempt to run away. I furthermore promise to remain faithful and loyal and obedient to Dr. John de la Howe and the laws of Lethe or of whatever territory in which I may find myself, and that I will faithfully discharge my duties as I am instructed. To all of this I promise without any mental or secret motives within my heart. This I swear before my brothers and sisters and before God so help me God."

Bacchus then leaned over and kissed the Bible as a token of his truthfulness and sincerity. I shook his hand and thanked him for being such a wonderful companion. Then each of the other slaves, one at a time, came forward and placed their right hand on the Bible and said "I do" and kissed the Bible.

I was a little worried about Tam-O. I was told that he blamed God for allowing his people to be enslaved. He had heard that General George Washington had sent an edict to his recruiters so that they were allowed to recruit freed slaves and free black men. Tam-O wanted to join the army. But he was not free. The British, on the other hand, promised freedom to any black man who signed up to fight for the Crown.

I was trying to remember if Tam-O was ever saved or baptized, but since the slaves went to a slave church on the west side of New Bordeaux, I would not know. If he had not been saved or baptized, then taking an oath on the Bible would have meant nothing, and he would not be bound by my words or his. I will have to see. That is one reason I am taking him to Charlestown to keep him close so Bacchus can supervise him more closely.

I dismissed everyone to go to the kitchen for supper and then for everyone who was leaving to get their gear ready for a prolonged stay in Charles Town.

So it was me and the seven slaves loaded the wagons and headed for Charlestown. On the ninth day of the trip, we came to Jacksonborough and I learned that Isaac had been given the rank of captain in the artillery and was off fighting in the Colleton Militia. He was also a state senator at the time. We have so much in common. He, like me, tried his best to remain neutral in this war, but when pressed into making a choice, he first joined the English, but when the war began he switched to the American side.

I was sorry to hear that Elizabeth Hutson Hayne, his wife, and their daughter Mary had died of the smallpox from which I had treated them a few years ago on my first trip to Jacksonborough. I am happy that the other six children survived the epidemic, so at least my treatment was not in vain. I spent the night in Hayne Hall and arose the next morning to continue my trek to Charlestown.

I came into town on the Savannah to Charlestown trail and took the Ashley River ferry boat past the first pier, Gibbs Wharf, to the second wharf which is Blake's Wharf. Blake's Wharf is located at the foot of Legare Street. We unloaded the wagons and carriage and since there was a large lot with a guard, I asked if I could store my medical supplies therein the wagon until I could retrieve them in a day or so to take them to my office. Mr. Gibbs owned the lot and agreed to guard my things for a nominal fee. He told me not to leave them very long because the British are expected to attack the city at any time and if they did, my medical supplies would be confiscated.

We had just traveled twenty miles from Jacksonborough and it was getting dark. Thank goodness Mr. Laurens had another carriage there to take me to my new home at 25 Tradd on the corner of Tradd and Church Streets.

I boarded the carriage and put Cecelia and Phyllis on the seat with the driver and told Bacchus to take Sam, Jack, and Tam-O with him.

We drove two blocks north on Legare Street and turned right on Tradd Street. I knew that the street was named after the first child born in Charles Town, but the driver told me that Tradd is the only street in Charlestown in which you can stand in the middle of the street and see the Ashley and Cooper Rivers, and I did not know that.

We rode past King Street and past Meeting Street to Church Street. On the far left corner is 25 Tradd Street.

I noticed that these English style buildings were built close together and fronted the street. The house in which I will reside was built in 1748. It has a deep lot with a lovely garden in the rear between the main house and the slave quarters. It is not as large as my other house on Church Street, but it is in the same neighborhood, and it will suffice nicely because I plan to return to Lethe as soon as I have the money.

I entered the house. The slaves lit lanterns and candles and made the beds. Bacchus had lit a fire in the kitchen from the firewood that was left by the previous tenant and soon brought me hot water in which to bathe and to shave. I told Phyllis to cook something that would hold us until breakfast and went into the upstairs dining room.

The next morning, I took a tour of the house and found it quite adequate for my medical practice. This house did not have a piazza but the front door was right on the street. When a patient would come in there was a large room that would do for a waiting room and through a door is another large room that would be my treatment room. There were two rooms opposite these rooms on the other side of the hall that would be used for an infirmary and my study. All the living, entertaining and dining would be on the second floor. There are four rooms on the second floor; one for dining in the rear and one for entertaining in the front. On the other side of the hall is my bedroom in the rear and Bacchus' room in the front. I chose the rear room because it is furthermost from the street noise and smells.

Today is Monday, June 2, 1777. I instructed Sam and Jack to hang my sign over the front door while I went to the newspaper office. I wrote out an advertisement that read,

> The subscriber is removed to Charlestown and hath taken a house in Tradd Street, next to the corner of Church Street, where he will practice Physick as before.
>
> John de la Howe

This advertisement will run in the June 5 paper. While I was there, I bought last week's paper and a few older papers to catch up on the local happenings. In the advertisement section, I saw and advertisement that read where Ann had leased out Fairbanks to David Kaylor for the sum of 450 pounds. The lease was signed by Edward Martin and Ann de la Howe. Ann must have given Edward Martin, her former husband's partner, power of attorney for this transaction. The reason both names are on the lease is because I see they leased 530 acres when Ann's Fairbanks is only 245 acres. I know that when a woman marries, her property becomes her husband's property. Legally, I could protest the lease and secure the land; however, I shall let it pass and not bother Ann. I know that she will die on Fairbanks and I wish her well. If she is leasing out Fairbanks, where will she live? The only place I can think of is in Charlestown. I am comfortable seeing Ann again, but she has made no attempt to contact me in three years. I decided it would be best to leave the situation as it is. Maybe by her turning fifty-one this year, she is not able to manage Fairbanks like she used to. I can't believe that little Elizabeth will be going on sixteen this year.

I think that the most astounding thing in my life is the brevity of life. Here I am sixty years old getting ready to start over. I am still very rich in land holdings, and I will make my money back because too many people are depending upon me. It seems like yesterday that I was meeting Ann and little Elizabeth instead of almost twelve years ago.

My next stop would be Mr. Wish's house on Mazyck Street. Mazyck is an old name in Charlestown and Mazyck Street is at the west end of Broad Street. Rebecca Woodin lives two blocks off Broad to the right on the corner of Mazyck and Beaufain Streets.

At the door I used the large iron knocker to knock on the large oak door. I looked back and saw that Bacchus had tied the horse to a statue of a little Negro boy holding a ring in which to tie horses or boats. Some of the streets in Charlestown still had creeks running alongside. One block from my house is a street named Water Street. A seaman can row his boat right up to his front door and enter the house from the boat.

This little Negro boy horse ties abound in Charlestown. There is one outside of most houses in town.

The door opened and there stood a very attractive woman a little younger than me. She said, "May I help you, sir?"

I said, "Madam, I am Dr. John de la Howe. I read in the gazette that you had advertised for a Negro wench to do cooking and housework at your boarding school. I have a perfect fit for you. I have a Negro wench named Matilda who has just gotten married to Sam. I would be willing to allow Sam to come along at no additional expense to you if you would like to take Matilda. She is a good cook with a delightful disposition, and she would make you a fine servant if the position has not been filled."

She asked me to come into the study and have a seat while we talked. She offered me tea and crumpets, but I declined and told her that I had just moved back to Charlestown, and I needed to return to my home on Tradd Street to set up my medical practice.

She sat down in a large quilted leather chair that would accommodate her bustle. I could not help but notice her grace and charm as we conversed. She replied, "Doctor, she sounds like just what I need. I have been using my father's house in Saint Michael's Parish downtown for my boarding school, but he is in poor health and I do not expect him to live much longer. He is under the care of a live-in nurse right now, and I have started looking elsewhere for a house large enough to accommodate a boarding school. I have been teaching school for many years and I hope I can continue when my father passes on. I fear that my father might leave me in quite a bit of debt because of his prolonged illness, and I do not know when I could pay for Matilda. I have rented this house on a year's lease to see if it is suitable to be used as a school for young ladies and gentlemen."

I said, "Ms. Woodin, you would honor me by taking Matilda off my hands and begin teaching her how and what to cook and how she and Sam may best serve you. For the first year's lease, I will charge you one peppercorn."

Ms. Woodin answered, "You honor me sir, but I do not know you well enough to accept such a gift such as this. Why, we haven't even been properly introduced."

"Madam, I introduced myself when you opened the door and you responded. Two adult people our age should not have to follow mannerly protocol so closely. Matilda and Sam were a gift to me from a very wealthy friend and it would please me greatly if you would accept my offer."

"I should like to meet Matilda and Sam as soon as possible. I will interview them and let you know my decision. I am most grateful for your offer. May I expect a visit from you soon?" she asked.

"I will bring them by tomorrow. I will have their things packed and if they do not meet your standards, I will take them back home, but if you can use them, then they will stay with you."

"You bless me, sir. I shall see you on the morrow."

I excused myself and bowed to her and said, "Good day, madam." To which she curtseyed replied, "Good day, Dr. de la Howe."

I left the house and climbed into the carriage. Bacchus smiled and said, "She be a fine lookin' woman."

"Yes," I replied, "and I noticed a good deal about her as we talked. On her bookshelves were books in Latin, German, French, and English. She had books on etiquette, mythology, history, mathematics, and philosophy. She speaks very well and she is confident and comfortable in her surroundings. She carries herself well and she is delightful. I am looking forward to seeing her tomorrow. She has a beautiful harpsichord in the center of the room with mounds of sheet music so she must play it often.

We arrived home and I saw my shingle hanging outside my residence. I think that when the newspaper comes out next Thursday that we will begin seeing customers again.

I go into the house and through the house out the back door to the kitchen. I see Sam and Matilda sitting at the table away from the large fireplace. They both stood as I entered the room. I then asked them to please have a seat.

I started off, "Matilda, you have been a faithful servant for me now for over thirteen years and you know the rumors that have circulated about us. You and I know that they are not true, but when a fire like that gets started, it is hard to extinguish. You and Sam mean a great deal to me and I would never do anything to hurt you, but I have an opportunity for you to work for a lady here in Charlestown who plans opening a boarding school. She needs a cook and a handyman, and I have offered you to her. I will always be checking on your welfare and if, for any reason, you want to come home, I will come and get you and Sam and bring you home."

"Will dis hep you Doctor?"

I said, "It would help in many ways and now that you are married, you and Sam could live by yourselves and be together. By leasing you, I will not sell you so I can get you back at anytime if you are treated unfairly. I have met Ms. Woodin and I find that she is a remarkable woman. She is smart and she is very nice. You would be helping her in her ministry of teaching young girls and young men in the ways of polite society. Would you like to talk it over with Sam before you both decide?"

She looked at Sam and Sam nodded and she looked to me and said, "You has never lied to me. If dats what you want, den dats what will be."

I told her to get her things ready and tomorrow we would go to her house and talk to her to see if it is a mutual agreement. They both answered, "Yessur." And then they hugged each other. Matilda was crying at the aspect of leaving her home she had known for such a long time. At least, she was assured that she could come back if she wanted. I have to admit that I had a tear in my eye and find myself somewhat surprised to have such feelings. I will endeavour to keep my commitments to them.

MEETING REBECCA

The next morning, we loaded up the carriage and I sat in the back with their things and Sam, Bacchus, and Matilda sat on the driver's seat. It was a beautiful spring morning in Charlestown. All the flowers were blooming and the sea breeze was blowing and it was just a grand day. Matilda was humming some church hymns on the way. It was only eight blocks to Ms. Woodin's house. We went to the corner of Mazyck and Beaufain Streets. We arrived about 9:00 a.m., and Ms. Woodin opened the door and greeted us as we approached her home.

"Good morning, Dr. de la Howe, How are you this fine day?"

I replied, "Very fine, thank you. It is good to see you looking so well."

"I feel well and happy. Is this Matilda and Sam that I have heard so much about?"

I introduced Matilda and Matilda curtseyed. Then I introduced Sam and he bowed. They did not speak because by law they were not to speak unless they were spoken to and given permission to speak back. I was surprised that Sam and Matilda remembered this because we did not follow these principles at Lethe unless we had guests. I have to admit, I had forgotten all about such things, but I would brush up because I am still an active judge for Saint

Bartholomew's Parish in which Jacksonborough is located as well as the Ninety-Six District.

I was relieved when I heard Ms. Woodin say, "Oh fiddlesticks, don't be so formal. If we are going to live together you may address me at anytime. Call me Rebecca when we do not have company and Ms. Woodin when we do have guests and in front of the students."

I knew that "fiddlesticks" was a word that came from France during the reign of King Henry IV in 1620. I had no idea that Rebecca was probably the only other person would know that.

"Yessum," replied Matilda. "Dis heah be Sam, my man."

Sam bowed and said, "Mawnin mam."

Rebecca told Matilda how pretty she was and asked them and me to come into the parlor to have a seat where we can talk.

We went into the parlor and Sam and Matilda waited for Rebecca and me to sit. Rebecca motioned for them to sit facing her. Rebecca said, "Matilda, I hear you are a good cook."

"Yesum, I is. My Mammy teached me good fo she died at Mepkin."

"Sam, I hear you are good around the house, is that true?"

"Yessum, I speck I is. I ben wid da Doctor fo a long time. Wez don goot togedder."

"How would you both like to come and work for me?"

Sam spoke, "Wez talkd hit over wid da Doctor, en he say wez gwine wourk fo you en we 'gree."

"I think you will like it here. You will be my only employees and Dr. de la Howe has told me that if you are not satisfied, he will come and take you home. Dr. de la Howe feels the same way about slaves as I do. I would never hurt you and as long as you do your jobs, I will not interfere in your lives. There are comfortable slave quarters and the kitchen behind the house that will be all yours. There are storage buildings for yard working tools and necessary outbuildings there also. Matilda, I think we would become good friends, and I would love for you to come and help me build a great school for children."

Rebecca asked me if I were agreeable to our arrangement and I told her that I was and that they could move into the slave quarters right now. She told Sam to take Matilda and go get their things and told me to stay for a while because she wanted to talk to me.

Sam and Matilda went outside to Bacchus, and I heard them getting their belongings and carry them around back through the whistle way.

"Dr. de la Howe, did you notice the glow in Matilda's face, how long has she been with child?"

I did not know she was with child, she did not say anything to me."

"Just like a man, and a Doctor to boot. I am surprised at you."

"I am surprised at me too," I said. "How did you know?"

"Being a girl's school teacher for thirty years has taught me. I have to know these things. I also know when someone is lying to me or insincere. I found Matilda honest and refreshing to talk to. I hope she will be happy here and don't worry about the baby; I will take care of that situation when the time comes. Right now, we need to see that she maintains good health and has a strong healthy baby. Will you volunteer to come and deliver the child?"

"I would be most honored, Ms. Woodin."

"Call me Rebecca, we are both over fifty and we need not stand upon such propriety. Do you not think that I have heard the rumors about you and Matilda? Now don't get excited, I know from whom they came and I don't believe a word of it. So many good folks have vouched for your integrity that you will never know. They do not appoint judges who have checkered pasts. And besides, if Henry Laurens is your friend, that is good enough for me. May I call you John?"

"Of course, you may call me John or any other thing you care to call me. I am so happy to make your acquaintance and I pray that we will become great friends."

"I believe with all my heart that we will. I will keep you posted as to their progress, and I may even bring them over once in a while to visit if that is agreeable with you."

"They are like family to me. I would appreciate your indulgence in keeping me in the loop. You are welcome at my house anytime. Please visit often."

"What would your wife Ann say?"

"Ann and I have been estranged for ten years. She has her life on Daniel's Island at Fairbanks and I have mine here. I will soon find a house in Jacksonborough and live there and commute to Charlestown during the week to maintain my medical practice. I will leave my other slaves here, and Bacchus and I will commute between weekends."

"It sounds like an arduous regimen," she said. "Why would you want to do that?"

"Ann will probably come to live with her sister-in-law Elizabeth Lesesne who lives just around the corner. I do not think we would have any problems although it may be an awkward situation", I replied.

Explaining that as a surgeon in the Seven Year's War I had seen all of war that I cared to see. I had been to see Mr. Laurens last week when I arrived and he told me that he had been elected to the Second Continental Congress and John Hancock was stepping down as president and the consensus of the congress was that Mr. Laurens would succeed Mr. Hancock. Mr. Laurens and his committee have drawn up the Articles of Confederation, which effectively creates the United States as its own entity, a break from Great Britain which most assuredly will mean a long and hard fought war.

"I am not a coward, but I refuse to take sides until I am forced to, and if I stay in Charlestown, I will be forced into service with one or the other. Can you understand what I am trying to tell you?"

"Of course I can understand, and I agree with you completely. I wish you well in you endeavors."

"Will you consider visiting me some weekend? I asked.

"We will see," she said.

"Would you like to go with me this weekend to look for a house?"

"No, we are new formed friends and we would have no chaperone."

I told her that Bacchus was my chaperone and my best friend, until now, and I thought she was gaining on him.

"Whoa, slow down there Doctor, we will have plenty of time to become friends."

It hit me then that I was being too forward but the more I talked to her, the easier it was to express myself. I have already told her more than anyone else besides Bacchus. I rose and asked for her pardon and she smiled and told me to think nothing of it. I excused myself and bowed and she curtseyed and told me that she enjoyed our tête-à-tête. She held out her hand and I did not know what to do. *Do I kiss her hand or shake her hand?* I thought that she knew that I am French so what the heck, I am going for it. I gently kissed the back of her hand and she said, "Please come again soon."

I asked if I may talk to Matilda and Sam and she agreed. At the slave quarters and kitchen at the back of the house I knocked on the door and Matilda said, "Come in." I found Sam and Matilda unpacking.

I let Matilda know that I was aware she was going to have a child and I wanted to make sure that she knew that I would take care of her. I asked her if she would let me be her doctor throughout the pregnancy and she nodded her head. I asked her, as her doctor, when she had her last menstrual period and she said it was at Lethe last January. I knew that babies will deliver

270 days after conception so if I added two weeks to her best recollection, we will have a close time of delivery. I will not be more than two weeks off either way. According to what she told me, she will have Sam's baby about nine months and twenty minutes after they got married. She was about five months along and I did not have a clue. I was ashamed. I ask her why she did not tell me. She said she was scared what I might say or do. Since she was going to work for Ms. Woodin, she was going to wait to see what happened. Assuring her that I understood, I asked her if I could examine her with Sam present and she agreed. I found her to be a healthy young woman who should have no trouble having this baby at all.

I walked out the door and I saw Bacchus with that sheepish grin on his face. I asked him what he was grinning at and he said, "I never seen your face so red. Is you embarrassed or is you in love wid Miss Rebecca."

"Not much gets by you does it Bacchus?"

"No Suh, it don't wheres you is concerned. I done talked to Matilda en she en Sam say day gwain like hit heah, en iffin it please you den it please dem. Is we gwan see dem again?"

"I think we will see a good deal of them, Bacchus. I thought I had really strong feelings for Ann, and I did, but I have a feeling deep in my heart and in my gut about this woman. She is the most graceful and intelligent woman I have ever met. I was not struck at first, but the better I got to know her, the better I felt. I do not want to rush into anything and God knows that I am still married and I would never ask Ann for a divorce, it just isn't done in this society, so I need to be very cautious in my actions so as not to offend anyone. I would hate to come out of one nasty rumor situation into another, but at the same time, I need to think of my happiness. Like she said, we shall see."

Bacchus did not say another word except to correct the horses all the way home. But I saw the glint in his eye. It dawned on me that Bacchus had never made company with a woman, so I asked him why.

He answered, "Cause you is my woman. I takes care o you and dat don't leave time for no woman. Iffin one come along dat I falls fo, den I tell yo, but ain't none come by dis way yet. Ise git all da compny Ise need from de odder slave girls en da ain't no reason fo ta jump no broom."

I smiled and thought that Bacchus was a gift from God. I would like to think he would treat me like I treat him if our positions in life were reversed.

I explained, "We are going to open the shop next Monday, but for the next four days we are going to visit Jacksonborough. I am a judge in St. Bartholomew and that is where I need to spend most of my time. Charlestown will be the site of many battles and we should try to avoid this war as much as possible."

He agreed and asked me who we were going to take with us. I told him that this trip we would familiarized ourselves with the area and stay at the Hayne Plantation. Later, if we find a house we will bring Tam-O and Phyllis and leave Jack and Cecelia to manage the Tradd Street home. He was not to ever worry, he would remain by my side. He gave me a smile in response.

"See, I told you was my woman."

I smiled because I knew what he meant even if it did sound strange. He was telling me in his own way that he loved me like a brother and felt blessed to have come into my life. He said that things could have been much worse for him if he was in different circumstances, and he was right.

I knew he knew about Matilda, but he was not going to say anything to me about it. He was going to wait for Matilda to tell me and I admired him for his discreteness. I have always known, since our ship ride that he knew when to speak and when not to speak. A quality that most men lack even learned men of distinction. I think, with the proper schooling, Bacchus could have been anything he wanted to be. I consider him my equal in every way except the circumstances in which we live and in which we had no say or part.

We rose the next morning and Cecelia had made me a good breakfast. Bacchus had already eaten in the kitchen. Cecelia was about our age and she has seen it all. She has a good sense about her and she had helped me bring many children into this world. She takes no sass from the men or the boys. They all mind her and respect her. I have heard her say, "Boey, git out my kitchen fo I snatch a knot on yo head. I'll tan you till day won't be nuff skin on yo hide to make a hummingbird a pair o britches. What ails you? You best gwain now fore I tells yo ma on ya!"

No one will ever know if she means it because she gets her way every time. The other slaves will run out of the door and go to work. Then there are times when I see her tending to a child or a hurt slave with such tenderness and emotion. She has never turned anyone away. The first time I caught her, she was tending to a runaway slave who had been horsewhipped. I came into the kitchen and she looked very surprised and then worried. I turned around and went and got my medical bag and came back and told her to rip a linen sheet and make some bandages. I gave him some painkiller and treated his wounds with a soothing salve and wrapped him in linen bandages. When I got through, I left and told Cecelia to keep him quiet for a week and give him plenty of food and liquids. She knew that I meant not only water but also some wine and whisky to help the pain. I do not know what happened after that and I never put Bacchus in the position of telling me because I really did not want to know. Ever since that time twelve years ago, Cecelia has been more comfortable around me and I am glad for that.

As Bacchus was pulling the carriage to the front of the house, Cecelia came to the front door and called to me. Slaves were not allowed on the streets without the master's escort or a pass. She handed me a big sweetgrass basket that she had woven. It was full of fried chicken, bread, fruit, and wine. I knew that she had stayed up very late making all this for me and Bacchus. I thanked her and told her we would be back late Sunday evening.

She smiled and said, "Godspeed, Doctor, I'll have supper ready fo ya." And she turned and went back into the house.

I climbed into the carriage and off we went to the ferry and on to Savannah Road to Jacksonborough. I called on Isaac Hayne, who was home on leave. He has been promoted to the rank of Colonel.

"Jean, It is a pleasure to to see you", he greeted me enthusiastically. "I hope all is well with you in Charles Town."

"It is an honor to see you as well Col. Hayne. I am seeking a residence here in Jacksonboro. In a effort to avoid getting involved in the war I feel it would be best to stay in Charlestown only during the week days when taking care of my medical practice. Thus far I have not been forced to take a stand with either side as you have."

Col. Hayne told me that Mr. Thomas Radcliffe had a nice house in the town section for sale or for rent. I asked where he lived so I could see the house. Isaac told me to get in his carriage and he would take me there.

We rode back toward Charlestown about a mile before we got to the Edisto River; we turned left into a planned community. We went to the second street to Market Street to lot number 21. The lot measured 100 feet by 218 feet with a large house. It was fenced in and had all the necessary outhouses and a well.

"I offer you a lease, for one year, at an allotment of the ten shilling filing fee and one peppercorn payment. At conclusion, I would require payment of three thousand pounds for the property," Mr. Radcliffe advised after our talk.

"That will fit my needs most handsomely. When might I be able to take up residence?" I inquired.

"I will be ready to vacate the first of December, we can sign the proper documents at that time," Mr. Radcliffe responded.

With my appreciation, I offered my hand and a gentlemen's agreement was formed. Bacchus returned to Isaac's plantation for the night.

While I was there, Mr. Joseph Dobbins came to Isaac's home and asked for me. He asked me if I was still the judge for Jacksonborough and I confirmed that I was. He informed that he had a horse stolen or strayed from his property and asked me to put an advertisement in the gazette for its return. I wrote the advertisement while he was sitting there. It came out in the June 19, 1777 issue of the gazette. It read,

> Stolen or strayed out of Mr. Joseph Dobbin's plantation on the Round-O, between the 9th and 10th of this instant sure, a Chestnut gelding, 13-1/2 hands high, he is a natural trotter, but canters also, hath half a star on the left side of the forehead, a small white spot on the side of his neck about four inches below the ear, one ditto in the middle and forepart of his neck, and one of the forelegs partly interspersed with white hair, is branded on the mounting shoulder with a blotched P, and on the buttock of the same side OO. Whoever will deliver the said gelding to Mr. Joseph Dobbins or to the subscriber in Charlestown shall receive a reward of twenty pounds current of money of this state and all reasonable charges, from John de la Howe.

I thought it ironic that I read in the paper just a while ago that I was reappointed as JP for Saint Bartholomew Parish and Ninety-Six District.

We decided that we would stay another day and see the beauty of the Edisto River and maybe take a boat ride. There is a sloop in the river being used to bring supplies from Savannah and Charlestown. It runs at night to escape the British blockade. It has a captain and his partner who schedules pickups and deliveries. They are looking for an investor. It is fairly risky, but the profit potential is very good. When I get back to Charlestown, I will talk to Mr. Valk to see how much money I will have after I purchase my house and if I am able, I probably will invest in the boat.

The next morning, we left Jacksonborough early after breakfast. I thanked Isaac for his hospitality and he said that he was looking forward to a long friendship with me. It was Sunday and such a beautiful day. As we crossed the Edisto, I could not help but wish that I did not have to leave, but I missed Lethe most of all. I pray that someday Rebecca and I may live out our lives at my dear old Lethe Plantation.

All the way back, Bacchus and I discussed the move and who would come and who would stay. I told him that I hoped that I could move completely out of Charlestown soon and if my practice in Jacksonborough improves, I would do just that. I also thought that I had six months to see Rebecca and get to know her better. I think this will be the start of a wonderful relationship, or at least I hoped it would.

We arrived home at twilight and sure enough, Cecelia had fixed a grand supper. Rebecca still calls it breakfast, lunch, and dinner but to call it supper or dinner is a matter of choice. Either is correct.

The next day, we had patients who showed up and I was pleased to have some patronage again. I promised myself that I was going to be more frugal with my money from now on. I never had to worry about such matters before I took on so much responsibility. I could easily sell my slaves and relieve myself of all burdens, but for me, that is out of the question. My trust being in God, it is well founded and I am not worried at all. I am confident in my ability.

For the next three months, I saw patients on a daily basis and very often I would go to see Rebecca under the pretense of treating Matilda. She must have thought that Matilda was the most treated pregnant slave girl in the world, but I know that I am not fooling her one bit. She puts up with me and even seems to enjoy my visits. When I visit, we have tea and sometimes we share a meal and she will play her piano for me. She plays beautifully and skillfully. She plays Mozart more than any other music. He is her favorite composer and every time he produces another song, she buys it.

We have been very proper in our relationship, but I feel that I am falling deeply in love with Rebecca. It is unlike any feeling I have ever had. My mother always told me that I would know when I met my soul mate and now I know what she meant. I loved Ann, but there is no comparison between the two. I am looking for a lifelong companion versus a physical relationship. I am able to discuss things with Rebecca that when I tried to discuss them with Ann, all I got was a blank stare. Much of the time, Ann was condescending to me because she thought I was weird. Rebecca is as smart as I am and we enjoy the same things. I now know what the preacher meant when he said that you and your soul mate would become one flesh. We love the same food and share taste in music and languages. We feed off each other and I have wished a thousand times that I had found Rebecca before I found Ann.

One night in mid September, there was a knock on my door. It was Sam telling me that Rebecca needed me because the baby was coming. I hurried to get dressed and told Sam to wake Bacchus. We did not take time to hitch up the team of horses so we rode with Sam. I was surely glad that it was night and we had the street all to ourselves because Sam had gotten excited and I was afraid that he was going to turn us over. I told Sam to stop and Bacchus to take the reins and dive us quickly but safely.

We made our way through the gas-lit streets to Rebecca's house. Looking for Matilda I entered the slave quarters but Rebecca had moved her into the spare bedroom in the house. I found her and Rebecca had already done everything that I would have done. I asked why she sent for me and she said, "For two reasons. First, just in case we need a doctor, and second, I thought you would like to be present when Matilda delivers."

I examined Matilda and saw that her water had broke and she was in labor with labor pains about three minutes apart. I told Bacchus to go sit with Sam and the baby will be here shortly. I hollered to Bacchus to get some cigars out of my bag and give them to Sam to pass out.

After a few minutes, the baby started crowning and I was amazed at the bravery of Matilda. She grabbed the bed sheets and refused to scream out. She had assisted other slaves in child birth and they all tried to keep calm and in control. I have even seen slaves in the cotton field squat on a pair of blocks and another slave woman would catch the baby as it fell out and the mother would hold her baby and go back to work.

Soon the baby was out and I laid it across Matilda's stomach when it caught air and cried. I told Matilda that she had a fine baby boy and asked her if she had a name picked out as I cut and bound the umbilical cord. I refuse to spank a baby when it is born. It is unnecessary and cruel. It is almost as bad as circumcision. The child will see enough violence in the world without beginning life with a slap.

Matilda composed herself and said, "He be called Sam, like his Daddy."

Rebecca cleaned the child up and handed it to Matilda who instinctively put the child to her breast for its first meal. I washed my hands and went into the parlor and told Sam that he had a fine healthy boy and his name was Sam, like his Daddy. Bacchus slapped Sam on the back and said, "Gemmie my ceegar Sam." And they laughed and Sam gave me and Bacchus a cigar which we smoked as we sipped on a glass of whisky.

I started to leave with Bacchus and I thanked Rebecca for being such a good midwife and said good night. She came up to me and kissed me on the lips and said, "You are amazing. Thank you for being a part of my life."

I smiled and we left. It was about 3:00 a.m., and all the way home I tried not to analyze the evening. It was what it was.

The delivery went good and Rebecca kissed me. How could life be better?

I was thinking of how many lady slave owners would go to that extreme for their property. Rebecca was a special lady who is earning my respect and admiration more with each passing moment. I am flabbergasted by her knowledge and ability to handle every situation with grace and dignity. I find myself wanting to spend the rest of my life with her. I just have to find a way.

I kept a check on Matilda for a couple of weeks which gave me a reason to spend time with Rebecca. One night I came to the house and Matilda came to the door and invited me to the parlor. Rebecca was crying and told me that her father had taken a turn for the worse. Upon seeing him I realized that he had suffered a stroke. His breathing was shallow and he was turning pale. I suggested that Rebecca say her last good-byes while we made him as comfortable as possible. She hugged her father and held back her tears and told him she loved him and thanked him for being such a good father to her. Then he deeply sighed and he gave up his spirit. Rebecca kissed his forehead and told her father to go with the angels and that she would see him soon. Then she turned to me and held me for a long time. When she composed herself she pulled the covers over her father's head and thanked me for being there to support her. I assured her that I would be here for her for the rest of our lives.

I asked Bacchus to go and get the funeral director and to let the pastor at Saint Michael's Church know so he could get with Rebecca and make funeral arrangements.

When I returned to Rebecca she said, "Isn't it amazing this cycle of life? One child is born and one dies. Even though I have been anticipating this for quite some time, it doesn't hit you until it happens. Maybe he will find some peace now. His suffering is over, thank God!

We sat there on the divan for quite some time after that. We did not say much. I held her hand as she snuggled into my shoulder and whimpered. At times like these, all my medical expertise cannot prepare me to comfort Rebecca. I wish that I could take it all away but one must let the grief run its course. Eventually, love will triumph over grief.

For the next month, I practiced medicine and visited Rebecca and checked up on Matilda. One day I was examining Matilda and I looked at her and she smiled. She knew that she was pregnant again. She said, "dis time its gwain ta be a girl, en her name be Liza."

"That's a pretty name," I said.

I knew that she was asking my permission because the owners have the privilege of naming their slaves; even though the slaves give their children their own names, they legally are bound by the slave owner's name. Since Mr. Laurens first gave me those nine slaves and I named them after Greek mythology gods, I realized that they would be happier using their own names. They had never heard of Greece or any of its gods. To them, the names must have seemed strange indeed.

I saw no problem with them using their own names, but I did need to know which names they were going to use because of their ignorance they may choose an inappropriate one.

"Is there a reason you picked Liza," I asked.

Matilda said that she had talked it over with Sam. If it were a boy, she was going to name it John after me and if it was a girl, she was going to name it after my stepdaughter Elizabeth because she used to keep Elizabeth and play with her when they were both very young. She told me that she loved that name and decided long ago that if she ever had children, she would use that name if it was all right with me.

"You do Elizabeth an honor, Matilda. If I ever see her again, I will tell her of the honor you have bestowed upon her. I handed her the ear part of the stethoscope I was using and said, "Listen."

She put it in her ear and asked, "What dat is?"

"That's your baby's heart beat, which means she is healthy and kicking."

Matilda was fascinated. She grinned and listened in awe. I allowed her to listen as long as she wanted. Eventually, she called to Sam and told him to listen.

Sam asked the same question and Matilda told him, "That's our baby's heart." Sam smiled and told Matilda, "Dis child has three hearts, youse, mine en hers."

Matilda and Sam laughed and listened.

In my mind, I was wondering how she got "Liza" from "Elizabeth"? Would she not have known how to spell it? Could Matilda have been more observant that I thought or was Rebecca teaching her to read along with the other day students? Maybe she would listen in on school lessons or sneak books out of the house to learn to read. Who knows? I will not ask and I do not want to be told. I have known for some time that these people are not the savage stupid race some whites believe them to be. Alas, for the present they must suffer and abide by the laws of the land.

Rebecca walked into the room and asked, "How is my best girl today, Doctor?"

"She is fine and healthy and the baby has a strong heartbeat. I let Matilda listen to the baby's heartbeat through the stethoscope, and she and Sam are listening to it."

Rebecca said, "I know that as Justice of the Peace, you have published many articles in the *South Carolina Gazette* that goes out all over the state. Would you consider helping me place a notice in the paper informing the public of my father's death and to contact me if they have any debts or money owed to them?"

"Of course, let's sit down right now and write it out. The next issue will come out on October 2, 1777."

"Don't forget to mention my school. As long as I am going to pay for the advertisement, I may as well make the most of it."

I wrote,

> All persons any ways indebted to the estate of John Woodin, deceased, late of St. Michael's Parish, are desired to call and settle the same as soon as possible; and those

who have any demands on the said estate are ordered to bring them in properly attested in order to have them settled by Rebecca Woodin, administratrix, who proposes opening a boarding school for young ladies as soon as she can meet with a house.

"If anyone comes, hold the paperwork until I can review it so I can make sure the claim is legitimate."

She said, "Thank you again for your help. You have been a comfort in my time of need. I will do as you say." She kissed me to seal her expression of appreciation.

I had gotten a note from Mr. Laurens that my old office at 5 Church Street was available again. I informed him that I would be moving to Jacksonborough as soon as the paperwork went through and this would be very serendipitous for me. I told him that I would move my practice and move my medical supplies back in the Church Street office, and I would maintain an office at my house in Jacksonborough and in Charlestown. I did not think that the local population in Jacksonborough would support me in the manner in which I needed. I would schedule appointments that would allow me to commute two days a week and live at Tradd Street three days a week and Jacksonborough two days a week. I know this sounds ludicrous, especially while maintaining my plantation at Lethe, but I do not know how the winds of war will blow and I need to be prepared for anything.

Every once in a while, John Lewis Gervais will come by the office or come to my house when he is in Charlestown and have supper with me. We will talk of New Bordeaux and Hillsborough and his plantation Herenhousen. He would always send a note to me informing me of his visit so I could go to my lawyer, Mr. Valk, and get enough cash to send to Lethe to keep Anna and the farm supplied. I am pleased to learn that Rev. Gibert is keeping an eye on Lethe for me and that Lethe is starting to become self-sufficient. Soon it will be making a profit.

Another of my friends, and probably my best friend, according to whom I care for, is Capt. Francis Charles Worley. I miss seeing him for as long as six months when he is at sea, but when he comes into port; he brings his family by to see me. His daughters—Patricia, Cheryl, and Tonya—are growing up to be quite pretty young ladies. I have been designated as their godfather and I try to keep up with them. He had a brother, who has since passed away, and Patricia has gotten married and Cheryl is getting ready to enter the College of Charlestown in the spring. All three have been students of Ms. Woodin as Tonya is now. They have been schooled in the ways of polite society. All three are gracious and beautiful, and I love them all very much. They are the closest thing that I will ever have as a family. God has richly blessed me by having them in my life.

Today, December 11, 1777, I became the owner of the house I purchased from Mr. Thomas Radcliffe. I plan to move there as soon as I am able. I would love Rebecca to come with me but she teaches school every day in Charlestown and unless she closes everything, she is obligated to stay on the corner of Beaufain and Mazyck Streets. I will be able to visit her during the week and we will share meals together and I can keep a watch on Matilda.

There are several advantages about living in Jacksonborough. If the war comes to Charlestown, and it surely will, I will be twenty-five miles away and also being in Jacksonborough, I will be near to most of my friends. I will also be away from Ann who has not tried to contact me all these many years. She had made her feelings known by her absence, and I would spare her the embarrassment of a chance meeting at a social or any other public gathering. I am sure she has heard of my affair with Rebecca, and she is comfortable allowing us both to carry on with our individual lives. I think of her often and I pray that she has a good life.

I was appointed as Justice of the Peace for Saint Bartholomew's Parish, in which Jacksonborough is located, last May and I will resume those duties when I get home in Colleton County.

THE ADVENTURES OF TAM-O

I have been commuting from Charlestown to Jacksonborough for about three months. The year is 1778 and things with the war have settled down a bit for this area and for Charlestown. I think the British are beginning to amass an army to move on Charlestown. Since Bunker Hill, the French and the Spanish have pledged their support for their long time enemy Great Britain. This war is costing the British a great deal and I think they will have a final big push all over America and especially South Carolina because of the Port of Charlestown. The blockade has not been very effective due to nightly sorties of blockade runners. Throughout the course of the American Revolutionary War, over two hundred battles were fought within South Carolina more than in any other state.

The presence of the British camped at different locations around the state has caused trouble for slave owners. Slaves have spread the word that if they can make it to a British outpost and are in good health and physically strong, the British will enlist them and give them their freedom.

When I moved to Jacksonborough, I brought all of my remaining slaves with me. There was Bacchus, of course, Phyllis, Cecelia, Jack, and Tam-O.

Tam-O was about seventeen years old now and quite an intelligent young man. I have sent him on errands and he drives the wagon very well. He has had no trouble in getting the supplies I needed including medical supplies. Before he leaves to go to Charlestown or to go to Walterboro or even to Round-O or wherever what I need is located, I read the list. Sometimes there are one or two things and sometimes there are several things on the list and he has to make several stops. I often wonder if Tam-O can read or if he just has a good memory. At first, I sent Sam or Bacchus with him to make sure he knew where to go and who to see so that the merchants would recognize him. I eventually gave him a pass in case he is stopped by a constable to check to make sure he is not a runaway. As Justice of the Peace, I have a stamp which I make an impression in hot wax which would be recognizable by most residences of this parish.

Tam-O is the logical choice because he is the youngest of my slaves who is able to carry out these duties. Jack is a little younger, but I keep him near to help Cecelia and Phyllis do the kitchen chores and yard and besides Tam-O is much more intelligent than Jack. Tam-O is also good friends with Sam. Sam took over the fatherly duties and took care of Tam-O when he first came to me from Mepkin when Tam-O was only about five years old. I had named him Charles Town but Sam named him Tumminy because he was always so active that he was hard to keep up with. Sam said that it was like trying to watch many children at once and he was like "too many" children to watch, so he named him in the Gullah Tumminy. Since that time the other slaves shortened his name to the familiar Tam-O which nearly everyone calls him. He prefers Tam-O. It is almost like a title to him.

There are several names in South Carolina named by the Gullah. Daufuskie Island is an eight-square island located near Hilton Head Island ninety-five miles south of Charlestown was the first island the Gullahs came to from Sierra Leone. The Spanish were the first to control the island and their word for island was "cayo" from which the Gullah used the word "key." So they referred to it as "Da fust Key." If you say it all together, you get Daufuskie and it has been the name of the island ever since. Hilton Head was named for Capt. William Hilton in 1663 who noticed a headland near the entrance of Port Royal Sound. It is situated thirty-two miles north of Savannah and ninety-five miles south of Charlestown.

There is a small settlement just south of Jacksonborough named Pocatalico. When the first plantation was settled there, a hunting party of slaves and whites came upon a large snapping turtle. The turtle retracted his head and tail into his shell and one of the white men asked how you make the turtle move. One of the slaves said, "Poke he tail he go." And from that we have Pocatalico, South Carolina.

I came home from Charlestown one night in late April; Bacchus was with me and Cecelia came out of the house and told me that Tam-o had not come home from an errand. Cecelia said, "I knowed youse was cumin home and I needed vittles fo da kitchen. I sent Tam-O to da market in Jacksonborough dis mawnin an ain't seed um since."

I made Cecelia aware that we would send Bacchus and Jack to the market and ask around if anyone has seen him, but Bacchus and I were tired and hungry and Tam-O is probably lost. We had supper and Bacchus and Jack hitched up fresh horses to the carriage and left. They came home about 10:00 p.m. and told me that they had talked to some folks who had seen him and who had sold him some groceries, but that is the last they had seen of him.

Bacchus said that the store owner said that he took off going north away from Jacksonborough, but he thought he was going on another errand. Bacchus said that he followed the road all the way to Walterboro but found no sign of him.

I thought of the possibility of him running away, but I preferred to believe that he was lost or confused.

During the wee hours of the morning, there was a knock on the door. There were two constables holding Tam-O on each arm. He was in chains and they had him tied to the back of the wagon and made him walk back to Jacksonborough.

One of the officers spoke, "We found your boy going the wrong way from where he was supposed to be. We think he was trying to get to the British outpost in Perrysburg near Augusta to join the British Army but he tells us he is lost. You as a judge know the penalty for a runaway slave. We need to whip him and cripple him as a deterrent from running away again. We need to do this with all the other slaves watching so they won't get any ideas."

"I will give him the benefit of the doubt this time. I will brand him on his cheek in case it was no accident. That way, I will have a means of identifying him if he tries it again."

"We ought to hang him with the others watching," or at least lay open his back with a bullwhip. We can't be too harsh once one has the urge to run. We have to whip it out of him."

"Thank you," I said. "I will take care of punishing him in my own way."

"We will not leave until you at least brand him as a runaway, the constable told me."

So I got down a needle and some ink and told them that I would do it right now. The constable threatened me that if I did not heat an iron rod and brand him like the wild animal he was, he would report me."

I started getting angry, but I thought it best to hold my temper. This situation is bad enough without getting the community into a panic. I asked the constable, "To whom will you report me?" I am the judge for this area and you work for me. If you know what is good for you, you will suffer me to conduct my business as I see fit."

With that the constable held his peace, but I could tell just how much he was irritated by my unwillingness to conform to his way of punishing runaway Negroes.

The constables stayed while Bacchus held Tam-O down and I tattooed him with the initials "DH" on his left cheek. This was a common practice among slave owners who were worried that a slave may try to run away. I tattooed the initials on the lower part of the jaw out of sight of anyone not knowing that it was there. I did not want Tam-O branded for the rest of his life. This was a common place to brand a Negro because we needed to have some standards to which people in authority would know where to look to see if this was indeed a runaway.

Tam-O was defiant and refused to cry or to groan from pain. He just stared at Bacchus with a determined tenacity that he would not give his white captors the pleasure of seeing him in pain.

When I was through, Tam-O wiped the tear from his eye and I told Bacchus to go with him and unload the wagon and go to bed. The constables got on their horses and left. I looked at Cecelia and she had a worried look on her face. I tried to clam her fears by letting her know that I did not blame her. I knew that if Tam-O had run away that she did not encourage him. She respected me too much for that. I have no doubt that Cecelia has helped other slaves run away by giving them food and shelter but this is an occasional thing and it does not happen when I am nearby, to my knowledge. I do not believe Bacchus would allow something like that to become an open practice of which I would be responsible.

The next morning, I summoned Tam-O to the house. I asked him what happened. He told me that when he finished with the errands that he fell asleep on the wagon seat and the horse carried him until the constables stopped him.

Although I had my doubts I accepted his explanation but made it clear that if there were to be a next time, I may not be able to stop the authorities from imprisoning and torturing him. I did not want to see that happen.

He left my presence and began chopping firewood. I asked Bacchus if he would know any reason why Tam-O would want to run away and Bacchus said that there were some in the parish who were loyalists or for religious reasons were determined to see the slaves freed. They would harbor slaves and take care of them until they could be led to a safe haven. There were underground railroads and villages set up around the state that would help a slave find freedom. British soldiers would entice slaves away from their masters with promises of freedom and a trip to a northern state that is slave free. Some loyalists would do anything to disrupt the lives of Americans. They hoped that their mini-battles would add up to a major offense eventually.

I asked Bacchus if he thought Tam-O would try to run again and Bacchus said. "He got rabbit in um, dats fo sho. I hope he don't cause you no mo trouble."

Two weeks later, I received a note from Isaac Hayne informing me that Tam-O had disappeared and had been gone for two days. I wrote out a notice and took it to the *South Carolina Gazette*. The notice was published on May 18, 1778 and read,

> Run away on the first day of May instant, a Negro boy named Charles Town, his country name Tam-O; he speaks very plain, is about 17 years of age, of slender limbs, black complexion, and large lips and eyes; had on homespun jacket and trousers, with an Oznaburg shirt, and having heretofore offended in the same way, is branded on one check DH. He is supposed to be gone to Charlestown. To be inveigled by some of those who lately have made a practice of that in those parts, or to be harboured in the neighborhood of this Borough; Five pounds currency will be given, besides reasonable charges, to him who will deliver the said Negro boy to the subscriber to Jacksonborough, or to the Warden of the Workhouse in Charlestown, and One-hundred pounds currency for convicting any white person, or twenty pounds for convicting any Negro of having harboured said boy, by John de la Howe.

I prayed that Tam-O was safe and yet I was angry that he took advantage of me again. I knew now that he was a liar and he would never be trusted again. I did not want this! I did not want to be put in a position of having to punish Tam-O and I worried for a week about what could I do to make this go away. If I sold him, he would be beaten or worse and if I crippled him I could not live with myself. It would be against my Hippocratic Oath of doing no harm and it would go against every grain in my body.

One night, I went over to Rebecca's house to have supper with her and check on Matilda. I knocked on the door and Rebecca hollered, "Get up here, John! Matilda is delivering her baby. I entered the house and saw Sam in the parlor and I instructed Bacchus to wait with Sam. I found an all-too-familiar scene. Matilda was in the main house upstairs in the in the spare bedroom in labor. We repeated the same procedure as before and Matilda was a true trooper this time as last time. She delivered a beautiful baby girl and as I laid the baby across her stomach, I said, "Here is your beautiful Little Liza." Through the sweat and pain, she smiled and held Liza as I cut the umbilical cord and Rebecca cleaned the afterbirth off the child.

Rebecca and I left the room with Liza breastfeeding from Matilda. They both needed rest and time alone. Finding Sam downstairs I asked if he would like to go up and meet his daughter Liza. Bacchus grinned and patted Sam on the back and said, "We gotta quit meetin like dis. I needs to have a talk to yo to be sho youse know where day cum from."

I requested of Sam, "Come back down to see me after you have a chance to meet your daughter because there is an important matter that I need to discuss with you."

After a few minutes, Sam came down the stairs and into the parlor. He said, "Days sleepin now. Thank yo Docter fo you hep."

I thought of how close Sam was to Tam-O. If I ever saw Tam-O again, I would put him under the supervision of Sam and that should solve the problem. I asked Sam if he would be agreeable to accompany me, Bacchus and Tam-O back to Jacksonborough and try to talk some sense into his head before he was killed. Sam agreed.

A week later, I got word that Tam-O had been delivered to the guard house in Charlestown. He was in jail and I am sure he was being treated harshly. I had Bacchus drive me to Rebecca's house and asked to see Sam. Sam and Matilda were in their quarters behind the house. I knocked on the door and Sam came to the door. I knew that slave owners had the right, by law, to enter any slave house at anytime without knocking or making his presence known. I tried to not be so crass and I always tried to treat my slaves with respect.

I told Sam that they had found Tam-O near Perrysburg almost at Augusta and was looking for a British outpost, but he had approached a rebel regiment thinking it was a British Regiment. The Americans captured him and put him in irons and brought him to the guard house in Charlestown where he was now.

I asked Sam if he would go with me and Bacchus to pick him up and take him back to Jacksonborough and if he would stay for a while until he was satisfied that Tam-O would not try to run away again. I know Sam could not promise me but he could advise me. Sam agreed and we drove to the guardhouse and barracks just two blocks from Rebecca's house at the end of Queen Street.

I asked Sam and Bacchus to hitch up the wagon because the surrey may not have enough room if Tam-O was not able to sit.

At the guardhouse where the jail was located I entered with Sam and Bacchus to get Tam-O. I did not know what kind of shape I would find Tam-O, so I had Bacchus and Sam come with me in case he needed to be carried to the wagon.

I was pleasantly surprised when they brought Tam-O out of the jailhouse. He was tired and hungry, but he was otherwise unmolested. The jailer informed me that a squad had left Augusta to come to Charlestown for supplies and had Tam-O locked in shackles and rode in the wagon with other prisoners.

The jailer asked me what I was going to do with Tam-O and I replied that I had not made up my mind yet. I told the jailer that I would send over plenty of rum and tobacco for the men who captured him and brought him to Charlestown. I thanked and we left with Tam-O still in shackles.

We were well outside of Charlestown when I finally asked Tam-O why he ran away again. Tam-O told me that he had met some British troops on the road, and they told him that he could go to Perrysburg where the British were encamped and become a British soldier. They would grant his freedom and he would be safe forever and never have to be a slave again. Tam-O had no idea that these troops were tricking him and having fun at his expense. The troops from Perrysburg were on the March and were coming into this area for a bivouac to reinforce the contingent to subdue the surrounding areas of Charlestown and eventually attack and occupy Charlestown.

I was really in a quandary as what to do to Tam-O. I knew that he needed discipline and he needed to be taught a lesson, but I did not have it in me to hurt another human. I did not know whether to believe him or not. He makes just enough sense to believe that it could have happened that way, but wrong is wrong and crime is crime, and it is a crime for a slave to leave his master without permission. Tam-O has been told this over and over. It maybe that he had rather died than to remain a slave.

Sam and Bacchus knew that when I got quiet that I was thinking about what I need to do. We drove for a good ways when Sam finally spoke up and said. "Doctor, Ise gwain take Tam-O en stay wid em till he quit runnin, iffin youse llow me."

"I think that would be a good idea. We will keep him locked up for a week or two until he calms down and then he can work for you. Can you stay with me here in Jacksonborough for a couple of weeks? I will have to go to work in Charlestown half the time and you will stay here and take care of him. After two weeks, I will take you back to Matilda in Charlestown."

"Yessur, I tak care o Tam-O lack he wuz un o myown chrurin. I git dat rabbit oudder em."

A week later, I was notified that Tam-O was missing again. I got a visit from one of my neighbors who told me that Tam-O had slipped off his shackles and escaped. He must have heard that the British were camped nearby and thought this would be the time. He had just left early this morning and Sam had gone looking for him.

I had Bacchus to get my carriage and I stopped by the newspaper office which was going to publish the paper in the morning. I wrote out another notice which was published June 11, 1778. It read,

> The subscribers negro boy named Charles Town, branded on one jaw DH, but not observable without attention, and lately advertised in this gazette, again ran away, on Sunday May 13. He pretended to have been inveigled by a soldier, and did actually follow as far as Perrysburgh; he is supposed to have been again inveigled by a fellow lately of this neighborhood. Whoever will deliver him to the subscriber in Jacksonborough to the warden of the workhouse in Charlestown, or any of the keepers of the common goals, shall, besides reasonable charges, receive ten pounds currency reward.
>
> J. de la Howe

Bacchus and I loaded up the carriage and left for Jacksonborough. We arrived a little after dark. Sam had just come home to eat and rest for an hour and then go back looking for Tam-O. Sam is sure he is hiding out in the woods near the Edisto River. He will probably wait until later and look for fires and try to contact the British, or he may be being hid and protected by those who are trying to disrupt the Americans in any way they are able. Col. Isaac Hayne has brought some militia with him and some hound dogs to track him.

We left home after taking one of Tam-O's shirts for the dogs to recognize Tam-O's scent. They started howling and tracking immediately. They came to the Edisto Bridge and went under the bridge where Tam-O had waited for darkness. The dogs lost the trail there so they split the dogs and men into two parties. One party went upstream and the other downstream. Sam reckoned that Tam-O probably caught a log and floated downstream. There is a road that follows the river going south. I told Bacchus and Sam to get in the carriage, and we would run as fast as we could to try to catch up with Tam-O. About two miles down the road, I saw a British encampment. I stopped short of the encampment as close to the river as possible. Sam jumped out of the carriage and went downstream toward the camp and Bacchus went upstream to try to head Tam-O off if he hadn't made it that far yet.

I tried to follow Sam but he was much faster than I. Suddenly I heard, "Tam-O, Stop! En da name o God, pleze stop bouy."

Tam-O had seen the campfires and was making a last chance dash to get to the British. Just then I heard a loud voice holler, "Halt! Identify yourself!" I heard some more bushes rustling and then a shot rang out. My blood ran cold as I quickened the pace. Then I heard a yell as someone in agony and wailing.

I neared the camp and I yelled, "I am Dr. John de la Howe. I am a judge for Saint Bartholomew's Parish. For God's sake put away your firearms."

The sentry told me to advance and be recognized and called the Sergeant of the Guard. I arrived at the guard's picket and showed him my credentials and told him what was happening. The sergeant told me to advance and take care of my business. They would not fire anymore until I assured them that we have left the area.

I hollered out, "Sam, can you hear me?"

Bacchus yelled, "Over heah!"

I arrived and Sam was lying on the ground and Tam-O was over him begging Sam to wake up. The Sergeant of the Guard held his lantern near and we saw that a large part of Sam's skull was shot off. He was dead before he hit the ground. Bacchus and Tam-O wrapped him in a blanket and carried him back to the wagon. Tam-O was sobbing profoundly and talking to Sam.

"Oh, Sam! Please don't be daid! I loves yo and I needs yo. Pleze forgibe me Sam. Youse da onliest daddy I ever knew. I be so sorry, Sam. Please wake up en come back to me."

I said, "Tam-O, Sam is gone. He is at rest now and no one can bring him back. He will have to live in our memories from now on."

Bacchus held Sam in his arms with tears streaming down his face he said, "Don't worry bout dem chrin, Sam, wese gonna take care of um. You jest go wid da angels en rest now."

We got home and Cecelia and Phyllis saw what had happened and started wailing. I guided them inside so we would not disturb the neighbors. Isaac called in his men, and before leaving for home, told me that he had a beautiful burial plot made for slaves if I would like to bury Sam there.

I thanked him for his kindness and advised him of our plan to carry him to Charlestown and have a ceremony there with his wife and children. That night, Bacchus and the others made a coffin and prepared the body for the trip to Charlestown.

The next morning, I was eating breakfast and Bacchus was preparing for the trip to Charlestown with all the other slaves when I saw Tam-O peek his head around the porch door and stood there with his head bowed. I did not really want to face Tam-O. I was angry and terribly hurt, only I did not realize how hurt he was.

"What is it Tam-O?" I asked.

He answered and said, "Pleze sur, May I speak wid jew?"

"What do you want?"

His eyes started watering and he threw himself at my feet and asked for my forgiveness. He said that he never meant to hurt anyone and what happened to Sam was his fault. He told me that if I took him back that he would take any punishment that I deemed necessary. He said that he deserved it and expected it. He then said that if I did not kill him, he would devote his life to taking care of Matilda and her children for the rest of his life. He told me that he had finally learned his lesson and he promised that he would earn my trust and he would never consider running away again.

I saw that his heart was breaking and that no punishment I could dole out would be as bad as he is punishing himself and besides, I just did not care what he did. If he was not sincere and lying again, I did not care. If he took off at some later date, good riddance!

I simply said, "We shall see. Go now and help Bacchus. You will work for him from now on. Stay away from me and leave me alone. I now have to face Matilda. What am I going to say to her?"

With his hat in his hand, he left the room. Bacchus came in and said that we were ready to go to Charlestown. He would drive the carriage and Tam-O asked if he could drive Sam and the other slaves. I told Bacchus that he would be Tam-O's boss now and to keep him away from me.

Bacchus just nodded his head and we were off to Charlestown.

We arrived at sundown. I hated to go to Rebecca's house and face Matilda, but a man ought to do what a man needs to do when he needs to do it. I judge a man more by how he handles his hard times rather than how he lives day to day. The mark of a man is bravery tempered with gentleness. I guess you could say that it all comes down to how much you love your fellow human beings.

I knocked on the door and Rebecca answered and looked at my face and asked, "What's wrong?"

I explained the situation to her and she said, 'Oh my Lord, that poor girl. I had better go with you."

We walked around the house to the slave quarters. I motioned for Bacchus to come with us and told him to bring Tam-O. I wanted Tam-O to see the heartache he had caused.

I knocked on the kitchen door and Matilda said, "Come in."

She saw me and smiled and all of a sudden she had the strangest look on her face. She knew something was wrong. She asked, "Where Sam is?"

I took a deep breath and told her that Sam was dead. Matilda screamed and fell to the floor. Rebecca, Bacchus, and I ran to help her up. She screamed and cried and ran outside to the wagon and climbed up in the wagon and lay across the casket crying and hollering, "Oh. God! Oh, God! Do Jesus hep me and my chrin. My main is dead, Oh God! Please!"

Bacchus tried to calm her down, but I told Bacchus to let her grieve for a while. We stood by her. I put my hand on her shoulder, Rebecca hugged her from behind, and Bacchus kneeled by her side. We let her stay for as long as she needed. Then she stood up, composed herself, and told us that it was feeding time for Liza and then she and Rebecca went inside. I asked Bacchus to take Tam-O and find the black Methodist preacher and make arrangements.

The next morning, we took Sam and Matilda to a graveyard across the street from Magnolia Cemetery where the blacks were buried. We had a beautiful ceremony during which I was wondering what color was a soul. Is there one heaven for blacks and another for Indians and another for Jews and another for whites? I think we turn our earthly bodies in for spiritual bodies when we will be raised at the rapture, and there will be no color in heaven just as there is no time or distance. The wisest things on earth are folly to God. We cannot begin to comprehend things he knows. We just need to live the best we can during our probationary lives here on earth.

Henry Laurens was elected to be President of the Second Continental Congress held in Philadelphia, Pennsylvania this year and on November 15, 1777, he signed the Articles of Confederation effectively making him the first president of the United States. May God truly bless Mr. Laurens and the United States of America.

JACKSONBOROUGH FOR
TWO MORE YEARS

During the first week of December, one of my neighbors, Mr. Peter Cooper, came to me and told me that one of his slaves found a horse and would I place a notice in the gazette? I told him that it was part of my job and to describe the circumstances to me. He did and on December 10, 1778, this notice came out in the gazette.

> Peter Cooper informs me that a boy of the plantation in which he is the overseer of, at Wilton, belonging to the estate of the deceased Dr. Reed, hath taken up a stray old dark bay gilding, about 13-1/2 hands high, branded on the mounting shoulder and buttock JS or CS, much saddle spotted, having a scar on the forehead, both hind feet white. The owner must prove is property within the time prescribed by law.
>
> John de la Howe

Mr. Cooper was one of the men with Col. Hayne who searched for Tam-O. Mr. Cooper told me that he was sorry about the way things turned out for Sam during the hunt. He told me that he had never experienced such a change of emotions. One minute, he and the men were angry and ready to hurt or kill the runaway and the next minute they felt sorry for the poor lad who got his friend killed. He told me that he never thought that he would get caught up in that mob mentality, which he had always thought for himself and did not think that peer pressure would have affected him; however, he said that we all learned a little something about ourselves that night. Then he did a remarkable thing. He asked me about the welfare of Sam's wife and children. Here, this man was a professional overseer of a large plantation whose owner had died, and he was keeping the plantation running and disciplining slaves and working slaves every day and yet, this incident motivated some spark of humanity within him that, I think, we all have, this momentary emotion of grace to your fellow man that comes out in times of despair that makes us all human. I don't know if he will treat his slaves differently or not, but things will never be the same as they were at his plantation.

The year ended with me dividing my time between Charlestown and Jacksonborough and during holidays, I would visit Lethe. I visit friends when I am home in Jacksonborough and I visit Rebecca in Charlestown. There have been rumors about Rebecca and me, but I am over sixty years old now and if they think that this is just a sexual relationship, I say more power to them or to be perfectly frank, more power to me!

Tam-O has been a model slave. He has not gotten out of hand one time and he is still reeling from the incident at the Edisto River with Sam. He has asked me to give him to Rebecca so he could tend to Matilda and Little Sam and Liza, but I will not burden Rebecca with this for now. If this war for American independence will ever end, we will all move to Lethe and live happily ever after.

Jack has grown into a fine young man and has taken up with Phyllis. Phyllis is older than Jack but that does not seem to matter to Jack. Phyllis helps Cecelia in the kitchen when she is not performing nursing duties. She travels with me and Bacchus on our weekly commute to Charlestown and back. We see patients in both places. I take Phyllis whenever I visit Rebecca. Which is as often as I am able, and Matilda and Phyllis visit and play with the children.

I asked Rebecca if she minded having the babies around the house and Rebecca said, "Absolutely not. I have fun with them and I love Matilda. Even with a toddler and a baby, she does everything she was hired to do. She cooks for the day students and I have taught her how to serve the young ladies and gentlemen in my school. The girls are always asking to see the baby because in their house it is usually forbidden for a white girl to touch a black anybody much less a baby. All the students love Matilda and I hope she will be with me for a long time. Do you want her back?"

"No, in fact I would like to make you an offer. I would like to make Matilda a gift to you to have forever. I do not know what this war will bring in the next few years, so I thought that no matter what happens, you and she would legally be together and no one could take her away unless you sold her."

"Oh John, what a delightful thing to do, that would make me very happy and I think Matilda would be happy also, but I would not enter into this agreement without her approval."

"She is a slave, you don't need her approval. She is legal property and you may do with her as you please."

"Only in this country," Rebecca answered.

I could see that I had struck a nerve.

"How would you like it if someone captured you and made you go to Africa and become a witch doctor? They could sell your children and legally rape you and when they had your child, the child would become their slave also. They could tell you who you could associate with and marry. You could not own property nor even go onto public property without being beaten and castigated."

She drew a big breath and I said, "Hold on, calm down. I was just feeling you out to see if you felt about them as I do. I am satisfied as to how you feel and I love you the more for it. Will you take her?"

"Let's go ask her feelings," Rebecca replied.

We walked to the back of the house to the slave quarters, and I asked why she never moved Matilda into the main house like I did Bacchus. She told me that Bacchus did not have two babies that cried when they were hungry or soiled. She said that her house was filled with very high-class students who were children of the Charlestown elite, and she did not need for stories of a slave living in my house like a sister to circulate. Rebecca said that no matter what her feelings toward Matilda, she would have to be very careful as to her attitude and treatment toward her. Even though the girls and boys may say one thing in the school, they will go home and say something different to their parents.

"During school hours, I treat her like a hired help and at night I treat her like a daughter. We have discussed this and Matilda understands. I am astonished at how much she has picked up just being here and waiting on the girls. I think she can read and write and decipher arithmetic. Just the other day I asked a question to a young lady about etiquette and she answered. I watched as Matilda was pouring tea to the girl, Matilda shook her head ever so slightly that I knew that she knew that the girl was incorrect. I wanted to have Matilda give me the right answer, but prudence kept me from doing that. The girl would have gone home and told her father that I had a slave to correct her and it would have escalated into a major scandal. So, I maintain sort of a 'separation of powers' during the school days."

Rebecca went on to say, "I have purchased her some fine clothes so she would present herself well during the school day. She attends to the student's needs and pretty much runs the day-to-day chores. I pitched in after school since Sam is gone. Her workload doubled when Sam died. Around the students, she is calm and collected and presents herself very well. I have even seen some of the boys making eyes at her and then looking at the other boys and smiling. She is perfect for my school. She is light skinned, lovely, graceful and intelligent, and I would not trade her for anything."

We knocked on the kitchen door and Matilda said, "Come in."

I noticed that she has lost much of her Gullah accent. I think the school of polite behavior is rubbing off on her.

We opened the door as she was pinning a diaper on Liza. Little Sam was sitting on the floor with some small pot and pans and a wooden spoon making noise as a little boy should. She saw me and smiled.

"How are you today, Doctor?" she said.

I knew that she was trying to impress me and she had. I answered, "I am fine. You speak very well. How are you?"

"I miss my man," she said, "but de Lawd done took him away. We is...uh are learning to live wid dat."

"My, these children are growing like weeds. You are a good mother, Matilda."

"I got hep. Ms. Rebecca hep me a lots. She give me everything I need."

I asked Rebecca if she would excuse Matilda and me for a moment. Rebecca said she would go into the house and make some tea for her and me. Bacchus was with me and I allowed him to stay in the room with me and Matilda.

"Tell me and Bacchus how you honestly feel about living here and how you like Ms. Woodin. I told you when I brought you that this was a temporary setup and that you could come back anytime you wished."

"I lack it hear," she said. "I lack da kids, and da learnin en da work is easy for me to handle. Ms. Rebecca loves me en she love my chirin. Please let me stay Doctor, dis my home now."

I asked her how she would like it if she became Ms. Woodin's property which would allow her to stay with Rebecca forever and nobody could ever change that.

She answered, "What Ms. Rebecca say?"

"Miss Rebecca loves you and she loves your children, and she thinks of you like a daughter instead of a slave, but you have to be careful around the students, you know what I mean."

Matilda was beaming at her newfound good fortune. It is just what she was praying for and she was grinning from ear to ear.

"No one will ever take Sam's place in your heart, but Rebecca will help you live with your hurt. She will eventually become a part of your family and you a part of hers. I hope that someday soon we can all move to Lethe for good and live there together. I promise you that from this day forward you belong to Ms. Woodin, and you will go to her from now on instead of me or Bacchus."

Bacchus spoke up, "See honey, yo dreams do come true, Ms. Rebecca will take good care o you and yo chirin. I hopes yo kin be as happy as me."

I left Bacchus playing with the children and went back inside through the back door. Rebecca was sitting on the settee with her tea. I leaned over and kissed her and told her what Matilda said and Rebecca smiled and said, "God bless her."

I told Rebecca that we did not need to draw up a legal agreement. My word is my bond, but just in case, I would sign a bill of sale for one peppercorn in payment for Matilda.

Rebecca said, "Thank you John, you have been another blessing to me and to Matilda today."

We are settling into the new year of 1779. I read a very interesting article in the gazette yesterday which was February 10, 1779. It said,

> Run away, a stout young fellow called Marcus, of yellow complexion; he had on when he went away, a brown surtout coat, works frequently on board vessels. All captains are desired to take notice, and do not employ him or carry him off. Whoever delivers him to the warden of the workhouse or to Ann de la Howe, shall be well rewarded.

I thought to myself that I must have fixed his foot very well indeed. I called Bacchus in the room and read the notice to him. Bacchus smiled and said, "Well, bless my soul. Teach a man to fish en he will eat for a day, teach slaves to sail, en he'll sail away." We both laughed and I realized that I had no longer had feelings one way or the other for Ann. I hate that she has to go through this, but it would be the same for anybody. It did not matter to me what she did.

If Marcus took the sloop, he could be in the Caribbean by now or in Novel Scotia or anywhere within a two-thousand-mile radius. If he was hired by a French or English ship, he could be anywhere in the world. I fear that Ann will never see Marcus again.

I thought it interesting that on March 20, 1779, Washington responded to Henry Laurens's March 16 letter on the possibility of raising a black regiment for the defense of the south. Washington wrote Laurens that he would rather wait till the British first raise such regiments before the Americans do so. He also expresses some general reservations. But "this is a subject that has never employed much of my thoughts," and he describes his opinions as "no more than the first crude ideas that have struck me upon the occasion." Henry Laurens is now a past president of the Continental Congress and is presently serving on a committee charged with forming a plan of defense for the south. The committee issues its report March 29, urging the formation of regiments of slaves for the defense of the south, for which Congress will compensate slave-owners and the slaves will receive their freedom and $50. Henry Laurens's son, John Laurens, is appointed to raise the regiments. South Carolina and Georgia reject Congress's recommendation. Successive commanders of the southern army, Benjamin Lincoln and Nathanael Greene, support the formation of slave regiments in the south but to no avail.

It is the old problem of money. The letter did not say how much Congress would reimburse slave owners. Would they pay for the loss of production work that slave could earn the plantation owner? No, and who would reduce their free work force to win a war that the plantation owner could profit from either side? It is not the money, but like the Bible says, it is the love of money that is the root of all evil. The large plantation owners control the money and the money controls the politicians.

On June 30 of this year, there was a battle at Stono Ferry just a few miles from Jacksonborough. This was the same British company that killed Sam. It seems that a force of 6,500 Continental soldiers, led by Maj. Gen. Benjamin Lincoln, launched a poorly conceived and executed attack against a 1,200-man British rear guard unit commanded by Lieut. Col. John Maitland. The American losses were 146 killed or wounded and 155 missing in action. The British losses were only 23 killed and 104 wounded. There was nothing to be gained by either side in this battle. It just goes to show you that war is ludicrous. Here as in other battles, over 500 men were killed or hurt for no reason whatsoever. They killed each other because they were on opposite sides.

The only good thing that happened this month is that on the next day after the Battle of Stono Ferry, Spain declared war against Great Britain. Spain was persuaded by France by promising to assist the Spanish in recovering Florida. This will certainly help the American cause.

All these battles and plans are leading up to the siege of Charlestown. If this were to happen, it will be the greatest loss in the history of the Americans. I am still trying to remain neutral, but I am in a bad situation. I have treated wounded on both sides and I will continue to do so. People in Charlestown are trying to prepare for the worse. They are stocking up on food and ammunition to defend their homes. We have about 6,500 militia men inside the city to defend it. I am sympathetic to the American cause because most of my friends are, but if the British win, I can live with that also. I think that one of these days, my mind will be made up for me.

On July 21, I placed an ad in the gazette which read,

> Wm. Kenny of Ashepoo informs me of two stray geldings, one a flea-bitten grey, about 13 hands high, judged to be 8 years old, branded on the mounting shoulder RW and on the buttock T; the other bay gelding, about 8 years old, 12 hands high, branded on the mounting shoulder H.
>
> Mr. Osterman tolls of a bay mare, taken from a runaway negro, with a small star on her forehead, about 6 years old, and 13 and a half high, branded on the mounting shoulder T. The owners must prove their properties before John de la Howe.

I receive a fee for being a judge in Long Canes and Jacksonborough. They keep electing me every two years and I wonder what will happen if the British take control. Will they produce their own judges? Oh well, I cannot change a thing by worrying about it.

Again, on December 1, I placed another advertisement in the gazette as a JP.

> Mr. John Logan informs me of the following horses being strayed into his inclosures. A sorrel gelding, about 13 hands and a half high, with a blaze face and snip (between nostrils), branded on the mounting shoulder 3, is about 7 years old, paces and gallops.
>
> A white mare, branded on the mounting Shoulder B, and R or B on the off shoulder, is about 7 years old, with a star and snip, branded on the mounting shoulder with the likeness of a fishing hook, and is a natural pacer.
>
> The above strays appear to have been exceeding ill used and very low, and much galled. The owner or owners must prove their property before John de la Howe.

Rebecca read the advertisement and asked me, "Do you really know all these horse terms or do you just put in the paper what they tell you to write?"

"I have to know. As a judge, I must have the owners prove their property and sometimes they have to describe the horse."

Rebecca asked, "What is a sorrel?"

"Of a reddish brown color."

"How high is a hand?"

"Four inches."

"Gelding?"

"Castrated!"

"Blaze?"

"A strip or a stripe of white or light color on the forehead running between the eyes to the nose."

"Snip?"

"That little piece of soft meat between the nostrils."

"Which side is the mounting side?"

"The left side."

"How do you know all these things?"

"Growing up and in the army and living and studying in general. I never forget anything I read or study. I do have some trouble with people's names, but I remember a face. I don't know how, but I have a great memory. I had very little trouble in school. I easily learned languages, mathematics and chemistry and the other subjects came easy to me. I have always enjoyed my intelligence. I am almost as smart as you."

She laughed, "Well, I certainly hope so."

I told her that by her being intelligent, we are more compatible. She understands just about anything I may talk about whether very complex or something trivial. She has a good deal more common sense than I, and I am learning to depend upon her to help me see things more clearly.

I firmly believe that God has endowed different people with different gifts. Individually, these gifts do not mean much; however, when we use them together, we form a chain that Satan himself cannot break. No one gift is better that any other gift.

I told Rebecca that I bet we would have had very smart and beautiful children. She answered that we already do. I smiled because I knew what she meant. We have a family that has been together for fifteen years, and we are growing and prospering.

Later near Christmas, Captain Worley brought his family for a visit. We all gathered at Rebecca's house. I took Bacchus, Phyllis, and Cecelia to be sure that we had enough cooks to have a good time. Captain Worley's two daughters that still lived with him, Cheryl and Tonya, were in attendance and were as beautiful as ever. Tonya reminds me a good deal of Ann and her tomboyish ways. They will make some gentleman a fine wife some day. We had supper and the ladies went to the slave quarters to see Matilda's children; Chuck and I went into the parlor to smoke our pipes and enjoy a glass of fine wine.

"What will you have?" I asked.

"What do you offer?" Chuck asked me.

"I have my favorite Madeira; I also have Vidona, Fajal, Lisbon, and Oporto."

"I like Madeira also, let us toast a glass of Madeira."

Bacchus poured us a glass of Madeira and we toasted each other. Then Captain Worley started, "I am worried every time I cross the Atlantic. I am at the mercy of the British who may fire on me at anytime and sink me and my crew. Mr. Laurens is asking me to ready the ship for a trip to Holland next year. I know it is political and he has never asked me to prepare the ship so early before. I am really worried."

"What will you change by worrying?" I asked.

Charles told me he understood what I was trying to tell him. We lit our pipes and talked on several subjects like what happened to Sam and Ann, and how Rebecca and I are getting along as a couple. I explained him that we were deeply in love, but we would have to suffer it to be so for now. I told him that I did not need a piece of paper to certify my marriage or divorce. Rebecca and I are married in the eyes of God, and he will bless our union. As soon as this war is over, we intend to move to Lethe. I hope you will visit me there. We talked into the night and finally he went his way and I went mine thankful for what time we have together.

I believe one of the most moving events of the war so far has been an encounter with the USS *Bonhomme Richard* when it fought the HMS *Serapis*. It was September 23, 1779. The *Bonhomme Richard* was an unseaworthy former merchantman commanded by a young naval officer named John Paul Jones. He had the audacity to attack the 44-gun frigate *Serapis* commanded by Capt. George F. Pearson. The far more powerful British ship had Jones on the verge of defeat when he asked Jones to surrender and save his men. John Paul then uttered the words, "I have not yet begun to fight." These words stirred the crew and they rallied to defeat the Serapis with the loss of one-half of his crew while capturing five hundred British seamen. The next day, the *Bonhomme Richard* sank and on October 3, Jones sailed the damaged *Serapis* into Texel in the Netherlands.

This story really moved my heart and if a man can be so dedicated to the American cause, so can I. From now on, I will do all I can to further the American fight for independence.

Captain Worley smiled and said that he was pleased that I finally came around. I also told him that I would still honor my Hippocratic Oath. He said that he understood.

Captain Worley told me that I would be tested soon. He said that General Sir Henry Clinton was leaving New York this week with eight thousand men. He plans extensive campaigns in South Carolina and Mr. Laurens tells me that they are going to launch an all out attack on Charlestown. General Charles, Earl Cornwallace will assume command when they arrive even though Clinton is his superior and General Clinton will return to New York to fight a French expedition which is heading this way. I fear Charlestown is in great danger. He asked me why I didn't go back to Lethe?

"I thought of that, however, it was insinuated once a while ago that I was a coward because I would not commit to taking a side. Many of my friends defended me and I would like to uphold their honor and not let them down. I would rather die than be treated as a coward at Lethe. I have lived a good life for sixty-five years now, well past the average. I believe that when your time is up, it is up and you are predestined as to when you will die. On the converse, I believe that no power in hell or on earth may cause that to change. God willing, I will survive. I would like to spend a few more years with Rebecca."

Captain Worley lifted his glass and said, "Then sir, allow me to toast your conviction and pray for your safety."

We clicked glasses and I said, "Fare thee well also, my friend."

We finished our toast of mutual admiration and threw our glasses into the fireplace. The glasses shattered which was a token of a truly mutual friendly bond between us and that no other toast would ever be made from the same glass.

The year 1780 started off peaceful enough but Cornwallace is amassing troops all around Charlestown. He has about fourteen thousand troops and ninety ships poised to capture the city. I have been in Jacksonborough, and I think that I will stay here until I see what is going to happen.

Jacksonborough is almost a ghost town now and just a few of us remain at home. I shall have to go to Charlestown soon if I am to survive and make enough money to support me and nine slaves.

On Wednesday, the twenty-second of March, a doctor in the British army wrote in his diary,

> We moved on about three miles through a swamp and over an exceeding bad causeway. This day Coll. Tarleton with his dragoons joined us from Beaufort where he had been to mount his men, having lost all his horses on the passage from N. York. We took up ground about ten o'clock at night.

Wed. 22nd, we got in motion at ten o'clock in the morning and marched ten miles to Horse Shoe where we were again detained to repair the bridge. After crossing, continued our march four miles to Jacksonburg, a village containing about sixty houses, situate on Pon Pon River. The most of these houses are very good, the people tolerable well to live, some large houses for rice, from which they convey it to Charles Town Market. In short, it is a pleasant little place, well situated for trade. The inhabitants are all violent rebels, not a man remaining at home except two, one of whom was so sick he could not get out of bed. The other, a doctor who had got the name of a friend of government. The women were treated with tenderness and the utmost civility.

I remembered this doctor because when the rest of the army moved out of town and crossed the Pon-Pon in boats and flats due to the bridge being destroyed, stayed in town to dress Colonel Ferguson's wound. The doctor himself was sick and came to me for treatment.

I have been assured that Rebecca will be all right. She is at the north west end of the city which would be away from any shelling, and she teaches many of the rich loyalists' children. If I thought it would be any safer, I would bring her to Jacksonborough; however, it is just as bad here as it is there.

On April 8, the British began their attack. They brought their ships up the Stono and landed at James Island. They stationed troops around the city and demanded that the commander of the American forces, Maj. Gen. Benjamin Lincoln surrender. Lincoln held a war conference and was advised to surrender because of the inadequate fortifications in the city, but Lincoln refused and Cornwallis shelled the city. On April 12, Cornwallis compelled Lincoln to surrender. The loss of the City of Charleston and her five thousand troops was the worst American defeat during the revolution.

By June 3, General Clinton issued a proclamation abrogating the articles of Charlestown's surrender. He requires all male residences of Charlestown to take an oath of allegiance to the Crown. He also demands that they take up arms against their former comrades. I hope I do not become involved. I always knew the moment of truth would come and here it is. Should I pledge allegiance to America or to the Crown, who seems to be the victor at this point.

I continued my medical practice in Jacksonborough as often as I could. Then in May, a contingent of troops came to my house and busted in. The lieutenant said, "Dr. John de la Howe?"

"I am and by what right do you enter my home uninvited?"

"I enter by the authority of the king and my commanding General Sir Clinton. You have been charged with crimes against the Crown. Please come with me."

I asked if I may have a moment with my manservant Bacchus. The lieutenant said he would allow me to speak with him briefly, but that I was under arrest and he could not leave me.

I gave Bacchus the option of staying at the Jacksonborough house or going to Rebecca's if it got too rough. I explained that it was a doctor's obligation to treat the sick and wounded without regard to which side they were fighting on, and he was not to worry, that I would be home soon.

The lieutenant asks for my word that I would not try to escape during our trip or he would have to shackle me. He understood that I was a distinguished doctor, a judge and gentleman, and he wished to treat me as such. I said, "You sir, have my word."

The troop took me to Walterboro, the seat of the parish. There I was processed and put in jail.

While I was in jail, the regimental commander, Colonel Ballingall, came to me and told me that they knew that I had treated American prisoners. He said that if I were to pledge my allegiance to King George that I would be let out of jail, and if I joined the British Militia, I could go back to, somewhat, my normal life; however, if I did become a loyalist, I would be obliged to treat British troops only.

Colonel Ballingall is a Scot who had been Mr. Edward Fenwick's manager of his plantations. Ballingall is in command of a British Militia post called Fort Balfore, north of the Santee River at Pocotaligo (remember? Poke-he-tail-he-go?). Pocotaligo was the old capital of the Yamasee Indians. Col. Ballingall is a ruthless man determined to see the British win this war. He is so close to the British that the plantation of which he was the manager served as headquarters for General Clinton at the Battle of James Island.

Colonel Ballingall said, "Sir, you are inevitably to become a British citizen. We have conquered Charlestown and now it looks like we shall capture the whole colony and as the colony of South Carolina goes, so goes the other twelve colonies. Why do you not take advantage of this unfortunate situation you find yourself in and volunteer to work for me? I have need of another surgeon. Please do not make this any harder on yourself than necessary. We have other means to "entice" you to serve with us, but I had rather see you come voluntarily. It will look good on your record after the war and you will be rewarded."

"I know the British have taken Charlestown; however, there are losses in every war. Having served in the Seven Years' War, I know that to lose a battle does not mean that you have lost the war. I know that "The Swamp Fox" Gen. Francis Marion and General Washington's close friend Gen. Nathanael Greene is in the area and wreaking havoc on the British troops all around Charlestown and the low country. Colonel Ballingall, with the caliber of men of the likes of these who believe so strongly in the cause of freedom, I appreciate your offer; however, I think that I shall remain allied with the Americans and men such as these."

I am most impressed with Nathanael Greene. The first thing I remember is that most people spelled his name Nathanael; however, his father named him after the prophets Nathaniel,

Daniel, and the Angel Michael hence the spelling of his name is Nathanael. The thing that I was most impressed with was the fact that when the Revolutionary War started, he joined the Continental Army as a militia private, the lowest rank possible. He has since attained the rank of major general and has the reputation as George Washington's most gifted and dependable officer. He is like me in many ways, especially him being a Quaker. All Quakers are pacifists, just as I am; however, General Greene is known to his men as "The Fighting Quaker."

Col. Ballingall then said, "Then you shall remain in jail and we will confiscate your property and we may even hang you. I will give you some time to think it over. We paroled your neighbor Isaac Hayne and when he swore allegiance to the Crown, we released him. I talked to him last week and offered him the command of the Colleton County Loyalist Militia, but he refused and now he considers the terms of his parole invalid because of my offer and has taken a command for the Americans. I shudder to think what will happen to him if he ever gets caught again. Would you rather become a wanted man like him or would you come with me and treat loyalist soldiers?"

"The treatment of Isaac Hayne gives me all the more reason to remain neutral. I have treated wounded on both sides and I will not take sides now. I will not treat your wounded unless you allow me the freedom to treat American wounded also."

"Then we are at an impasse sir. I will take leave of you now and give you time to think it over. I will come back in a week to see if jail life has weakened your resolve."

Jail life was not pleasant in Walterboro. The keepers are neighbors who have pledged loyalty to the Crown and are fighting to remain as they were before the war. They believe that the British will win and they will be rewarded after the war is over. They believe with all their hearts that England is the most powerful nation in the world with the mightiest navy and army, and they will be the victors and retain ownership of America and bleed the colonies dry with taxes and they would control exports and imports which would make the king wealthier than King Solomon.

I have pledged allegiance to America, but if we lose, I will be in terrible circumstances.

One week later, Colonel Ballingall came to see me and asked if I had made my decision. I told him that in the words of Paul Revere that I will continue my stand as an American and take my chances.

I could see Colonel Ballingall's face redden with anger. I think that if I were a common prisoner that I would have been executed then and there. "Then you leave me no choice, sir. You will be hearing from me again."

A few days later, the cell door opened and Col. Ballingall was there with the guards. I have lost weight and they have not allowed me any water to bathe or shave. I am weak and sick, but alive. Colonel Ballingall informed me of the Battle of Camden that had taken place on August 16, 1780.

Col. Ballingall said, "This battle is a major defeat for the Continental army. Gen. Horatio Gates seriously overestimated the number of soldiers he had available for combat. When he realized his mistake, it was too late to withdraw and, like you, he would never surrender. As a result, over 900 Americans died and another 1,000 are captured. Additionally, 22 wagonloads of equipment, along with 2,000 muskets and a large amount of ammunition, fell into our hands. We were led by Lord Cornwallis and our losses were only 68 killed and another 245 wounded in this lopsided victory. This should tell you that we are superior and we will win this war."

Then to my shock he told me that on the third of September my friend Henry Laurens, a member of the Continental Congress, departed Philadelphia on August 13 for a mission to Holland on the brig *Mercury*. He was captured off Newfoundland by the British frigate HMS *Vestal*. Laurens threw his confidential papers overboard, but they were recovered by the British and later used as a pretext for declaring war against Holland. He was taken back to England and incarcerated in the infamous Tower of London, and he will be there for a long time if we do not hang him first.

He emplored, "Please do not procrastinate, won't you join my army and be part of the winning side?"

"Have you any news of the captain of the *Mercury*," I asked. "His name is Capt. Francis Charles Worley, he is a close friend."

I was told those who did not get killed in the skirmish were taken to England.

"Sir, my mind is made up and if pleases God that I die here, then so be it. I will not fight in your army."

Colonel Ballingall became very angry and rose, bowed and said, "Sir, I admire your tenacity and your resolve, however misguided as it is. You may sit here and rot. If I had the authority, I would hang you. This is nothing as compared to what is going to happen to you after we win this war. After all, I only want you to do what you would normally do anyway."

By this time, I had made up my mind to become a full-fledged American patriot regardless of what happens to me. It finally felt good to be a loyal part of something noble and good. I feel like God is on our side and if he is for us, then who can be against us. This time of trouble is just a time to reflect upon my religious principles, and I will either crumble or I will fall.

In October, Bacchus came to see me. I was surprised when the guard was told to allow him to speak to me. I did not know it then, but this was a part of Colonel Ballingall's overall plan.

Bacchus came in and said the Ms. Rebecca had sent him to tell me that my neighbor Dr. John Mackey, a true loyalist and Justice of the Peace, had been ordered to confiscate my property and sell it at auction and the money would be given to the British. Bacchus told me that when I was put in jail that the Americans who were retreating from the British advance on Charlestown had confiscated all of my medicines and equipment for their use in the war effort.

Now is the bleakest time of my life. I am in jail with no home and no property. I am at the bottom of the pit. I would soon learn that the pit has no bottom. No matter how much you may think you have reached the bottom of life, you can always go deeper into despair. The British offered the men slaves' freedom if they would fight for the British, and they just told the women to get out with no plan or prospects for the future.

Bacchus remembered what I had told them that if it got too rough in Jacksonborough that they were to go to Rebecca's house and wait for me.

Bacchus handed me a loaf of cornbread that Rebecca baked for me. He gave the guards a basket of bread and wine and rum as a bribe. I opened the cornbread because I was starving. I took a big bite and as I started to chew, something inside my mouth felt like I was chewing paper. I took it out of my mouth and unfolded it. It was a note from Rebecca telling me not to give up and to do whatever they said in order that may I be released from prison. She also said that she loved me with all her heart, and she was praying for me every day and every minute. She said that she needed me and for me to please come soon. I asked Bacchus to get the guard for me. The guard came and I requested to see Colonel Ballingall because I was ready to talk terms with him. I told Bacchus to salvage anything that was left and go back to Charlestown, and I would see him there soon.

Colonel Ballingall came into the jail cell. I must have looked pitiful. I was weak and pale from rickets and had not shaven or bathed in a month. I informed the colonel that he had won and that I have finally seen the light. I told him that I would be a surgeon in the British Army.

Colonel Ballingall smiled and said that I have lasted longer that he thought. He said that his forces were in skirmishes all around Charlestown and I could be of help right away. He told me that I had taken the oath of Allegiance to the Crown when the British had captured Charlestown and that I was still bound by that allegiance. He then ordered the jailer to remove the shackles from my feet and unchain me from the wall. I told Bacchus to return to Charlestown and Bacchus told me that he was fine just where he was with me. When the jailer removed my shackles, I slowly stood upright for the first time in a good while. Every muscle in my body ached and I fainted into Bacchus' arms.

I woke up in a tent at the camp of Colonel Ballingall's Charlestown perimeter guard. The colonel sent me some meat and potatoes, and greens. I ate them very quickly and told Bacchus to get me some fresh fruit to combat these rickets. Bacchus came back with some oranges, pears, and apples. I ate them and laid back down for I was too weak to sit up. I closed my eyes and thought of Rebecca as I drifted off to sleep.

The next day, Colonel Ballingall asked me when I would be able to treat patients. I responded that I was recovered sufficiently enough to do some light diagnosing and treatment, but the heavy work of moving bodies and cutting off arms and legs would have to wait for now. It would probably be best if I assisted another surgeon for a week or two. The colonel then told me that since I had been a Justice of the Peace for the colonies, and since the British had taken over the Charlestown area, that he has nominated me to become a Justice of the Peace for the British.

"Do I have any choice in the matter," I asked.

"Not really, we need justices to take care of business and keep peace and order in the parish. You will be doing what you have always done. You should be pleased that we have chosen you."

"I will serve because I have no choice," I said.

I am recovering well and keeping up with the news of the Americans. On September 4, Francis Marion "The Swamp Fox" routed a force of loyalists. This battle broke the loyalist in the area and many of them joined the patriot cause.

I thought it amusing that on September 17, I was brought before the Colonel Ballingall. He had me to sign a report that I was a refugee from Colleton County in indigent circumstances. He told me that I was now on the roll as a private in the Colleton County Militia and that I would now be paid for my services.

The biggest news so far came October 7 when Major Ferguson and his force of 1,100 loyalists were killed, captured, or wounded at the Battle of Kings Mountain, South Carolina. The Americans were led by Col. William Ferguson with 1,400 men in his command. Ferguson was the only person in the battle that was not an American. The loyalist forces relied, as they always do, on massed fire from volleys and the bayonet while the Americans, remembering lessons learned by "the Swamp Fox" used long rifles from cover to pick off the loyalist, including Ferguson who was shot off his horse while leading a charge.

Being in a British camp, I was pleased to hear of the victory, but I was cautious not to reveal my true feeling. The talk in the camp is that this was not the most glorious day for the Americans because they killed many loyalists trying to surrender as Tarleton had done earlier to the Americans. This was a payback to the British. This battle forces Cornwallis to abandon his invasion of North Carolina.

In December, there was an interesting engagement at Rugeley's Mills. A force of Continental dragoons commanded by Col. William Washington, a cousin of George and one of my neighbors in Charlestown, obtained a surrender of loyalist forces by guile. He used the "quaker gun trick," where they fabricated cannons from pine logs. The forces under Rugeley surrendered rather than face bombardment.

I am busy treating British wounded and I take care of prisoners of war often. I am not supposed to do this, but when I see an injured man, I do my duty. So far no one has stopped me, and I will continue to bide my time until circumstances change.

My big day came five months after I was intimidated to serve in the British Army. This was a great way to start the New Year. In January 1781, Colonel Ballingall called me into his tent and told me that there had been a big battle in the upstate out in the countryside. The place had no name so they called it "Cowpens" because of the fields and cattles there. He told me that Brig. Gen. Daniel Morgan of the Continental Army defeated British Lieut. Col. Banastre Tarleton and his British Legion and supporting regulars. It was a thousand against a thousand going head to head. The Americans were repositioning themselves and Tarleton thought they were routed. He charged only to run into a hail of gun fire. The British lost 100 men who were killed and 229 wounded and an additional 600 were captured.

Colonel Ballingall told me that the American rifles, scorned by the professional British Soldiers, proved devastatingly effective. The Americans only lost 12 who were killed and 60 wounded.

Colonel said that this lopsided victory has proved to be uplifting to the patriots' morale and has caused many to join the rebel cause, and that he has been ordered to evacuate the area and join up with General Green's army moving to Eutaw Springs for a battle there.

"Will you reconfirm your allegiance to the Crown and promise to treat only British troops?" He asked.

"Sir, I have stated many times that my Hippocratic Oath supersedes any other oath in my life. I cannot and I will not give you my word that I would not treat anyone."

He pulled out a paper that paroled me to the Americans. He told me that he thought that I was too old and feeble to make the journey and since there is no contingent of British left in the low country, would trade me for a British prisoner. I thought to myself that I am only 61 years old. I am too young to be called old and feeble, but I dare not tell him that. He said that he hopes that I would consider his actions if the tables were ever turned.

I thanked him for his granting me a parole. I wished him well and I bowed to avoid shaking his hand. I let him know that I respected his position, but not the man.

The next morning, the troops marched past me and I watched them go. I thought to myself, *Where shall I go? I have no hope and no money. I have no horse, no carriage, and no means of making a living, and no one here to help me.* As the dust cleared and the fog lifted, I saw the silhouette of a horse and carriage with a man in a tattered old panama hat and the most beautiful sheepish grin I had ever seen. It was Bacchus. Such a sight I shall never take for granted again. He had been the liaison between me and Rebecca all these months. Even though he was not allowed to see me, he kept a vigil of my movements every day. He effectively never left my side.

He said, "Need a ride?"

I said, "I surely do. Do you know where I may get one?"

"Come on up heah, en let's leave this place."

I climbed up and we left for Charlestown. I was so relieved. I did not think that I would ever see Rebecca again or any of my extended family, my slaves who have kept it all together in my absence. Bacchus told me that Lethe was doing well and the plantation was even making a little profit.

With no labor costs except room and board, a plantation would have to be sorry indeed not to make a profit.

We went to Charlestown and straight to Rebecca's house.

We arrived about suppertime and Rebecca came running out to the carriage and hugged my neck and kissed me. I felt that I was at home. We went inside and I told her, "I hope you do not mind if I stay here for a few days, it seems that I have no place to go except Lethe and now is not the time. I need to stay and help the American cause and treat American soldiers. I have learned how the British treat citizens and I have had enough of that. I never want to see the inside of a jail again."

"You need to rest a while before you make any decisions, John. You are tired and emotionally spent. Let us just relax and enjoy your freedom for a while."

"It is because I know the harshness of bondage now that I associate myself with the patriot cause of freedom now. I shall do all I can to assist the Americans come what may."

After a warm meal and some wine and my pipe which I had missed so much while I was in jail, I felt so drained that I simply put them down and fell asleep in the chair. Rebecca covered me with a quilt and kissed me on the cheek and said, "Good night my love. You deserve a rest."

I learned that Henry Laurens served fifteen months as a prisoner in the Tower of London before being released, in large measure, because of the combined efforts of Benjamin Franklin and Edmund Burke. He was released in February 1781.

This is indeed good news. I hope he comes home and I find my friend Captain Worley alive and well.

I had been recuperating at Rebecca's house for about a week. I was stronger and I felt the need to become active in the American war effort. I was not sure how to help being that all of Charlestown was still under siege. The British position has weakened a bit and they are concerned how much longer they can hold on to the city. I was pondering how I could get to an American outpost when I was surprised by a visit from my friend from Jacksonborough. It was Isaac Hayne.

We went into the parlor and sat down. Isaac had just come from being paroled, as I was, from the British. He began to tell me his story. He said that on the invasion of the state by the British, he served in a cavalry regiment during the final siege of Charleston, and being included in the capitulation of that place, was paroled on condition that he would not serve against the British while they held possession.

I told him that the same thing happened to me.

This year, when the fortunes of the British began to decline, he, with all the others who were paroled on the same terms, was required to join the royal army or be subjected to close confinement. I told them, "as they [the British] allow no other alternative than submission or confinement in the capital, at a distance from my wife and family, at a time when they are in the most pressing need of my presence and support, I must, for the present, yield to the demands of the conquerors. I request you to bear in mind that previous to my taking this step, I declare that it is contrary to my inclination and forced on me by hard necessity. I will never bear arms against my country ...I do not mean to desert the cause of America."

Isaac told me that he would gladly have accepted imprisonment, but his wife and several of his children lay at the point of death from smallpox. He went to Charleston and being assured by the deputy British commandant, Patterson, that he would not be required to bear arms against his country, took the oath of allegiance. After the successes of General Greene had left the British nothing but Charlestown, he said that he was summoned to join the royal army immediately. This, being in violation of the agreement that had been made, consequently released him from all his obligations to the British. He went to the American camp and was commissioned colonel of a militia company. He told me that he needed a surgeon in his regiment and asked if I would take the job.

"I would be honored to serve you and the American cause, sir. Thank you for your faith and confidence in me. Please allow me to make ready my things. May I bring along my man servant?"

"You mean Bacchus? Of course you may bring him along. We will be in for some heavy action if we are to free Charlestown, and we will free Charlestown and all the rest of the colonies. You may rest assured of that."

We stood and toasted to our agreement and to the United States of America. We bowed and shook hands. And he told me to meet him on the Savannah Road about six miles outside of Charlestown. He would be off the road in a community named Ravenel. He said that the British send out patrols daily, but they have learned not to get too far from Charlestown. Ravenel is just outside of their comfort zone and is unknown to them.

I told him that I knew it well and that I would find him there.

He asked if I would accept a commission in the Continental Army, but I responded that due to my age I felt I would be better to serve him as a civilian doctor.

I worked for several weeks patching up wounds and amputating limbs from all the skirmishing going on around Charlestown. I feel as though these Americans are filled with such a resolve that they will fight to the last man. I felt a sense of pride in my newfound allegiance. Now, for the first time since I left France twenty-five years ago, I have a country and a home. I will live as a free American or perish defending my right to do so.

Today is March 1, 1781. Today is a grand day in the history of the United States of America. The Articles of Confederation were ratified by all thirteen states today. They were presented by Richard Henry Lee on June 7, 1776, and sent to the individual states the following year. Every state accepted the articles except Maryland and Virginia who were squabbling over land claims. Finally as of today, they are all in agreement and we are officially a country. We must still defeat the British for our survival, and I know that we will, for the Americans are fighting for an ideal and the British are fighting for money. The average British soldier has no feelings one way or another except that they get paid to be here. We will always remember that we tried to succeed peaceably, but the British invaded our country and they are here trying to take away our homes, our land, and our birthrights. I think that any one of us would fight anyone who tried to enter our homes and tried to hurt our families. That is precisely what the British are doing.

In July 1781, we made an incursion to the Quarter House, a precinct within five miles of Charleston and captured Gen. Andrew Williamson, a former patriot, who had gone over to the British service. It was feared that Williamson would be hanged as a traitor and the British commandant at Charlestown, Col. Nesbit Balfour, ordered out his entire force in pursuit. Hayne's party was surprised and scattered; he was captured. The British soldiers came to the camp and arrested everyone in the camp and took the officers and me to the Provost dungeon.

It appears that I will be incarcerated again, but this time it is for a reason. I was told that I would be tried for my life on a double charge of suspicion and charge of my attachment to the American interest.

Colonel Hayne was called to a room upstairs over the dungeon and after a brief examination before a board of officers, without trial or examination of witnesses, was sentenced to be hanged by the joint orders of Colonel Balfour and Lord Rawdon. Hayne protested against this summary proceeding, which was illegal whether he was regarded as a British subject or a prisoner who had broken his parole.

He is sentenced to hang without the benefit of a trial. He will be an example to the other rebels who may be thinking about renouncing their oaths to the Crown.

I fear that I shall be next to go to the gallows. If I go, I will also show the world how a true patriot should die. I pray that my life does not end here. It is an enigma. I do not wish to be hung, but if it is inevitable, I will accept that it is my time. None of us will get out of this life alive anyway. I have lived sixty-five years and if it is my time, I have lived a long and productive life doing good where I was able and living life to the fullest. I leave my fate in the hands of God and whatever he deems fit for me, I will accept with courage and humility. I wonder where I would be interred. I will leave that to Rebecca and Bacchus.

The citizens of Charlestown united in petitioning for Isaac's pardon, but the court was inexorable. A respite of forty-eight hours was at first turned down by Clinton but later he relented under pressure to allow Isaac to take leave of his orphaned children. His son Isaac came back to the Provost with his father.

The British allowed me to accompany my friend to the gallows. As we walk down the steps of the Customs House, I thought of the parties Ann and I attended in this same building. What a difference a war can make. It was a delightful place to have fun, hear good music, and entertain friends. Now it is a place of doom and agony. Whole families are in the Provost Dungeon in the basement. They have lost everything they own to the British who are intent upon teaching those innocent wives and children a lesson in humility. America welcomes its citizens' loyalty while England demands it.

After the execution, I felt the need to remember what happened so I returned to my cell and wrote these words describing the day, "The streets were crowded with thousands of anxious spectators... When the city barrier was past and the instrument of catastrophe appeared full in view, I as a faithful friend by his side observed to him 'that I hoped he would exhibit an example of the manner in which an American can die.' He answered with the utmost tranquility, 'I will endeavor to do so.' He ascended the cart with a firm step. He enquired of the executioner, who was making an attempt to get the cap over his eyes, what he wanted. Upon being informed of his design, the colonel replied, 'I will save you that trouble, 'and he pulled it over himself. He was afterwards asked whether he wished to say anything to which he answered, 'I will only take leave of my friends and be ready.' He then affectionately shook hands with me and two other gentlemen—recommended his children to their care—and gave the signal for the cart to move."

Isaac was thirty-five years old. His son wrapped the body in a blanket and carried him back to Hayne Hall for burial in the family cemetery plot.

Isaac told me that he would show the British how an American should die and he did. I will always remember him and our mutual brotherly love.

I stayed in the Provost Dungeon for what seemed like eternity. This time my incarceration was not so severe. Rebecca and Bacchus were allowed to see me and bring me personal hygiene items and food. I would always share the food with others who were less fortunate than I. I was so thankful that Rebecca maintained her teaching throughout the war and we always had some income coming in. I had lost everything, but if we will win the war, it would have been worth it.

It is now September and I have been here about three months. Rebecca and Bacchus have been here every day that they were allowed to be here. There were several days when troops were moving that they were not allowed in the building for fear of espionage by the American families of those imprisoned.

Today I heard of a battle in Eutaw Springs, a small community north of Charlestown located on the banks of the Santee River. This is where Ballingall was ordered to when he released me from the Walterboro jail. I thought it would be an insignificant little battle until I realized the importance of the outcome. When Ballingall and other commanders reinforced General Green, he assumed offensive action against Lieut. Col. Alexander Stewart. Green had approximately 2,200 men compared to less than 2,000 for Stewart. The Americans lost over 500 men while Green lost over 700 men. This action forced the British to withdraw to Charlestown in one of the hardest fought battles in the revolution. It turns out that this was the last major engagement of the war in the south. American control of the southern section is now virtually assured. It appears that I may be going home soon.

The next month, the battle that will eventually end it all was fought in Yorktown, Virginia. General George Washington aided by the French had seventeen thousand men compared to nine thousand led by Cornwallis. The Americans surrounded the British and the siege began. They bombarded the British day and night for almost a month. The British supplies began to dwindle and on October 17, Cornwallis proposed the terms of surrender. Cornwallis proposed that he would surrender his war material and avows that his men will no longer engage in war against the United States or France.

Cornwallis did ask that his officers be allowed to keep their side arms and their personal baggage. This was agreed to by Washington and the next day over seven thousand British marches off into captivity to the tune of "The World Turned Upside Down."

However, the British still have a stronghold on Charlestown. General Clinton knows the surrender at Yorktown was decisive American victory, but he is determined to hold onto Charlestown at all costs. He still thinks that the British will regroup and turn the tide of the war.

I now know that I was right in choosing to cast my allegiance. I know and I think everyone else knows that the war will be won by the Americans. As I am here in the dungeon, the Americans are busying themselves with all the necessary things to establish a new nation. We are designing a Great Seal, establishing an official flag, and drafting a permanent Constitution among many other duties of Congress. I am proud to be an American and to be veteran of the revolution.

Washington will travel to Paris to set up the "Treaty of Paris" which will set the conditions of surrender of all British forces in the United States. It will take almost a year before the British will sign a treaty and in the meantime, Tories and the patriots were still fighting fiercely, particularly in South Carolina. The hostilities will probably not end until late next year when the Treaty of Paris is signed.

On January 8, 1782, Jacksonborough enjoyed the distinction of being the South Carolina state capital. The selection of Jacksonborough as the state capital was more or less a matter of expediency. With the British forces in control of Charlestown, General Green, head of the Continental forces in South Carolina, had set up headquarters at Sanders Hill which is about eight miles south of Jacksonborough on the road to Round-O. Round-O got its name from the Indian chief of the tribe settled there. He had a large "O" tattooed on his left shoulder and his Indian name was so hard to pronounce that they called it the place of the Round-O and the name stuck. From this position, Green thought he could better protect the Senate and House members, so he advised the General Assembly to meet there.

The people were trying to find buildings large enough to house this illustrious body of some one hundred men. Finally, the Masonic Lodge and tavern were converted to its purpose. The tavern was owned by Peter DuBose who was a neighbor and a good friend. He removed the partition between the two rooms to make the proper space. He was sure that he would be reimbursed for his trouble after the war; I know that I certainly hope to be. If not, I will make it, but I will have to start from scratch.

There was much excitement in Jacksonborough during that time. There were so many prominent men milling about and so many important events taking place. First, there was the election of a new governor because John Rutledge had served out his time. Gen. Christopher Gadsden was offered the position, but he refused the office citing old age and infirmities. The General Assembly then elected John Matthews of Charlestown.

Their next action was very concerning to me. The Assembly started debates over the dreadful Confiscation Acts, which if approved as presented, would prove very costly to British sympathizers. These acts would banish those people decreed disloyal to the American cause and deprive them of their property as a punishment for their actions. As General Green wrote, this action affected "known loyalists, those who joined the British Armed forces, who had failed to surrender to the Americans after the prescribed date, February 20, 1779." He went on to include those who congratulated Gen. Clinton in public and Admiral Arbuthnot upon the conquest of Charlestown, those who congratulated Cornwallis on his victory at Camden; those who held commissions of the king; and those whose activities manifested their attachment to the British cause generally."

This is me! They do not know my heart. They will only know that I served in Col. Ballingall's brigade as a surgeon and that I was on the rolls as a loyalist. My god! I even became a judge for the British right there where they are meeting. I hope they realize that I am now in prison for fighting the British. I don't know what I would do if the tables were turned.

Regarding this matter, Aedanus Burke wrote a letter to Arthur Middleton in which he said, "Bills before the House that merit attention are, one regulating the militia, for raising two Continental Battalions, circuit Court Laws, etc., and a confiscation bill. This will make a great noise and will bring so many families and their children to beggary and ruin, that I most devoutly detest it."

The assembly received a list of over 700 names and the Commissioners of Confiscation added 240 more. My name is near the top. Much of the confiscated property would be given to war heroes as a payment for their services.

Jacksonborough had grown to a population of about twelve thousand inhabitants and about ten thousand slaves. So at that time and when I lived there, it was a thriving little metropolis. Now that the British were restricted to the vicinity of Charlestown, Jacksonborough was the perfect place to hold the assembly.

The rebels confiscated all of my medical supplies and the British confiscated my land and property, so if I am amerced or taxed as a penalty, I will not have much to pay; however, if they find out about my land at Lethe, which is on the Register Mesne Conveyance public records at the court house in Charlestown for anyone to read. Being amerced would be better than banishment. Where would I go, back to France? France was allies of the Americans, so how would I be received if I were even allowed to come back? If I were banished, would they give me anything to live on? What would happen to Rebecca? What would happen to my slaves? Would they be sold to individuals and families broken up and mistreated? How would I be able to start over at the age of sixty-five? I think that I had rather died than to face banishment. Even though I fit all the qualifications and requirements for banishment, I must somehow appeal my case to the assembly so that they would know the circumstances of my dealings with the British.

Something came out today that did not help my cause at all. I received a notice that I was being paid for being a private under Ballingall. The Public Records Office in London from the Treasury dated September 17, 1780 volume three, book 11:287, I was the second private mentioned that I had served 148 days of continuous service and I was due three pounds, eight shillings, and two pence. Mine was one of the few that did not show "Paid" by his name. I thought it amusing that the British were so magnanimous with their money. They confiscated my home worth about £5,000 and my medicines worth another £5,000 pounds, and here they are paying me a surgeon's fee of £3 for five months of service. Why, I may even retire on that. It would be about $7.00 in American money. I have to make fun out of this because the consequences could be devastating. This is worse than sitting in this Provost Dungeon. I was listed on the same date in volume five as a refugee from Colleton County in indigent circumstances. There I was number one with a rank of "refugee" my name and under remarks it said "Practiced phisick in Jacksonborough. They have confiscated all my possessions and my ability to support myself with no prospect for the future. The rest of the list included old and sick or dead men with large orphaned children. This may help me in my argument to be released from the Provost Dungeon; however, it will not help me in my banishment case with the Americans.

Later that week, a jailer came and called my name. I thought I was going to hang just as my friend Isaac had been, we were in the same circumstances. We both swore allegiance to the Crown and we both swore not to take up arms against the British, then we both violated that agreement by taking up arms and fighting the British and disavowing our allegiance.

I could see no hope. I thought that I had rather be dead than suffer at the hands of my country. Maybe it was for the best for all concerned that I get it all over with. I walked into the room upstairs where General Clinton's court was convened. The senior officer spoke up and said that there was a lengthy discussion concerning me and my status. They gave me the benefit of the doubt that I was a rebel spy and that they thought that I practiced medicine and gave aid to the enemy only when I had to. They said that I was a surgeon in the British army and a judge for the Crown in Saint Bartholomew's Parish and that my home was confiscated by the British. All that said, they told me that they were satisfied that I had been punished enough and I was free to go home.

My knees almost buckled in relief. It was a joyous occasion, but short lived. What now? I went back to my cell, actually my place on the floor that I had claimed. All the prisoners were in one big room. I administered to many other American prisoners while incarcerated. There were all kinds of sickness and wounds and babies born. If there was a disease in the city, the prisoners would get afflicted with it.

I cleaned myself up as well as I could and I thanked the sentry who let Rebecca and Bacchus visit me, and I walked up the stairway to the front of the building facing the harbor. I walked into the sunshine and the glare hurt my eyes. I was pale and weak from being in prison for so long. I will never forget the feeling of the sun and the wind on my skin. I stopped and took a long deep breath and closed my eyes and I thanked God for giving me the strength to withstand another war and imprisonment. I opened my eyes and there was Rebecca in the carriage driven by Bacchus. Rebecca jumped out of the carriage with a move I didn't think possible and ran to me and hugged me and kissed me. She said, "I pray that we will never be parted at any time again. Together we will endure. It is like being a child of God. You and God are a majority in any circumstance. I will never leave you as long as you will have me. I am afraid that you are stuck with me."

"I wouldn't call it stuck with you, but I would call it being blessed."

"Let's go home, John and enjoy the rest of our lives together. We still have a lot of living to do."

I looked at Bacchus and he said, "Need anodder ride, sir? We gotta quit meetin like dis." He smiled that big toothy grin that I swear would glow in the dark. He extended me his hand and pulled me up into the carriage and then he pulled Rebecca in and I heard that familiar, "Well, gwan dare, mule." Then he would laugh.

Of course, we had fine horses to pull our carriage, but every animal that pulled a carriage was a mule to Bacchus. Actually, mules are much stronger than horses, but they are much uglier. A horse is much calmer in battle but a mule will out pull a horse almost two to one. In battle, the men must take the mules to the rear to keep them from having heart attacks where most horses will just sit there calmly. That's why you hear the term "war horse" and not war mule.

We got home about noon and I held Rebecca's hand as we went into the parlor. "Is it really over?" I asked.

"It is really over and you will never have to endure war again, nor will you be thrown into a jail or a dungeon. We will buy the basic medicines you need to start your practice over and when you are ready, we will move to Lethe."

After a week's rest, I decided to travel to Jacksonborough and see if I could get representation for when I was punished by the Commissioners of Confiscation. I also wanted to check and see what happened to the Schooner in which I had invested several years ago with Captain John Driffle and a neighbor, Mr. Campbell. I was told that the Schooner was captured by a British whale boat in the Dawhow River. I will try to find out who is responsible and get restitution.

Jacksonborough was beginning to be a thriving town again. The British had destroyed almost everything they could not carry off but they were rebuilding. The Hayne Plantation was still there so I stopped by and paid my respects to Isaac Jr. and stood by the grave of my friend. I thought what a waste. What possible good could have come from such a tragedy? Then I thought of all the men who had become inspired by the manner in which he met his maker. His martyrdom has inspired thousands of patriots who rallied to the cause once they saw the British display their true colors. I prayed that his death was not in vain.

It was February 26, 1782, and the South Carolina General Assembly was adjourning. Inside the Masonic Lodge room I saw my old friend John Lewis Gervais. I was surprised to see that he had grown into a fine looking young man. He was still working for Mr. Laurens and had made quite a lot of money in his trade. He still owned and managed Herenhousen Plantation. I called his name and he turned, saw me and yelled, Dr. Jean! How are you? I am so glad to see you are out of the dungeon. Are you well?

"I am recovering well. I am not as young as I use to be and it takes me a little longer to recover these days. I am happy to see you are well and happy."

"Ah, mais oui, Monsieur, Je suis heureux de vous voir également."

ANTHONY NEIL WARREN SR.

I said, "Speak English, we are American citizens now, but when you come and visit me, assuming I have a home, we may speak in any language we wish without offending anyone."

I asked him if there was a place we could talk, informing him that I was in need of his assistance. He asked what it was about and I revealed that it was about my banishment. He asked me to wait saying that he would return shorly.

When he returned, he had Mr. Henry Laurens, Thomas Bee, and Patrick Calhoun and Benjamin Simons with him. All close friends with whom I had close ties.

We all decided to meet at Hayne Hall and talk over my situation.

We arrived at Hayne Hall about one hour later. Hayne Hall is four miles from the center of Jacksonborough. We assembled in the parlor, and Isaac Junior welcomed us and offered us pipes and drinks. I explained my situation to the gentlemen and Mr. Laurens told me that he was familiar with the day's proceedings and was very concerned when my name was brought up. He told me that he did not believe that stories that he had heard, and he was glad to finally hear it from my own mouth. He and the rest of the representatives could rely on my word. He told us that the recommendations were already made to the committee and they would be published in the March 20 issue of the gazette. He and John Lewis had lobbied the assembly on my behalf, but they will not know if or to what extent their influence had on the committee members. We would all find out in a month.

Mr. Laurens told me to retain a good lawyer, one that has no political interest in the assembly but one of great statue that everyone respects and everyone knows is respectable. John Lewis spoke up and said that he was thinking about Mr. Henry Pendleton. In 1776, he was appointed as an assistant judge and has been active in his law practice and politics ever since. He would be a powerful ally for you. In the meantime, regardless of the outcome, you may always appeal to a higher authority. All the

238

time you are appealing, we will all be lobbying on your behalf. That is all we can legally do without someone asking us to recue ourselves for conflict of interests.

We all sat around the parlor discussing the day's events when Mr. Laurens came up to me and told me that he knew what I have been going through. He said that he was in the Tower of London for fifteen months. It was a dark, rat-infested, filthy place. In the fall of 1779, he said that he was named by Congress as minister to the Netherlands. He went there and negotiated Dutch support for our war effort and on the return trip, he was intercepted.

The British charged him with treason, transported him to England, and imprisoned him in the Tower of London. I found out that I had the distinction of being the only American to have been held prisoner in the Tower.

"Of course my imprisonment was protested by the Americans. In the field, most captives were regarded as prisoners of war, and while conditions were frequently appalling, prisoner exchanges and mail privileges were accepted practice. During my imprisonment, I was assisted by Richard Oswald and Benjamin Franklin, Oswald is my former business partner and the principal owner of Bunce Island. Oswald argued on my behalf to the British government. Finally, on December 31, 1781, I was released in exchange for General Lord Cornwallis and completed my voyage to Amsterdam. I then helped raise funds for the American effort", He related.

Bunce Island is also spelled "Bence," "Bense," or "Bance" at different periods. It is the site of an eighteenth century British slave castle in the Republic of Sierra Leone in West Africa.

Located about twenty miles upriver from Sierra Leone's capital city of Freetown, Bunce Island lies in the Sierra Leone River (also called the Freetown Harbor), the vast estuary formed by the Rokel River and Port Loko Creek. Although a small island only about 1,650 feet long and 350 feet wide, its strategic position at the limit of navigation in Africa's largest natural harbor made it an ideal base for European slave merchants.

Tellingly, the chief negotiator on the British side was Richard Oswald, the principal owner of Bunce Island, and Laurens' friend for thirty years. US Independence was thus negotiated, in part, between the British owner of Bunce Island and his American business agent in South Carolina. This reflects the wealth generated by the trade in rice and slaves.

Mr. Laurens told me that his son John Laurens, a colonel in the Continental Army and officer on Washington's staff, believed that Americans could not fight for their own freedom while holding slaves. In 1779, he persuaded the Continental Congress to authorize the recruitment of a brigade (three thousand men) of slaves, who would be given their freedom after the war. However, when he presented it to them, the South Carolina Provincial Congress overwhelmingly rejected the proposal, and instead voted to use confiscated slaves as payment to recruit more white soldiers. John Laurens was killed in a skirmish in South Carolina in 1782. He urged his father to free their slaves.

After the war, Henry Laurens manumitted all his 260 slaves.

I asked him about my best friend in the world Capt. Francis Charles Worley. He told me that he was sorry to have to tell me that Captain Worley was killed in action and buried at sea. He was killed defending his ship and defending me. He died a brave and gallant death, and his country should be proud of him.

Tears began to swell up in my eyes and it felt like someone had kicked me hard in the stomach, but I held my composure and I knew that his memory would live forever in my heart. It was hard for me to realize that we would never have a chance to enjoy each other's company again. I will keep up with his family and somehow make sure that they have everything they need. But for now, I have to exonerate myself to the Americans if I am to possess anything.

All the gentlemen visited and enjoyed each other's company. I talked to John Lewis and asked him about Lethe. He told me that Boze was doing a good job managing the farm and that James had asked Molly to marry him and Ben asked Becky to jump the broom. They are waiting for your permission. I explained that they would have to wait until I found out the status of the property at Lethe. If I am banished from America, they would be sold and maybe not as couples or even as a family. I am sorry, but I think it best not to allow any marriages right now. I hope they will understand what I am facing. Slaves are property and if I am banished, they will be confiscated and sold to the highest bidder or the property will be given to a patriot hero who may not be as amenable as I am as far as accepting them as human beings.

John Lewis informed me that the Lethe Plantation is actually making some money. It is self-supporting and the money is handled by Rev. Gibert. When Rev. Gibert takes his wine or other crops to market, he takes the yield from Lethe, especially the indigo, and sells it and puts the money in an account to support Lethe. He has managed the property very well. John Lewis said that he goes there as often as he is allowed and keeps the community informed as to my circumstances. "The whole district is anxious to hear of any news concerning you and they are very curious about Rebecca. I hope and pray that you will be allowed to return to your beloved Lethe and live the rest of your life in peace."

We all socialized for the rest of the morning and finally we knew that we needed to return to Charlestown, but now that the General Assembly has met, they are going to change the name to "Charleston."

Bacchus and I arrive at Rebecca's house at the corner of Beaufain and Mazyck Streets where we are welcomed by Rebecca and the staff. I see that Jack and Phyllis are together, and Tam-O is staying close to Matilda trying to make up for Sam's tragedy.

Matilda has forgiven Tam-O because she said that she understood his desire for freedom. She told him the she knew that he would have not gotten Sam killed on purpose. No one would ever take Sam's place, but Tam-O is trying his best. Rebecca tells me that Tam-O has been the best behaved slave in the house. He has had many opportunities to run to the British, but he comes home every time. Rebecca said that it was time to trust him again, and besides, if he runs away, we would just let him go. I agreed as long as he does not try to influence any of the other slaves. Bacchus will see to that.

I told Rebecca of the day's events and she smiled and said, "God's will be done. John, you are a good man with a kind spirit, and I do not believe God will allow you to be banished from this country. You have fought for its freedom and you have saved many, many lives for its cause. Surely, they will realize your circumstances."

"I really don't know. The legislature is made up of true rebels who are angry at anyone who was not 100 percent for the independence of the United States. They are banishing and punishing loyalists every day as an example to others as to where their allegiance should be placed. I have powerful friends in high places lobbying for me; however, there are many very prominent loyalists who will be banished or worse for their actions in the war. They are punishing some men for being obnoxious. I am really afraid the worse may happen. We need to make plans now as to what we will do. Listen to me, I shall not burden you with my problems. You are established here and you have a good business teaching young ladies and gentlemen. The war has not affected your business and it would be very unfair and selfish of me to expect you to follow me wherever I go."

Rebecca sternly said, "Stop right there, let me quote you from the book of Ruth, 'Intreat me not to leave thee, or to return from following after thee: for whither thou goest, I will go; and where thou lodgest, I will lodge: thy people shall be my people, and thy God my God: Where thou diest, will I die, and there will I be buried: the Lord do so to me, and more also, if ought but death part thee and me.' That is precisely how I feel about you and our relationship. I love you with all my heart, and I will not have you treat me as a separate person. We are united forever. I have never left your side, in any circumstance, and I never will. Don't you ever try to spare my feelings again. You are my feelings and we will face all this together or not at all."

"Yes mam, please forgive my doubts but it seems that my whole world is falling apart."

"I remember the advice you gave a friend, what you will change by worrying. Let's let what happens happen and we will deal with it together."

The weeks dragged on. I was just about over all of my health problems. I had gained back some weight and had rested. I returned to my old office and there were enough supplies to see a limited number of patients, mostly wounds and amputated limbs being treated to prevent infections. I was keeping a record of the American wounded that I was treating by suggestion of Mr. Laurens and my new lawyer, Mr. Henry Pendleton.

I visited Mr. Pendleton in his office last week and informed him of my circumstances. I paid him a retainer and he told me to keep quiet and see what the outcome of the Confiscation Committee recommendations. Once we knew where we stood, we could better appeal the decision. He told me that feelings were easing as to the harshness of the penalties. Gen. George Washington and others have met and recommended that we try to mend out fences and try to forgive our enemies and become one nation tolerant of religious and political beliefs. But still, there are those on the committee who have lost sons and fathers in the war and their sentiments have been hardened by the treatment of some by the British. We will just have to wait and see. Mr. Pendleton said that he would start making notes to prepare arguments for appeal for whatever negative decision the committee may make.

Finally, the day of reckoning was here. Today, I will find out my fate of being banished or worse. I had Bacchus hitch up the team immediately after breakfast and we went to look for a newspaper. The gazette was being printed in Jacksonborough because the British were still in control and would not leave until the signing of the Paris accord. They were very lax in their rules and regulations knowing that we will soon become their judges.

I finally found a newspaper boy and bought a paper. I did not open it, but I took it back to Rebecca so we could learn of my fate together. We sat down on the davenport and I opened the paper and saw the results of the committee findings and with Rebecca sitting by me side and started reading under the heading of "South Carolina Physicians 1780–1781, Loyalists,"

> Item 1. Confiscated Estates belonging to British Subjects Lying and Being in the State of South Carolina, 1780–1781:
> Crockett, Doctor – Heirs
> Gibbs, Doctor – Heirs

And upon reading the next item I thought, *Oh lord, they could group me in this category.*

> Item 3. Petitioners to the British Commandant of Charlestown to be Armed as Loyal Militia – Their Estates Confiscated and their Persons to be Banished from the State:
> Rose, Hugh, Dr.
> Wilson, Robert, Dr.

> Item 4. Congratulations of Lord Cornwallis on his Victory over General Gates at Camden on August 16, 1780, whose Estates are Confiscated and their Persons Banished from the State:
> Clitheral, James, Dr.
> Garden, Alexander, Dr.
> Perroneau, Robert, Dr.

> Item 5. Militia Officers and Magistrates Commissioned by the British commandant of Charles Town whose

Estates are Confiscated and their Persons Banished from
the State:
Lynah, James, Dr.
Fraser, James, Dr.
Fyffe, Charles, Dr.

My name was not there! I am really surprised.

Item 6. Obnoxious Persons whose Estates are Confiscated
and their Persons to be Banished:
Spence, Peter, Dr.

Item 7. Persons Refusing to take an Oath of Allegiance to
the Staate in the year 17— and in Consequence Thereof,
by Law obliged to depart the same by the aforesaid New
Act of Assembly, their Estates now Confiscated and their
Persons subject to Banishment:
Bull, Wm.- Lieut – Gov.
Baron, Doctor
Rhind, David, Dr.
Mackie, Doctor

I was not happy to see Dr. Mackey's name on the list, but he was
the man who confiscated my Jacksonborough property, evicted
me and sold the property, and gave the money to the British.

"Where am I?" I thought that I did not have a prayer to stand
on. Then I turned the page and read,

Item 8. Persons whose Estates are Amerced in a fine of 12
percent – Ad Valorem:
Delahowe, John, Dr.
Wells. John, Dr.
also Dr. George Carter
Dr. Moultrie
Dr. Farquharson

There it was. No banishment! I was ecstatic. Rebecca hollered
and we hugged and jumped up and down. I was to be an American

citizen and I would never have to move or leave again. I can finally put down roots at Lethe and live the rest of my life as a patriot.

Bacchus heard all the commotion and came running into the room. I explained what had just happened and his eyes got teary up and said, "Now, we goes home, en home it is!"

After calming down, we discussed my fine. I asked Rebecca exactly what 12 percent of my worth was. Did they include my Lethe property or was that not included? I had lost over £10,000 (about $2,000,000.00 in today's terms) due to confiscation of my medical supplies to the Americans and my property in Jacksonborough to the British, would they consider that or not? I would see Mr. Pendleton and help him prepare my defense. In any event, I could live with any judgment against me. I would gladly pay the fine and be at rest from now on if I have too. At least, I can go back to work and earn a living again.

I made an appointment to see my lawyer, Mr. Henry Pendleton, for the earliest convenient time. When we met, he informed me that the legislature would not meet again until January of 1783. Until that time, I was free to do whatever I wanted to do. He said that he had prepared a petition to present to the House of Representatives who had inherited the Amercement list from the committee and who are trying the individual cases. He told me that we had a fair chance of getting my name off the Amercement list. If we were able to do that, we could submit a claim for you to be paid for your treatment of American soldiers, of which they have records from the beginning of the war. He went on to say that I would not be getting my Jacksonborough property back and not to pursue that venue. It may cause discord among the members to know that you were a loyalist and a judge for the British.

They already know this, but we needn't flaunt it in their faces. The more they forget, the better it is for your defense. I agreed saying that I would be living at Rebecca's house but would be practicing medicine at my old address on Church Street. Any mail should come to my work address to keep any suspicions to a minimum. I I let him know that as soon as I could get clear of all my legalities that I was moving to Lethe where I would retire. If I could ever get there, I would never leave it again.

Mr. Pendleton told me to be patient. It will take some time to push all this through the House, but we should be through with it all in about three years.

I could live with that, I advised him, and asked that he do everything possible to clear my name. I would like to take a good name and a clean slate to Lethe. Maybe I could become a judge again and live off the land. We shall see.

Once at home I told Rebecca what was happening and that I was going back in the practice of medicine and try to lead a normal life or as close to it as possible until all this mess is settled and then we would go to Lethe.

For the rest of the year, I fell into the routine of going to work at the office every day. I was purging and bleeding sick people and healing wounds and fixing minor scrapes and bruises on little children. For the most part, I was pretty much living a normal life. I started making a little money and helping Rebecca with the expenses, but most of the money went back into buying medical supplies.

I adored Rebecca. We were so compatible and I thought how different this relationship was to any that I had known. Ann had to know that I was in the Provost Dungeon, but I never heard from her. She never once contacted me or had anyone else check on my welfare. I have found my happiness, and I sincerely hoped that she did the same.

I know the situation with Rebecca and me is one of controversy among my friends and the community; however, I have made my choice of how I will live my life. Many people think that we are living in sin, and at my age, there is not much sin involved; however, I believe that Almighty God knows your heart and he is a forgiving God. My sin, living with Rebecca, is no different than the murder and destruction done during the war on both sides.

God will forgive my shortcomings and like drinking from the River Lethe, my past will be obliterated and forgotten. I cannot marry Rebecca and I will not shame Ann by divorcing her, so I must suffer our current situation and I know that Rebecca will stand by me in any circumstance.

Today is Monday, January, 31, 1783. The House of Representatives are meeting at the State Capitol Building on the northwest corner of Broad and Meeting Streets. Today, Mr. Pendleton will read my petition for forgiveness for my amercement. I found a seat on the second floor overlooking the gallery. Several petitions were read and when they finished reading one for William Matthews by Mr. Gibbs, it was time for my petition. From the pages of the House Journal dated January 31, 1783, the following was entered,

> And Mr. Pendleton presented to the House a petition from Doctor de la Howe [setting forth that since the commencement of the present war, he has acted friendly to this state. That he has suffered much from the hands of the British and has assisted in distress several Americans wounded by the British. That he has assisted his neighbors at Pon Pon while the British passed thro' the country. That he conceives after the British had conquered the whole state, he was inevitably (to) become a British subject that he acted as a magistrate under them, not with a lucrative view, but only acted when he could not avoid it. That his life being threatened after being made a prisoner and on parole to the Americans, obliged him to take shelter in Charles Town, where he assisted many distressed prisoners. That he lost his medicines at Jacksonborough, said to be taken for the use of this state, which he values at five hundred guineas. That after coming to town, he refused acting in any employment under the British, and after being put into a dungeon in the provost, was tried for

his life on a double suspicion and charge of his attachment to the American interest, and praying to be relieved from the penalty of an Act for Amercing certain persons therein mentioned.

Ordered that this petition was read along with others, and they were ordered to be referred to a Committee of the Members of the Parishes and Districts in which the said Petitioners respectively resided.

The committee book, pages 37–38, gives specific committees to which these petitions were referred. My committee members were Colonel W. Skirving and Major Hyrne.

There it was! Now all I could do was to wait for the committees to meet and make their recommendation to the House of Representatives.

I found Mr. Pendleton and asked him how long before a decision would be made. He told me to be patient for a while. We would find out in due course. These things take a lot of time and we need to be patient. It could be a couple of years before the committee hears it. There are thousands of these cases to be heard and we will have to wait our turn.

The next two years seemed like forever. I was anxiously awaiting the verdict because if I am exonerated, I will be eligible to petition Congress for my services and war time loses. If this dream were to come true, I would have enough money to retire to Lethe and carve out an existence there with Rebecca and my friends in and around New Bordeaux. Could I be so blessed? At least, there is hope for me now where only despair use to abide. For the next two years, I can only dream of such an existence.

About this time in 1783, I collected all my saved bills and took them to Mr. Pendleton. He looked them over and told me that the books were in very good order. I had the time and date of my services, the patient's name, and the name of his commanding officer. Then in almost every transaction, I had the commander or the officer in charge to sign my invoice. These were for only

American wounded or sick and nothing was in there about my medicines that were confiscated. Mr. Pendleton carried the transactions paperwork to Mr. James McColl, Auditor General of South Carolina. Mr. McColl carried them to the Governor's Committee for approval and entered them on the books. I read a copy of the original Index Book showing the "Revolutionary Claims Filed in South Carolina" between August 20, 1783 and August 31, 1786 kept by James McColl, Auditor General on page 85; entry number 32 de la Howe, John; number of returns, forty-five.

What this means is that my bills are on the books of the Treasurer's Office of South Carolina to be paid. If I get paid for what I have submitted, it will be about ten year's salary, and Rebecca and I can afford to go to Lethe and retire. But again, we will have to wait.

Today, April 19, 1783, Gen. George Washington informs his troops that the Paris peace treaty is signed in France, formally ending the war and recognizing United States independence. John Jay, Benjamin Franklin, and John Adams represent the United States in signing the treaty. The treaty comprises nine articles that set the national borders, establish fishing rights and property of loyalists, allow the use of the Mississippi River by both British and Americans, and enable evacuation of British forces. He will officially inform his troops in person in September that hostilities have ended.

With the session of hostilities, Charles Town became Charleston and the British evacuated the city. The church bell rang and people danced in the street for days.

I kept working and living at Rebecca's house. I was happy and satisfied. I did manage to take a trip to Lethe to let everyone know that I was all right and that I was preparing my things and getting my business in order to move to Lethe as soon as I could close out all my accounts in Charleston. I had a good visit with Rev. Gibert and Mr. Moragne and especially with Anna Cook.

She has done a remarkable job holding things together as has Rev. Gibert. John Lewis Gervais has come by from time to time to check on everything and everybody.

While I was there, I officiated a triple wedding. James and Molly jumped the broom as did Ben and Becky, and Jack and Phyllis. They each picked out a cottage and life seemed worth living again. The plantation was cleared of a lot more land and we had a good crop of indigo as well as a vineyard and several vegetable gardens. My animals were procreating nicely and my pea foul were alive and well, and very noisy! But they were beautiful as were my sheeps, goats, and cattles. There were plenty of wildlife in the woods and fishes in the stream, how much better could it be? The only way for it to be better is that Rebecca and I live here. I wanted Rebecca to be with me, but she stayed in Charleston teaching her students.

With me, this trip was Bacchus and Matilda, Little Liza, and Little Sam and Phyllis and Jack. Cecelia and Tam-O stayed behind to help us move and take care of Rebecca's school until we return to Lethe.

I told Boze to have several rooms added to my home to accommodate Rebecca and her things especially her piano. People will come from miles around to hear her play. I do not know of another pianist in the whole district.

I congratulated Boze on a job well done. I told him that no one else could have done a better job in keeping the plantation in working order, especially through the revolution. I expressed my gratitude and made certain he was aware that he would have a special place at Lethe as long as I lived. Boze and Bacchus will be taken care of and I will see to that.

I left Anna and Boze some cash to use as they saw fit. I know now that I can trust them. Anna Cook has been true and faithful servants for almost ten years and Boze over twenty years.

Bacchus and I got home after spending the night in Jacksonboro, as it is spelled since the revolution. We stayed at

Hayne hall and visited with Isaac Junior. He has grown into a handsome young man and has furthered his father's wealth.

It is the summer of 1784. I have been working and saving all the money that I am able to save. Bacchus helps me with my medical practice and Rebecca has her Day School teaching the local wealthy children how to live in polite society. My thoughts are of Lethe and how much I am looking forward to moving there with Rebecca.

I received notice from the Rev. Peter Gibert in New Bordeaux and an executor of the last will and testament of my neighbor Jacob Bayland who had passed away. In his will dated September 23, 1784, he said, "I give full power to my wife to sign to Dr. Jno. Delahowe, the titles of a plantation of 150 acres joining lands of said doctor, the mill of Jeremiah Rogers, lands of Peter Bayle, Peter Boutiton."

I remember treating him and his family years ago, but I did not expect him to pay me. His fees were not that much when he came to bring his family during flu outbreak. Frankly, I had forgotten all about it. I do remember Jacob Bayland as one of the Huguenots who settled the area as being an honest and upright man and a good neighbor. I see now how much integrity this man possessed.

This brings Lethe to 2,200 acres. Lethe will be one of the largest plantations in the backcountry and with fifteen slaves to work it, Rebecca and I should have a good retirement. I will never retire from my medical practice as long as there is breath left in my body, but I have plans to keep and ideas to put into reality. One thing I wish to do is invent a silk-making machine. Silk was one of the premiere crops that were brought from the old country. The worms have found homes in trees here and I remember that a twenty-five-year-old man named Jean Aymerie who was one of the original passengers on The HMS *Friendship*—the ship that brought the Huguenots here from England—captained by Gregory Perkins who said of him "Lived with Mr. Gibert many years, built his house—was an ingenious man—lived sometimes with Dr. de la Howe. He married one of the natives but they lived together a very short time and she left him. He bound many books for Mr. Gibert and built a machine for making silk."

This young man and I designed and built a machine that would separate the silk balls from the strands, and lay out the strands and spin them on a spool for use in making garments. The machine required a few adjustments in order to operate properly, but I think it could be produced as a money maker. Mr. Aymerie stopped working on the machine when I left because he could not find anyone else to fund the project. I would like to see it completed. I hope he still lives in the area.

One day in November of 1784, Rebecca called me into her parlor and asked me to sit down. I walked over to her and bent down and kissed her on the cheek. "Is anything wrong?" I asked.

"No, I have made out my last will and testament and I wanted you to read it. John. You are the love of my life and I would like us never to have any secrets from each other. I hope to be able to go with you to Lethe and I know that someday you will, but if I do not make it in time, I wish you to carry out the terms of my will. If, per chance, we do go to Lethe, then you will be making all the decisions based on the circumstances at the time. I have left that completely up to you. You will never have to leave Lethe once you are there, and you may decide what to do with my things. Will you read my will and see if you agree with what I wrote?"

"Rebecca, I do not even want to think about such things. My money will be here soon and we will live at Lethe and be a happy and loving family."

"I know John, but this is important to my peace of mind and I need assurance of your support in this matter. I have visited Mr. Pendleton and he has instructed me on how to word the document so there will be no repercussions as to the legalities involved. Please read it and let me know your feelings."

"Let me see it," I said.

I took a deep and cleansing breath and braced myself for what was to follow.

"South Carolina."

"In the name of God, Amen."

"I Rebekah Woodin of Saint Philip's Parish in the City of Charles Town and the state aforesaid, being in perfect health of body and of sound and disposing mind, memory, and understanding, do make, publish and declare this to be my last will and testament. In manner and form following (that is to say) first, 'I principally when it shall please the Almighty God to me. Hence from this transitory life, do recommend my soul to his protection hoping for the remission of my sins, through the merits of my Lord and Savoir Jesus Christ, and my body I commit to the earth to be buried if I should die in Charles Town as near the remains of my dearly beloved parents and sister as possible in St. Michael's Church yard. "And what worldly estate it has pleased God to bestow upon me, I do hereby bequeath in manner and form following: to my most worthy friend and best adviser, Dr. John de la Howe, practitioner of Physics in the City of Charles Town and state aforesaid, my whole estate real and personal, except a few trifling legacies which will be here after mentioned, as knowing no one so justly entitled to my friendship and my gratitude as the above mentioned gentleman.

"In primis to that good Gentleman Wm. Daniel Bordeaux, I bequest a valuable rose diamond ring, set round with twelve brilliants to Mrs. Bordeaux three large table silver spoons and a pair of garnet drop earrings to Ms. Eliza Bordeaux (a little Chagrin case containing a pair of crystal pendant earrings, with three drops to each, a little out of repair, but easily mended and two silver needle cases, these I hope the family except as tokens of remembrance. 'Item' to Mrs. Matthews all my wearing apparel, two pairs of sheets, two pillows, a silver tablespoon and six silver teaspoons, not new ones, two dressing glasses in mahogany frames and a counterpane.

"But as I have met with the most solid friendship and disinterested from my very worthy friend, Dr. John de la Howe, I hereby name the said Dr. John de la Howe the sole executor and heir to this my last will and testament, revoking an annulling all former wills in witness whereof I have to this my last will and testament set my hand and seal, this twentieth day of November Ano Dom 1784."

"Signed, sealed, declared, and published by the said Rebekah Woodin, the testatrix for her last will and testament in the presence of us who were at the signing and seal thereof.

"W. Cunningham, Sophia Cunningham, Michl O'Brien, Rebekah Woodin."

I read it and said, "Except for a few misspelled words, I understand what you are trying to get across. It is plainly in black and white. What do you want me to do with it?"

"Put it in a safe place and see to my things after I am gone.

"What if I die first," I asked?

"Then I will deal with that when it happens," she answered.

"I shall see to it that your wishes are carried out. I hope that when your time comes, we will be together at Lethe and you will have many more things to give away."

"Then you can see that they are deposited where they need to be given. Will you promise me that you will see to my wishes and be the executor of my will?"

"Yes, as your life partner, I will attend to it. It is not a pleasant thing to contemplate."

"Death is a part of life. I will feel more at peace knowing my wishes will be met after I am gone."

What is with this 'Rebekah' spelling?"

"That is how the recorder spelled it when he recorded it. It was correct when I put an ad in the gazette about me moving to Mr. Murray's house. It is 'Rebecca' but most legal transcribers spell it Rebekah. As long as people know who I am, it is fine with me."

"Consider it done," I folded the paper and put it in my pocket to be deposited in my safe when I go to bed. I hated to even think of the time when we have to face the grim reaper. I pray that I die first. I know that sounds selfish, but I would not enjoy living in this world without Rebecca.

Today is Friday, March 14, 1785, and the House votes on the recommendation of the Committee on Amercement.

The following was reported in the House Journal, "The house took into consideration the report of the committee to whom the petitions of Sundry persons amerced were referred, which being read and the question put upon the first clause of the report the House divided." The yeas went forth. Teller for the yeas, Mr. Pinkney – 39 votes. Teller for the Nays, Mr. Minor Winn – 66 votes. It passed in the negative, and is as follows [Vizt,]

That they find there were originally forty-eight persons amerced by name, and that eighteen of that number have been released by Act of Assembly. See list No. 1 and 2 and thirty one now liable to Amercement, as the latter do not appear to your committee to have been distinguished from the former otherwise that by being more fortunate in obtaining a decision on their cases which could not be extended to all. Your committee think in order to be consistent with itself the house should release the remaining thirty see list no. 2 who were originally amerced from the Operation of the Law that is now before the House.

The list was in alphabetical order and my name was number seven on the list. My name has been removed from the Amercement list!

Again, I was elated and so was Rebecca. I was free of any punishment or fines from either side. I could start from afresh in my new country of the United States of America and live as a free man not beholden to anyone or anything. God Bless the United States of America.

Just a month later, I was notified that Mr. James McCall, the Auditor General asked me to come by his office at the State Court

House on the corner of Broad and Meeting Streets. I identified myself as I entered his office.

He said, "Sign here."

He handed me a ledger book which read, "Page 378 state of the Returns – 45; No. of accts – 68 – Letters, Aaw when sent out of the office on the twenty-fifth of April 1785 Amount. £4,431...19..0-3/4."

I nearly fainted. Mr. McCall was just matter of fact business like. I nervously signed the ledger as having received the bank draft.

I walked out of the office stunned and dazed. I was just handed a South Carolina Treasury draft for almost £4,500 sterling. (That's about one million dollars in today's money.)

That's it! I am done in Charleston. I love Charleston and the people, but I yearn for Lethe. I can't wait to tell Rebecca.

I told Bacchus to head for the house and don't spare the horses. He slapped the horse reigns on the horses and said, "Well, gwan dare mule."

Bacchus looked at me and smiled, "What yo grnnin bout?"

"I am sixty-eight years old and I have just been reborn. We have our money and we are going to Lethe as soon as possible."

"Well, git up mule, let's go home."

We arrived at Rebecca's house and I jumped out of the carriage and ran in the house. Rebecca was teaching a student to play the piano. There were other "proper" young ladies and gentlemen in the room. I ran up to her and she thought something was wrong and stood up. I grabbed her and hugged her and kissed her right there with no embarrassment of our audience.

"Rebecca, would you go with me to live with me for the rest of your life at our beloved Lethe?"

"You got the money!"

"Yes!" I opened my coat to show her the draft, then grabbed her around her waist, and spun her around and around.

The young people in the room first looked astonished, but I did not care. Then all the girls came and gathered around Rebecca and giggled and gossiped. The young men came up to me and shook my hand and wished me luck. Then they asked Rebecca if this meant that she was going to close her school. Rebecca said, "I am afraid so. I love you young people but I have to invoke the Latin phrase carpe diem which means to enjoy the day without regard for the future. I must seize the day and go with my heart. Let this be a lesson to you. Live your life, but above all, be honorable and seek happiness."

They all said that they would not know how to act in polite society without Ms. Rebecca's teachings.

Rebecca said, "School is dismissed, and I really mean dismissed. We are officially closed. Go home and live your lives to the fullest and think of me occasionally. If you are ever in the Hillsborough neighborhood, stop by Lethe Plantation and see me. I will miss you all."

The students filed out and she asked me when we were leaving. I said that I would have to put a sign on the office door on Church Street and pack up my things and collect some money that is due me, how about in a week? She said that she would do her best to be ready to go by then. She had two slaves to help her move her father's handmade furniture and she would wrap up her glassware and say good-bye to her neighbors. Then she said, "Are you not worried what people will say about you and me?"

"Not in the least. We will be two hundred miles from Charleston and in the wilderness. Our plantation will be our home and our refuge. If some people are shocked by our love, they can stay at home. People in the backcountry are busy worrying about digging out a living rather than the latest gossip. My true friends there will accept you and we will be happy, I promise to do everything in my power to make you happy."

Rebecca was beaming, "I was praying just last night during my daily devotionals that you would soon realize your dreams.

I decided to make your dreams my dreams also. I am so happy that God has seen fit to answer my prayers so soon. He will always answer prayers. Sometimes it is "Yes" and sometimes it is "No" or even "Not now" but he will hear and will always answer our prayers."

"I honestly believe God sent you into my life as a reward for all the good things I have done in my life. When I count my blessings, I always count you twice. Thank you for loving me."

At the office the following day Bacchus and I packed everything in the wagon. I put a sign over the window that said "Closed" and told Mr. Laurens the news. He said that John Lewis Gervais knew my circumstances and had gone to Ninety Six to cut Granville into several counties, one of which you will be living in. I asked what they are going to name the new county and he smiled and said, "You will see."

I thanked him for his friendship over the years and all the politics made on my behalf. I told him that if it were not for him my circumstances would be quite different. He shook my hand and bade a fond farewell and I left his office.

I returned home and Rebecca was packing and covering furniture so it would not be scratched on the trip. She was covering the piano and I said, "Are you planning to bring the piano?"

"Absolutely," she said. "I am holding you to your promise to make me happy and this is what makes me happy."

"Your happiness is paramount to me. I am so glad that we have Bacchus and Tam-O and Cecelia to help with the packing."

It is September 1785 and we are packed and ready to go. We have two wagons full of furniture and household goods, plenty of money, food, and Rebecca's piano ready for the ten-day trip.

Bacchus and Tam-O will be driving the wagons and I will be driving the carriage. This time Bacchus will be correct when he says, "Well, gwan dare mules."

The first night, we went to Jacksonboro and stayed with Isaac Hayne Jr. We had an excellent supper and Rebecca played his piano. We talked into the night. I thought about going to see who was living in my confiscated house; however, I decided to leave it alone and forgive my enemies and allow the tenants to remain. They will never know their benefactor.

I rode down the road next to the Edisto. The Edisto is such a beautiful river, forever flowing with its black waters which bring so many memories of Sam and my life at Jacksonboro.

The next night, we stayed in Walterboro. I drove by the jail to take one last look. I wanted to remember that feeling of hopelessness and forsakenness, so I would never take Lethe for granted. I will be forever thankful for the blessings bestowed upon me. I would remember being beaten and starved to be made to do something that I did not want to do. I will remember that feeling and treat my workers accordingly. I will never sell any of them and I will never mistreat them. I will provide a good home for all who live and work at Lethe.

We stopped and camped in the "sandlapper" part of the mid-state and on to Barnwell where I saw my friend Mr. Halford. We rode on past Purysburg where I had to come to pick up Tam-O after he ran away the first time. We went past Augusta on to Edgefield and then to Lethe. Home at last!

We drove up the country road to Lethe and came past the ornate wall there in front of the kitchen were what seemed like over one hundred people, most of which were friends, neighbors, and patients. They began to cheer and clap their hands and in the middle of them, I saw John Lewis Gervais, Rev. Gibert, and Mr. Moragne. I was overcome with joy. Rebecca smiled and waved.

We came up to the kitchen and a boy came out and held my horses, and I got out of the carriage and helped Rebecca down onto the carriage block. I turned and greeted everyone and yelled, "At my age it's good to be anywhere, but you have made it especially good to be home. Thank you for your welcome."

John Lewis said, "Doctor Jean, we all welcome you to your home and we hope you will never have to leave again."

Everyone cheered and clapped and danced around. John Louis held up his hands and continued, "But that is not our motive today."

Everyone got quiet, grinned, and poked each other.

"The reason why everyone is here today is to welcome you home and to inform you that we are in a new county. The people of the new county, your friends, and patients—most of whom you brought into this world—have taken a consensus and asked, since you are still the judge that to you be extended the honor of naming our new county."

"Thank you all for this great honor. I have thought of once naming my plantation "Abbeville" after the town in Northern France where so many of our brethren called home. It was the scene of some cruel persecutions and frightful tragedies in which the Huguenots, your relatives, were the victims. Least we never forget the awful religious persecutions we suffered and when we hear the name "Abbeville" may we pause to give thanks to Almighty God for finding a new nation, one that is tolerant of our beliefs and principles."

John Lewis shook my hand and said that he knew that we made the right choice in asking me to name our new county. We now lived in Abbeville County.

I invited everyone in to enjoy food and drink and told Bacchus and the other slaves to take the night off. Bacchus took some wine and moonshine to the slave quarters, and I heard some partying most of the night. Most of the party stayed the night, as was the custom, and left in the morning.

John Lewis Gervais came to see me before he left for his plantation Herenhousen. He reminded me that I was still a judge for the whole Ninety-Six District and he would make sure I would remain so for as long as he and Mr. Laurens was in the Senate. He wished me and Rebecca well and told me to come and visit when I could.

The rest of 1785 was blissful to me. We moved Rebecca's piano into the main house which had eleven rooms in it now counting the cellar. There is only one entrance into the house so that one would have to go through the treatment room to get to any other part of the house.

Rebecca has her own room and Matilda and her children are still her property. Matilda, Liza, and Little Ben are living in their old house by the creek and the other slaves have found themselves cottages to live in. Tam-O lives in the overseer's house with Boze and Bacchus, and Ms. Anna Cook comes in to oversee the kitchen duties.

Rebecca and I love to stroll throughout the property; 2,600 acres is a big place. When I first came here, I wondered about the term "acre." I found out that there are 640 acres in a square mile; (modern day folks can think of an acre as being slightly smaller than a football field). During the Middle Ages, an acre was the amount of land that could be plowed in one day with a yoke of oxen. I always wondered if you plowed all day with oxen if you would "ache" at the end of the day, therefore if you plowed two days, you plowed two "acres." I wonder about a lot of things.

Most of my property is in virgin timber. I could make a lot of money if I were to sell the timber, but as long as I am alive it will never happen, and I am going to make sure, as much as possible, to see that it is never cut. Nature's beautiful bounty such as this should be enjoyed by everyone for generations to come.

We have made lovely walking paths through the fruit trees and other trees we transported from Fairbanks and Jacksonboro. We love our home. We sit in rocking chairs and watch the flames in the fireplace when it is cold outside or we may play chess or read and very often Rebecca will play the piano. Neighbors will come from miles around to hear Rebecca play Mozart on her piano.

Our home is lavishly decorated with carpets on the floor. We have furniture made of walnut. Cherry and mahogany which was made by Thomas Woodin; Rebecca's father added to some we purchased. Rebecca dresses in silk, furs, and diamonds. At supper, we drink from wineglasses and porcelain cups and we eat off of nankeen china using silver flatware. We will never again take our blessings for granted, for what we went through during the revolution, we will enjoy every minute of our new surroundings.

It is now the spring of 1786. I will turn seventy this year and Rebecca will be almost sixty. We are leading a good life for a change. Rebecca and I have settled down in our good fortune. Lethe Plantation is supporting itself, and I am making a fair wage from my medical practice.

I read in the paper that my friend, State Senator John Lewis Gervais of the town of Ninety Six introduced a bill that was approved by the legislature on March 22, 1786, to create a new state capital. There was considerable argument over the name for the new city. According to published accounts, Senator Gervais said he hoped that "in this town we should find refuge under the wings of Columbia," for that was the name which he wished it to be called. One legislator insisted on the name "Washington," but "Columbia" won by a vote of 11–7 in the state senate.

I also noted that Ann's daughter Elizabeth was married to Thomas Lesesne, the little boy she used to play with at Fairbanks. Thomas is the son of Isaac Lesesne, Ann's sister's husband. Ann's sister is also named Elizabeth. Now Fairbanks and the Lesesne Plantations will be joined, and I hope Ann and her family will live out their lives in peace and harmony. I wonder what ever happened to Marcus. Marcus was the slave that simply sailed away and was never heard of again. He is the one that the carriage ran over and I treated when I first met Ann.

Then 1787 came and went with nothing eventful happening except Ben and Becky gave birth to Little Ben. Molly gave birth to Little Jim and Molly gave birth to Little Molly and Polly. I am so pleased that our family is growing. I have no offspring and it is good that life is abounding at Lethe.

Rebecca's health is failing. She is getting older and weaker by the day. She has difficulty breathing and any exercise is very hard on her. Her ankles swell a great deal, and I fear that she has heart problems inherited from her father. I dread the thought of living at Lethe without her. I had always hoped to die first, but then I realized how selfish I was acting. We limit our walks to the grounds around the house and we can still enjoy a carriage ride occasionally. She still plays the piano but only when she is feeling well.

I am reading an article in the April 1787 issue of the *Columbia Magazine* or *Monthly Miscellany*, a Philadelphia periodical. On pages 356 through 369, there is an article that I find most interesting and informative and may provide me with an answer to my dilemma about to whom to bequeath my land and property when the time comes. With Rebecca so sick, it is time I thought of these things.

The title of this article is: "A plan for establishing schools in a new country, where inhabitants are thinly settled, and whose children are to be educated with special reference to a country life."

I read, take any number of settlers, we will suppose sixty families collected in a village, and they will be able to support a schoolmaster and easily maintain their children at school for twenty shillings a year, paid by each family, will make up a competent salary for the master, and the children will be clothed and fed at home.

But if sixty families are dispersed over a large tract of country from twenty to forty miles in extent, how shall their children receive the benefits of education? The master's salary, it is true, can be paid as in the former case, but few parents will be disposed to incur the heavy expense of school. Hence, in such a scattered settlement, general ignorance will ensue; and the people consequently degenerate into vice, irreligion, and barbarism. To remedy evils of such magnitude will be difficult, perhaps it will be thought impracticable to attempt it, however, will be laudable;

and all those who have the dearest interests of society at heart, will give the measure their support.

If by charitable donations, or by grants of the state, adequate funds could be formed, to defray the expanses of the board and tuition of such children, the evils before mentioned would be remedied, but such funds are not to be hoped for. And if they could be obtained, it might well be doubted whether that would be the best mode of educating children destined for a laborious country life. There, the boys are to be the future farmers and the girls the farmers' wives. If both could, in early life, be well instructed in the various branches of their future employments, they would make better husbands, better wives, and more useful citizens. And if the mode of communicating such instruction could at the same time enable them largely to contribute to their own support, another important advantage would be gained. These reflections have given rise to the following plan of education for a country life.

1. Let three or four hundred acres of land be appropriated for the use of a school; let it consist of meadow, tillage, and wood land in convenient proportions.

2. Let a skillful and industrious manager be provided, who shall himself be a complete farmer and have two laborers— one acquainted with farming, the other with gardening— to assist him.

3. Let the farm be completely stocked, and all the requisite carriages and husbandry utensils be provided; such tools are designed for boys to be made of sizes suited to their strength.

4. Let the necessary buildings be erected for a school, a boarding house, a barn, and a workshop. These may be very plain and heap, and at the same time very comfortable. The necessary furniture and tools must also be provided.

5. A schoolmaster and school mistress must be chosen with much circumspection. The latter will be the housekeeper.

6. A cook will be necessary, and she should know how to dress the plain, wholesome food of the country in the best manner.

7. The childrens' beds and bedding, clothes, and materials for clothing must be provided by their parents.

The necessary foundations being thus laid; the school and farm may be conducted agreeably to the following regulations.

1. No boy or girl under eight years of age should be admitted.

2. Both boys and girls should be taught how to read, write, and cipher. The boys should also be instructed in every useful branch of husbandry and gardening, and the girls in every kind of work necessary for farmers' wives to know and practice.

3. For the purpose of working, let the boys be divided into such a number of classes as shall be judged convenient, distributing equal proportions of the larger and smaller boys to each class. Whenever the nature of the work to be done will admit of it, let equal portions of it be assigned to the several classes in order to excite their emulation, to excel in industry and skill, and for the reason each portion of land should be cultivated through a whole season by the same class to which it was first allotted. It will be obvious to direct several boys in the same class to perform such parts of the general labor required of it as shall be adapted to their several capacities and strength.

4. All the boys may be taught the methods of making and rearing nurseries of the most useful kind of fruit trees, shrubs and bushes, and of improving the former by grafting and budding. Each boy should have an equal portion of land allotted to him on which he should raise a nursery and when he has finished his course of education, he should be allowed to take home with him all the trees, shrubs, and bushes he has reared and cultivated; accepting only such a proportion as shall be requisite for supply the

school farm. In like manner, he should be allowed to take home with him a collection useful garden feds. In this way, the most valuable fruits and plants would in a few years be spread and cultivated through the whole settlement.

5. When orchards shall be grown, they may be instructed in the art of making and fermenting cider so as to produce a soft and pleasant liquor.

6. A small brewery may be erected on the farm and all the boys taught how to malt barley and oats; and both boys and girls may be taught the art of brewing, so far, at least, as the same might be practiced in every farmer's family. Perhaps by extending the plan of the malthouse and brewery, they might be able to supply that wholesome and nourishing liquor, good beer, to a great part of the settlement, and thus the use of pernicious, distilled liquors be superseded. Malt, at least, might thus be furnished and yield a small revenue towards supporting the school.

7. The management of cattle will be a necessary branch of their education, and the modern method of managing bees will well deserve their attention as well.

8. Tending the cattle and providing fuel and fencing stuff will be the principal employments of the winter. But the boys may also make the woodwork of all those utensils of husbandry which will be requisite for the ensuing season. The elder boys will be capable of handling axes and all the other tools used in those employments.

9. The girls will be taught how to sew, to knit, to spin, to cook, to make beds, to clean house, to make and mend their own clothes, to make the boys' clothes when cut out and to mend them, to milk cows, and to make butter and cheese.

10. That they may learn how to cook and perform all other household work. They should be divided into classes in the

same manner in which the boys were classed, and assist the housekeeper and cook a week at a time in rotation.

11. A collection of children from eight to fourteen or fifteen years of age thus regularly employed, on a good farm, would be nearly able to maintain themselves; and if the expenses of their schooling can thus be reduced as low, or nearly as low, as when, in ordinary cases, they live at home, the great obstacle to their education will be removed.

12. The winter will be the season most favorable for literary instruction of the children as then they will have but few necessary avocations, perhaps so no more than will occasion that degree of exercise which the preservation of their health may require. But their learning need not be wholly interrupted in the summer. Every morning, the boys may spend two hours at school and be ready to go in the field to work by eight or nine o'clock. And when they go out, the girls may enter and also spend two hours at school. Again at one o'clock (if they dine at noon), the boys may attend the school, continuing there an hour and half or two hours; and the girls may succeed them, as in the forenoon, attending the school a like length of time. Thus the same master might every day teach both girls and boys, and yet, in the whole, not to be confined above seven or eight hours in a day. An hour every evening might be allowed the children to amuse themselves in innocent sports.

13. The employments of a country life are so congenial to the human heart; the master of this rural academy could hardly forbear to engage in them in the intervals between school hours. He would naturally be led to read the best authors on agriculture and rural affairs and to get some acquaintance with botany. He would study theories, tracing useful practices back to the principles; and thus be able to communicate to the elder boys or youth, a degree

of scientific knowledge of the very important art of which, in the field, they daily learned the practice daily.

14. I hardly need mention what ought to be an indispensable part of education in every literary institution. That the children at this rural academy would be taught the plainest and most important principles of religion and morality.

15. It is to be presumed that the abler farmers would continue their children at school till they should be fourteen or fifteen years old. These children of both sexes might make further advances in learning. They might study geography and read some instructive histories, particularly the history of the United States, and a few of the best English moral writers, in prose and verse. At the same time, they might learn so much of bookkeeping as would be useful in the country, and the boys might be taught geometry, practical surveying, and the principles of mechanics.

16. Perhaps some useful manufactories might be established, in which the children, both male and female, might be very serviceable. Such an institution as that here sketched out, need not be confined to frontier settlements; though the first idea of it was suggested by a reflection on their situation. Rural schools or academies, upon such a plan, would perhaps be the most useful that could be established in the country towns and counties of this and every other state in America.

Numerous advantages would result from them. I will hint at a few.

1. The children would be taught the plainest and most useful principles and rules of religion and morality.

2. They would be well and uniformly educated in the most necessary learning and in the most important arts of civilized life, husbandry, and domestic economy.

3. They would acquire habits of industry.

4. Their manners and behavior would be formed and rendered mild and agreeable.
5. A few successive sets of scholars thus educated, returning to their several homes, would quite change the face of the country, in point of cultivation, and introduce a pleasing change in the knowledge, manners of the people, and abolish the invidious distinction of citizens and clown.

I will be sure to save this article and read it again. It is certainly one possibility of disposing my estate. I gave the article to Rebecca to read, and she thinks that it is a good idea. She and I have always stood for education—she as a school teacher and me as a physician. If we do this, we would possibly tend to the needs of hundreds or even thousands of children. We never had any of our own; however, this may benefit other children thereby making them an extended part of our family. Children with no heritage would have a home and a heritage.

It is summer of 1788. Rebecca is getting weaker and frail. As a physician, I have done all that I am able to do and yet she worsens. I fear that she is not long for this world. She has been my rock and my most worthy companion. No two people could have shared a more perfect love. It pains me to be around her. She is brave and smiles to reassure me to enjoy every moment we have left because there will come a time when we all must lay down this probationary existence for a more permanent one.

I am happy that she clings to her Christian beliefs. It is a source of strength and comfort to her.

The first day of October, she called me to her bedside. I knew that she had precious little time left. She told me that even though she had asked to be buried at St. Michael's with her parents, she wished to be buried here on Lethe so that she could remain by my side and wait for me here. I told her that I have prepared a place on the next ridge to the south which overlooks Lethe Plantation, and I could visit her there every day until we could be together in glory. She smiled and said, "Yes, I know the place well.

We can see the river and Lethe from there. That will be pleasing to me. And when you come to visit me and you kneel to be close to me, I shall say,

> And I shall hear tho soft you tread above me;
> And tho my grave will warmer be,
> And you shall bend and tell me that you love me,
> And I shall sleep in peace until you come to me.

I whispered to her, "You are like my Morning Star. When all the other stars have disappeared, you will still shine brightly in my heart."

She closed her eyes for the last time. I selfishly begged her not to leave me. Then I realized that she needed peace and on October 4, 1789, she breathed her last breath and drifted off into eternal sleep. I thought it appropriate that she died on a Sunday. She loved her Lord, and I knew that she would have liked it to end on his day. I held her hand until she was gone. I stayed and contemplated our lives together. All the hurt and agony in my life, all the prison time and torture, and death and despair rolled up into one and magnified a thousand times could not hurt as much as my heart is breaking right now.

The slaves have gathered outside the house in the front yard. There is a drizzling rain and just a dismal day. It somehow seems appropriate. They are singing hymns and praying as though Rebecca was one of their own. Bacchus and Boze have made a coffin and stuffed the lining with cotton and lined it in silk dyed in indigo.

I sent Tam-O to Rev. Gilbert's home to inform him of the events of the day and asked him to send messages to all of our neighbors and friends that we would have a funeral on Wednesday if they would like to pay their respects.

We had a large crowd at the funeral. Rev. Gibert conducted the service on the hill and the slaves hummed as someone played Rebecca's piano in the background. There were many handmade wreaths and flower bouquets, and Rebecca was buried with honor and dignity.

Except for my slaves, I was all alone now. I am seventy-two years old and I have no family. I will worry about that later, right now I must continue my life as normal as possible as a promise to Rebecca.

I had been putting off inventorying Rebecca's estate, but as a judge, I must legally do this task. I hope I do not embarrass myself with a mournful attitude in front of witnesses.

I grieved until July 1789 over nine months. I called upon my neighbors and friends Rev. Peter Gibert Peter Rogers and John Eymerie to be witnesses for the inventory. Her will must be probated and proved legally.

I wrote on the paper, "Appraisement of Sundries belonging to the Estate of Rebekah Woodin deceased, as produced by Doctor John de la Howe, Executor this 4th day of July 1789."

Item# – Description – Value (in British pounds)

1. One Forte Piano, with some music books 12
2. One feather bed, one black moss mattras with osnabrag cover,
3. Two pillows, one bolster, two old common rose blankets, and
4. One old gause pavillion, not compleat 4 /10
5. One Rose diamond Ring 15
6. One pair broken Crystal Earings, with three drops 14
7. One pair Silver Shoebuckles, two stones wanting to one of them 14
8. Three Silver hair pins, one Springed Do 6
9. Two Silver tablespoons 10
10. One Do childs spoon 3
11. Four Do teaspoons 5
12. One small plated Cruet stand with five small blue bottles 15
13. Two Japaned tin Canisters, and
14. Two Do waters,
15. Two Do candlesticks 18/8
16. Four Coarse China Coffee Cups with handles,

17. Six plain Do with Saucers, 10
18. Ten China teacups with Saucers, not _ported?,
19. Two coarse china bowls and
20. One small Do milk pot with handle broke of 10
21. Six wine glasses,
22. One common half_pint tumbler,&
23. One goblet 6
24. One pewter inkstand,
25. One gl? mugg,
26. One chamber pot with handle broke of, and
27. One wash bason (all old) 8
28. One pr of old Chamber fire doggs 5
29. One fire Skreen on a Mahogany stand 10
30. One old Common floor Carpet 7
31. One copper thea_kettle 10

Wearing Apparel
32. One Casimer riding_dress Compleat 3
33. One coarse white Summer riding dress 1
34. Ten pair of Stockings 5
35. Two pieces of whale bone 2
36. One pr of white leather, and two pr Do black shoes (wore) 9
37. Three pr of old Stays 14
38. Two white pockets 1
39. One paper fan & case 2/4
40. Three linnen under_petticoats 2
41. Four linnen aprons 16
42. Five shifts 8
43. Six white Ropers 8
44. Four cambrick pocket handkerchiefs (old) 3
45. Two night_caps & neck handkerchief 4
46. One striped holland riding coat 6
47. One worked? short dress_apron 8
48. Two plain muslim aprons 5

49. Two laicd dress handkerchiefs and two shawls hawk?? 1/18/8
50. Three Calico gowns 1/10
51. One Do with petticoat of the same 1
52. One laicd gown and petticoat 14
53. One red and yellow striped silk gown 15
54. One purple silk jacket and petticoat 2
55. One laicd Jacket and petticoat 1
56. One purple silk gown 1/10
57. One flesh Coloured Short Silk Gown} 2
58. One white silk petticoat}
59. One dress gause handkerchie}
60. One short gause apron} 6
61. One black silk cloak trimmed with white fur 2
62. One white silk summer shade 5
63. One grey old beaver cloak 10
64. One gown hatt, one white silk Do,and one gause Cap 8
65. One negro wench named Mathilda 60

The total estimated value of the appraisal is £123, 6 shillings, and 10 pence. (About $20,000 in today's money.)

These are to certify whom it doth or may concern, that we whose names are hereunto subscribed, have made and taken the above appraisement with care and caution, and assigning the back of both segments, given unto our hands this fourth day of July 1789 P[eter] Gibert Pierre [Peter] Rogers J[ohn] Eymerie.

So, there it is. Over sixty years of accumulations in a lifetime and nothing of value. She took everything of value to me with her to the grave. I will try to follow her wishes, but I know she will be satisfied no matter what I do.

Bacchus stood beside me at the funeral at my request. We did not show any emotion toward each other as that would have been crass to polite society. I knew he was there standing behind me letting me know his heart was with me and he is just as lost as I am. It was Rebecca who took care of everyone during my time in the Provost dungeon and in the Walterboro jail. The slaves were mourning just as I am.

I was reading the results of the 1790 census of the United States. I see that Ann is listed as living on Daniel's Island at Fairbanks with nine slaves. She never divorced me or remarried. I doubt if she ever had a gentleman again. I pray that she is well and happy. The same census shows me living at Lethe with one white woman, which would be Ms. Anna Cook and fourteen slaves.

My servants have been with me for over thirty years. I have kept them through the good times and the bad times. I have maintained the family unit and never sold any of them or split up a family. I will make it a point to see my neighbors and discuss with them my desire to insure my slaves are afforded good environs to live and work after my demise. I want to make plans now as to where they will go and be confident they will be treated well. It is of great concern to me that families will be allowed to stay together and I am sure Rev. Gibert will be able to assist me in making these decisions.

On Friday, January 20, 1790, I was notified that at age of seventy-two, I am to be appointed County Court Justice for Abbeville.

Lethe is a great refuge. I love the country and my surroundings. I was notified this year on July 29, 1792, that I was elected into the Medical Society of South Carolina on the first ballot. This seems to legitimize my work and my practice all these years. It is a grand honor.

I was very saddened to learn that Henry Laurens has died at Mepkin. He shall see his son again and I know his son will be happy that Henry freed all of his slaves. A few left his plantation, but most stayed on to work the rice fields and share in the profits. The man made a fortune selling humans and now has become one of the few that has reversed his outlook on slavery. Politicians will always listen to the people with the most money, but this action by Henry Laurens will have them buzzing for many years to come.

The year 1796 started off as usual. I am beginning to grow old and weak. I read a notice in the gazette that Ann had passed away on August 24, 1796. I was with her when she drafted her will and left all of her belongings to her daughter Elizabeth. Now, Elizabeth and Thomas will be the ones to play with the fiddler crabs and work the Fairbanks Plantation. I think it is about time I drafted my will.

It has been nearly ten years since Rebecca and I read the article in the *Columbia Magazine*, and I have decided to fashion my will after the article and establish the Lethe Agricultural Seminary. By doing this, I will establish the first Manual Training institute in The United States. As Rebecca told me many times, it is time we afford the backcountry inhabitants the opportunity to have the proper training to better equip them to thrive in modern society. Children in the country have grown up in ignorance and poverty too long, and I am going to see to it that at least some of them will have the same opportunities as the city children. I take pen in hand and write,

> Last Will and Testament of John de la Howe
> State of South Carolina
> Abbeville County
>
> In the name of God, Amen. I, John de la Howe, of the County of Abbeville in the State of South Carolina M: D: being of sound and disposing mind, memory, and understanding, do make, ordain, and publish this my last will and testament.
>
> In premis, it is my will and desire that my remains shall be buried as near as can be to the spot where those of the late Miss Rebecca Woodin are deposited on the hill opposite to the dwelling house wherein we both resided together, and I still do reside on my plantation or farm named Lethe, as the last mark and testimony of my

friendship and sense which I have retained of her merit. And it is further my will that as soon as it can conveniently be done after my decease a substantial brick wall shall be built around our sepulchers not less than ten feet square in the clear, eight feet above ground, and two bricks thick with a substantial door and lock and that the whole of it shall forever be kept up and in good order and the area within clear of bushes and weeds and that the following inscription in large iron capital shall forever be kept incased in the door: Rebecca Woodlin Obit 4th Oct. 1788. Johannes de la Howe Fundator Hujas Seminarii Agriculturalis, with the date of my decease.

I give and devise all my real and personal estate of whatsoever nature it may be, so in possession as in right (except what hereafter by this my last will otherwise disposed of) to the president and Agricultural Society of the State of South Carolina, now or lately holding their usual meetings in the City of Charleston, and to such of their members as the said society pro tempore shall name and appoint to take the Execution and Trust contained in this my last will and testament upon them, and to their successors is said appointment forever.

That is to say, in trust for the following intent, uses and purposes and for no other use, intent or purpose whatsoever—viz, for causing and procuring to be erected, established, organized, and forever kept up on that part of the plantation where I now reside or on any part between the springs and the mouth of the branch, which runs through the yard, and Little River, an agricultural or farm school in conformity as near as can be (*Mutates mutandis* as occasional circumstances may render advisable, and the wisdom of the Society shall suggest) to a plan proposed in the *Columbia Magasine* for the month of April, one thousand seven hundred and eighty-seven; with this difference—that this farm school is principally by me intended, for by the yearly income of the estate by me devised and bequeathed by this my last will, forever both educating in conformity to said Plan and also lodging, feeding and uniformly clothing twelf poor boys and twelf poor girls, whose Parents or who themselfs have resided in Abbeville County aforesaid not less than six years, and actually continue to reside within the compass or extent of said county; but that orphan children (*ceteris paribus*) shall have the preference. And it is my will that they shall manufacture such of their cloathing themselves, as can be made out of the produce of the farm, and that the trustees shall be pleased to procure out of the ready money which I shall leave at my decease such implements for facilitating labor, as may not only answer that purpose, but contribute at the same to facilitating the labour of the neighbors and making them more industrious; provided that not above one hundred pounds Sterling be employ'd in the purchase of said implements. And I do wish and recommend the use of Beach leaves, gathered before the frost and dried in the shade for bedding, as the leaves of the beach tree, cured as mentioned make as comfortable, and by far more healthy bedding than feathers, as they will remain good for four or five years, and may be easily renew'd and as being introduced amongst the poorer class of citizens, (whose bedding is now a blanket) they may thereby enjoy one that is comfortable and healthy.

And it is my will that such part of my personal estate as the Trustees shall not think immediately necessary or particularly useful for carrying on the farm and farm school, shall be by them sold, in such manner, and on such Terms, as they may think the most advantageous; but that in particular my surveying compass, chain, and instrument case, shall be reserved for the use of the farm school as likewise such books are in their Judgment may be useful to the Master and particularly, Shaw's Chymistry, so that he thereby may be enabled to comply with the following article, if unacquainted with the principles Viz.

That it shall be the duty of the Master that besides having the boys instructed in reading, writing, arithmetic, principles of Geography and of Geometry so far as to render them versed in practical surveying, and the Girls in reading, writing, and four common rules of Arithmetic, he will and shall instruct both boys and Girls (so as occasion offers) in such chymical principles as the success of their different operations depend upon as malting, brewing, distilling, baking, fixing different colors, making vinegar, soap, cheese, butter, etc., etc. And it is my will that such children as reside conveniently in the neighborhood for attending the school may be admitted to be instructed as the children of the farm school, those of parents not able to pay the schooling, Gratis, and those who can afford it, at such rate as they and the master can agree upon, but to such number only as the trustees shall judge that the master can conveniently instruct, provided that all children admitted into the said farm school, shall be obliged to conform to such rules and regulations, as the Trustees or master shall from time to time reasonably make for the government thereof.

And it is further my will, that in the choice of the master for the said farm school skill, industry, and morals, shall be the only qualifications attended to, and that in the admittance of poor children, no manner or regard shall be paid to what religion or sect they or their Parents profess; and that it shall be a particular charge to the master to teach and instruct them only, in the general, plain, and practical parts of religion and morality without meddling with speculative and controverted points, or with such as constitute the particular character of any sect.

In case that it should appear to the society that the yearly income of the Estate by this my last will given and devised should not be sufficient to carry immediately my above disposition into full effect, (which however is not expected) I in that case request them to make such beginning as the yearly income may bear the expense of in such manner that the stock on the farm as horses, mares in particular, horn cattle, & sheep may be kept up for the use of the farm, but as I shall leave a considerable sum in ready money, I recommend that such suitable but simple buildings in the way of my present overseer's house may be immediately erected to answer the plan to the whole extent, but that all the outward timber may be of Chestnut.

It is also my will that my tract of land, part of which I do now keep inclosed and reside on, made up of twenty-one original tracts, and by a late resurvey containing two thousand six hundred and thirty acres shall be forever so far indevisable as that five hundred acres shall be laid out for the farm, including what is under fence, and that one thousand acres shall forever remain in wood or forest in order to supply the farm with convenient range, and with fuel, and timber, and in process of time contribute to the support of the institution but the surplus land over and above the five hundred and one thousand acres before specified may be by the trustees to let to farm in such tracts as they shall think to the best advantage, provided that no tract of land by this my last will devised shall ever be let on a more extensive lease than that of fourteen years, and that every such lease shall contain a condition, that the Lessee shall not cut or willfully suffer to be cut any timber or wood from the said thousand acres reserved for the use of the farm school, unless by and with the express permission of the trustees.

And it is my will that in case the Agricultural Society of South Carolina, should against my expectation (the Plan being relative to the institution of the society) should decline or neglect appointing Trustees for taking upon themselves the execution of this my last will and testament or the trust contained in the same, or that the said society should at any time be dissolved or annihilated, that then and in each of those cases, the execution of this my last will or the Trust contain'd in it shall devolve upon such Trustees as the Honorable Legislature of this state shall please to name and appoint; and as the aim of this my last will and testament is to raise useful citizens, I do hereby humbly request Honorable Legislature that in the above case, they may be pleased in incorporate such Trustees as they shall think proper to appoint under such classes and regulations as in their Great wisdom shall seem meet; and for the same reason of intending to raise useful citizens to the State, many whereof would without such an institution be a nuisance, I beg the Honorable Legislature to graciously pleased to keep the Institution under their fatherly protection.

It is further my will, that whenever the yearly income of the estate by me bequeathed and devised, shall be adequate to it, such children as shall have completed their education at the farm school, provided they have not resided there a less time than five years, and behaved to the satisfaction of the Trustees during their residence, shall receive such gratification in cattle from the Trustees, as in their judgment they shall think expedient.

I give and devise to the heirs of the Rev. Mr. Samuel Frederick Lucius in his lifetime V.D.M., the immediately hereafter to be mention three contiguous tracts of land— Viz, one tract of one hundred and fifty acres, one Do. of one hundred acres adjoin the first, and one tract of fifty acres adjoining the two former making together a valuable plantation of three hundred acres more or less, situate on Savannah river and Swift creek in Edgefield county, below the mouth of Little River in compensation of such balance of a conditional bond, by me given to the said Mr. Lucius, as the heirs think unpaid. (No matter whether any is due by me or not) as the executrix and heirs have been unwilling or unable to produce the said bond though repeatedly by me required and solicited to it in order to verify the different receipts of the said Mr. Samuel Frederick Lucius for large sums on the back of the said bond by which, and such other vouchers as are in my possession, I believe that the Est. rather would be found in my debt. Provided nevertheless that the said executrix (now Mrs. Savannah Gibson of the Congarees) and the said heirs shall and do within one year immediately succeeding the date of my decease manifest, declare and make known to the President and agricultural society of South Carolina that they do accept of the said three tracts of land or plantation of three hundred acres or less in full compensation of what balance may possibly be due by me on the said conditional bond, but it is my will that in case the above-mentioned heirs, shall not manifest, declare and make known as aforesaid that they accept of the said plantation on the conditions above specified that then the said three tracts of land shall make part of the map and remain annexed to the bulk of the estate by me given and devised and that in that case, on the said heirs or executrix verifying any balance to be due by me, my said executors or trustees shall please discharge the same.

It is my will that immediately after my decease, my old Negro man, Bacchus, shall be free and manumitted as I have considered him to be many years ago and as that notwithstanding his voluntary services have been performed with equal honesty and fidelity. It is my will that all my common wearing apparel may be given to him, and that during the small remainder of his life, he be maintained out of the income of my EST. Both in sickness and in health, with every possible ease and comfort as his meritous services deserve every comfort in my power to procure him. I, therefore, particularly recommend this to my executors and trustees.

To my worthy and much respected friends Dr. Edward Jenkins, V.D.M., and his Lady, James Linar, M.D. and his Lady and Captn. Edward Linar, son of the said James Linar and to his Lady and to each of them, I give one mourning ring of the value of one guinea which I do request them to accept of me as a testimony that I have only lost the grateful sense of their friendship with my breath, knowing that in the circumstances as anything valuable would be beneath their acceptance.

To Miss Anna Cook, my present housekeeper, I leave ten pounds sterling in compensation for her services.

I do name, request, make, and point the Honorable President and South Carolina agricultural society and such of their members as they shall please pro tempore to name and appoint to take the execution and trust of this my last will and testament upon them and their successors in said appointment forever. Executors and trustees to this my last will and testament. And I do request Peter Gibert, Esq., of Mill Creek in said county of Abbeville to take the execution of it to himself until such of the members as the agricultural society shall please to name and appoint do take the same upon themselfs. And I do by this revoke and annul all former testaments which I may have made at any time previous to this seventh September in the year of our Lord one thousand seven hundred and ninety-six. Whatever ready money I shall leave at my decease (in case it pleases God it should be shortly) is known to my above named executor, Peter Gibert.

Signed, sealed, published, and declared by the said John de la Howe and the testator as his last will and testament in presence of P. Gibert, I. Emrie Anna Cook.

John De La Howe, L.S.

I now do hereby declare and republish my above will and in order of having the said will and testament more properly executed; I do name and appoint Mr. Willm Hulton of Abbeville County, planter, as a joint executor with Peter Gibert, Esqr. January 2, 1797, John De La Howe.

There it is. I have finished all of my business. I thank God that he allowed me to keep a good mind right up to the end. I hope the Agricultural Society of South Carolina will tend to the needs of Lethe, but being two-hundred miles and ten days each way from Charleston, I doubt it. The Agricultural Society is made up of the very rich and powerful plantation society men who get together and discuss the latest technology of farming. They swap variety of seeds and experiment with splicing. I hope they will hire an overseer and keep the plantation profitable until the school is established.

I have provided an out if the Agricultural Society thinks that it is too troublesome to travel and administer the daily operations of Lethe. I have asked that the Lethe agricultural seminar to be turned over to the State of South Carolina to perpetuate its existence. I cannot think of anything I have left undone.

One of the most important things to me is that I will have freed Bacchus upon my demise. I have arranged for him to live at Lethe in comfort the rest of his days. He has been my constant companion and intimate friend for thirty-five years, and I know that I shall see him on the other side. Rev. Gibert promised me that he would see to it that Bacchus will never want or need for anything. I have asked that Brister, who never married, be allowed to stay with Bacchus and do what he can for Lethe after all the other slaves have transistioned to their new homes.

I have arranged for Mr. Duvall to take James and Molly and their children Little Molly and Polly; Mr. Robert Foster will take Carolina, Matilda, and Little Liza. Sam is a grown man now and living by himself. Mr. John Gilbert, a neighbor to Mr. Foster, will take Sam Jr. and old man Pompy. Rev. Gibert will take Boze, Becky, and Little Becky. Mr. Forrester takes Beck; Mr. Patterson takes Ben; Sam Cowan takes Tam-O who will be allowed to check on Matilda next door. Mr. Thomas Lee will take Phyllis and Cecelia; and Brister will stay at Lethe with Bacchus.

I am satisfied that I can do nothing else except pray that my school will be a blessing to the children of South Carolina who otherwise would not have an opportunity to become educated.

I have left about $7,000.00 in assets in my account and at least a thousand acres that can be sold to benefit the school. Certainly, the state can start the school with that.

I am looking forward to lying next to Rebecca for eternity overlooking our beloved Lethe.

As I started this narrative, I spoke about vanity. I have contemplated if my life has been in vain. I think that if I have brought some happiness into another person's life, or healed their wounds and eased their aches and pains, or soothed their sadness, or made their burdens lighter, then I have not lived in vain.

A hundred years from now, it will not matter what my bank account was, the sort of house I lived in, or the kind of clothes I wore, but the world may be much different because I was important in the life of a child.

I lay here and my kidneys are failing. I finally drank of the River Lethe. I am oblivious to my surroundings. I see Hendricks and Capt. Worley. I see Ann and Mr. Laurens. I see Isaac Hayne and Sam. I see Rebecca playing Mozart on the piano and smiling to welcome me. I see them all and I see the angels coming to escort me to a place of rest and blessing. I pray that I shall one day meet all the children my life has touched. Good night, until we meet on the other side.

On January 18, 1797, this final notice came out in the *Charleston City Gazette and Advertiser*,

> Died, on the 2d, inst, at Long Cane in Abbeville County, district of Ninety-Six, in the 80th year of his age, Doctor John de la Howe. As a practitioner of physics, he was eminent in this country, for upwards of 30 years past, as a man of extensive learning he had few equals, and his benevolence endeared him to all who knew him. About twelve years ago, he retired to Abbeville County, of which he was made a judge; there his whole time was spent in assisting those who stood in need of his advice. By his last will, having no children, he has left his estate to support a public school in Abbeville County.